I0792939

IMAGES
of America

San Antonio's Historic Architecture

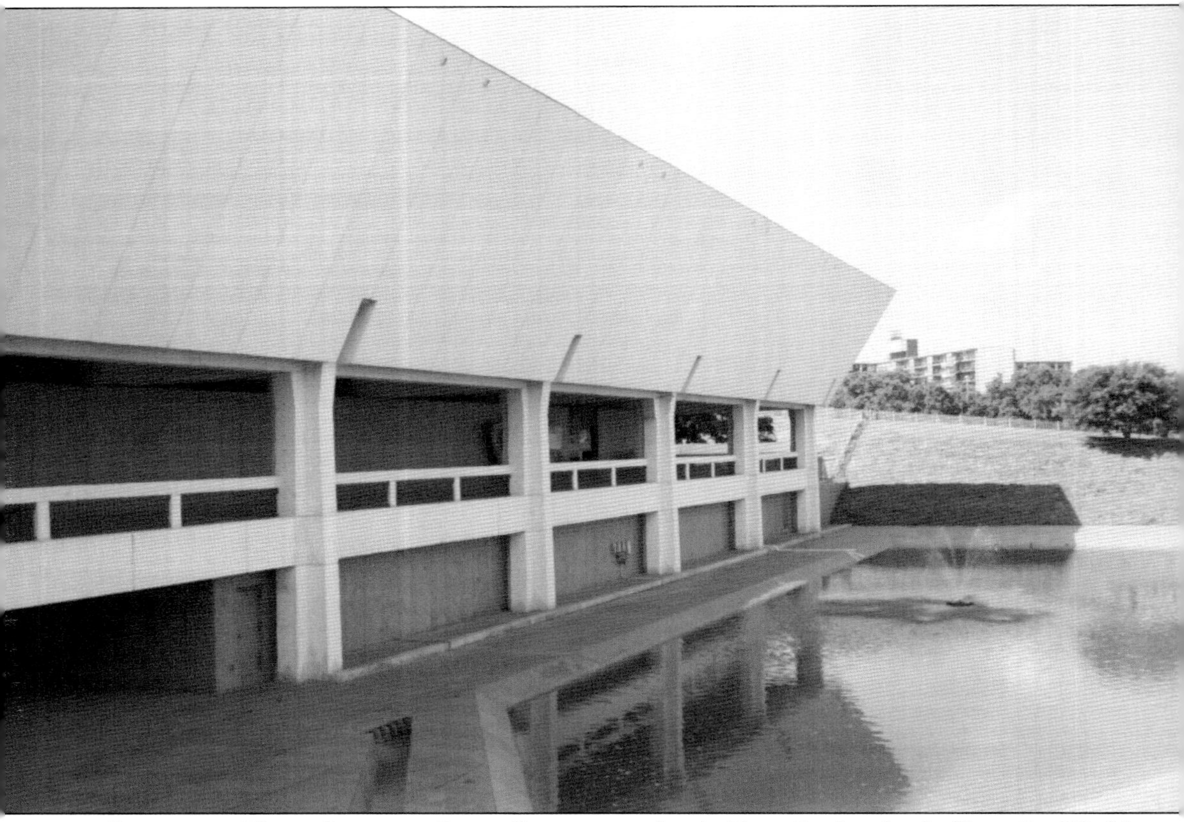

INSTITUTE OF TEXAN CULTURES. Originally constructed as the Texas Pavilion for the HemisFair World Exposition, held in 1968, the museum features exhibits that explore the cultural diversity and ethnic legacies of Texas. Designed by the Houston architectural firm Caudill Rowlett Scott, the museum captures the sculptural qualities and economy of Brutalism. (San Antonio Photographic Archive.)

ON THE COVER: Pictured is the Post Chapel at Randolph Air Force Base, as photographed by the US Army Air Corps in 1936. The Spanish Colonial Revival nondenominational church was constructed in 1931. Hundreds of the buildings at Randolph Field, most of which were completed between 1928 and 1933, are cohesive to this stylistic methodology. (Portal to Texas History, Tarrant County College Northeast, Heritage Room Collection.)

IMAGES
of America

SAN ANTONIO'S HISTORIC ARCHITECTURE

T. Irwin Sessions

ARCADIA
PUBLISHING

ISBN 978-1-4671-3483-5

Published by Arcadia Publishing
Charleston, South Carolina

Printed in the United States of America

Library of Congress Control Number: 2015943091

For all general information, please contact Arcadia Publishing:
Telephone 843-853-2070
Fax 843-853-0044
E-mail sales@arcadiapublishing.com

Visit us on the Internet at www.arcadiapublishing.com

For my children, who know and love San Antonio as I do

Contents

ACKNOWLEDGMENTS

Without the support of the following people and organizations, this project would not have been possible. Sincerest thanks go to Jane Lewis, executive director of Villa Finale Museum and Gardens; Sylvia M. Gonzales, Margaret Nowack, and Karina Serna of the Villa Finale staff; Tommy Adams and Don Kirk of the Building Arts Group; Tom Shelton and Carlos Cortez of the University of Texas at San Antonio Libraries Special Collections and the Institute of Texan Cultures; the San Antonio Development Agency, the San Antonio Photographic Archive; Jack Boucher, Brian Cary, Carol M. Highsmith, and Arthur W. Stewart, photographers for the Historic American Buildings Survey; Jose G. Jimenez and Charles E. Peterson, draftsmen for the Historic American Buildings Survey; and Martha N. Bradley, Linda Mercer, and Ann Russell for their generous contributions to the University of Texas at San Antonio Libraries Special Collections.

Key to courtesy lines for photographs:

FSHM – Fort Sam Houston Museum
HABS – Historic American Buildings Survey
HAER – Historic American Engineering Record
LOC – Library of Congress Prints and Photographs Collection
PTH/North Texas – Portal to Texas History, the University of North Texas Libraries
PTH/Tarrant – Portal to Texas History, Tarrant County College Northeast
SAPA – San Antonio Photographic Archive
USAF – United States Air Force
UTSA – University of Texas at San Antonio Libraries Special Collections and the Institute of Texan Cultures
VFMG – Villa Finale Museum and Gardens, Private Collection of Walter Mathis

INTRODUCTION

San Antonio is home to hundreds of historic structures that exemplify our unique heritage and active community involvement. Our city's enthusiasm for history has led to a remarkable collection of architecture that is exceptionally distinctive. For over 300 years, San Antonio has developed into a crossroads of cultures, producing multigenerational skilled craftsmen and artisans. Because citizens and local government care extensively about conservation, the city is privileged to have so much historical fabric remarkably intact.

Five 18th-century Spanish Colonial missions that collectively include over 80 structures, irrigation systems, and ranchlands are designated with World Heritage status. The United Nations Educational, Scientific, and Cultural Organization (UNESCO) nomination submitted in 2008 based the qualifications for the missions on three cultural criteria that exemplify exceptional universal importance. These include significant interchanges of cultural traditions and human values pertaining to architecture, town planning, and technology.

Instrumental intervention by local historic preservation groups, the US government, and the Catholic Church have protected the mission properties from deteriorating. Four of the mission complexes are part of the San Antonio Missions National Historical Park, managed by the National Park Service. Mission San Antonio de Valero, more commonly known as the Alamo, has been in the care of the Daughters of the Republic of Texas (DRT) since 1905. Collaboration between the DRT, the San Antonio Conservation Society, the Works Progress Administration, the Catholic Church, and local government in the 1930s was instrumental to their protection.

National Historic Landmarks are designated historic places recognized by the US secretary of the interior. These national parks, buildings, monuments, sites, and districts are advised by a board of trustees that fall under the jurisdiction of the National Park Service. The board members are nominated and selected based on their professional expertise and influence in archaeology, architecture, history, natural science, and related fields. There are over 2,500 National Historic Landmarks throughout the country—46 in the state of Texas, with 8 located in San Antonio.

Nationally known for the King William Historic District, this downtown neighborhood includes the Villa Finale museum, created by Walter Mathis. Mathis was a successful stockbroker who orchestrated a neighborhood-wide preservation movement, beginning with the purchase of the Norton-Polk House on King William Street in 1967. Not only did he purchase and restore multiple properties in the area himself, but Mathis was incredibly influential in promoting King William preservation to other prominent San Antonio citizens. Villa Finale is the only property in the state of Texas owned by the National Trust for Historic Preservation, and Mathis donated the fine art collection he amassed over his lifetime and the home he painstakingly restored to the National Trust in 2004.

Many historic residences have been rehabilitated to become restaurants as well as house museums, and several of them have been moved. Collections of these relocated, reconstructed, or replicated structures exist at the Witte Museum, the San Antonio Botanical Gardens, and La Villita Historic

Arts Village. Other house museums in the city are somewhat more traditional, if not unique, as they vary drastically in style, scale, location, and construction methodology.

The City of San Antonio has exhibited an incredible civic building program that includes not only administrative government buildings but also local public schools. Dozens of schoolhouses constructed between the 1880s and the 1930s are still in use throughout the city. Recognizing the multigenerational importance and community stability that develops with this archetype, San Antonio has continued to maintain, rehabilitate, or repurpose many of these buildings for over 100 years. Private religious organizations and local universities have also engaged in this process, allowing for a diverse collection during this era.

Lesser-known structures within the city include a variety of religious edifices that reflect the cultural evolution of local religious ideologies as they emerged within architectural building trends. Business and industry also shaped much of the city's downtown as we see it today. Numerous banks, offices, retail stores, and high-rises continue to serve as important centers of commerce, and the few remaining rail stations exhibit a unique regional style.

As the first civilian settlement in the state, San Antonio— once a part of the interior provinces of New Spain—has historically been an ideal strategic location for military activity, and conflicts with native tribes led to decades of civil unrest. The Mexican War of Independence relinquished control of Texas as a New Spain province in 1821, and it became an integral part of Mexico. Colonization of Texas by US citizens continued to be problematic for Mexico, ultimately leading to the Texas Revolution in 1836. The short-lived Republic of Texas was later annexed into the United States, concurrent with the Mexican-American War, which was sparked by a boundary dispute between Texas and Mexico. After the war, the US government established the San Antonio Arsenal in 1859, the first of many major federal military installations that would develop in the next century for the United States.

The late 19th century was a period of prosperity, and with it came large populations of immigrants. The development of a tourist industry blossomed soon thereafter, and a continuous influx of military personnel over the last century has fashioned one of the most distinctive cities in the American Southwest.

One

The Missions World Heritage

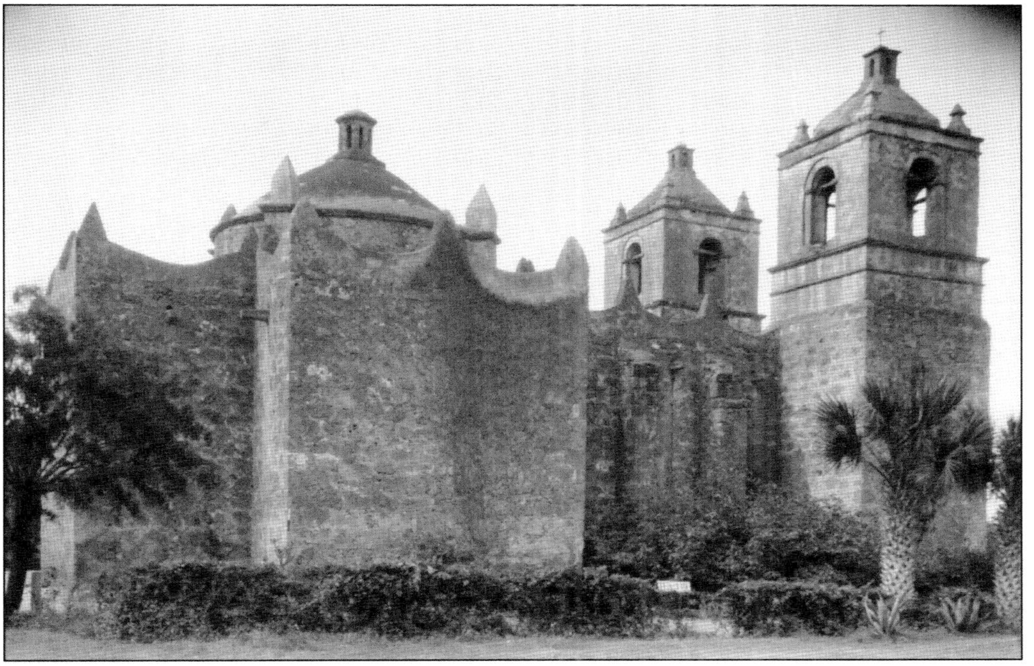

Mission Nuestra Señora de La Purísima Concepción de Acuña. Initial Spanish Colonial missions were established in east Texas in the early 1700s. After several trials at various locations, the area now known as San Antonio became the suitable permanent location from which successful settlements grew. The only mission church in San Antonio to have an intact roof, this north elevation view reveals the smooth surface of the dome at the center of the cruciform plan. Spires adorn the roof edges around the rear perimeter and cap the corners where the dome base meets the transept. (HABS.)

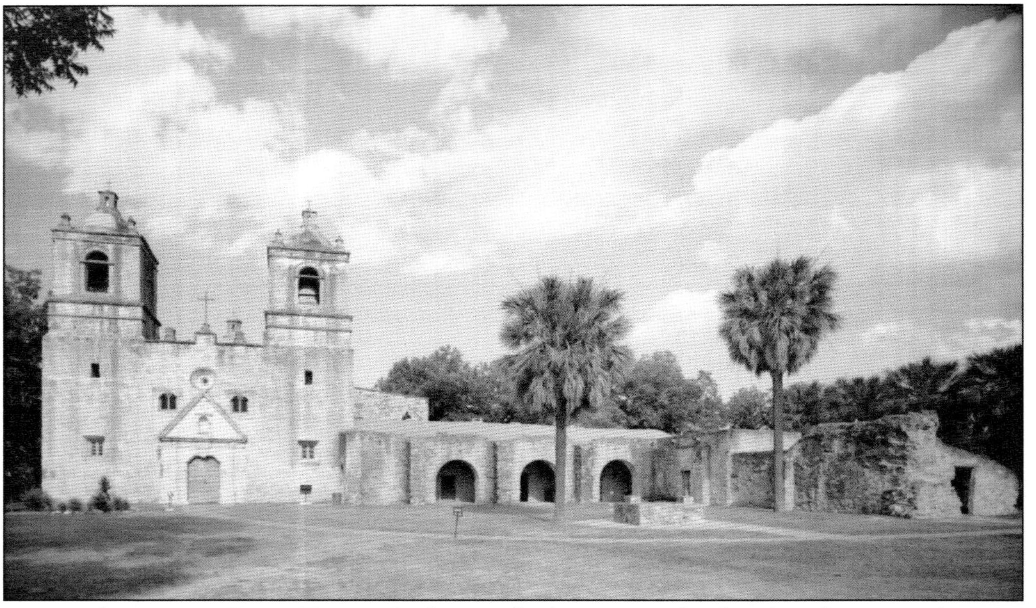

Mission Concepción Front Facade. In this view looking east at the church and convent, the main entry seen at left is adorned with simple geometry. The circular window just above the pediment illuminates the interior altar on the Holy Day of Obligation, celebrating the Assumption of the Virgin Mary. To the right of the arcade, the structure is in ruins in this photograph taken during the 1930s. (HABS.)

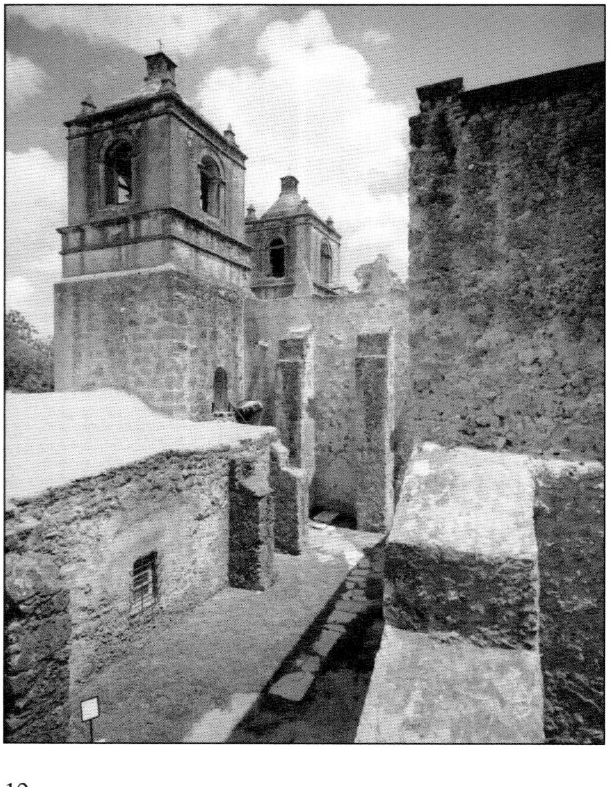

Mission Concepción South Elevation. This view from the south side of the structure reveals the need for buttressing along the nave of the church, as well as the wall supporting the barrel-vaulted roof to the lower left. Atop the nave buttresses, decorative pyramidal spires are more simply executed than their counterparts at the corners of the bell towers. (HABS.)

CHURCH DOOR DETAIL AT MISSION CONCEPCIÓN. Founded in 1731, the mission did not dedicate this structure until 1755. Intricately carved engaged columns flank the entryway, displaying delicate floral patterns and fluting. A decorative keystone crest rests directly above the door. The scalloped alcove in the center of the pediment is topped with a cross and also adorned with floral motifs. (HABS.)

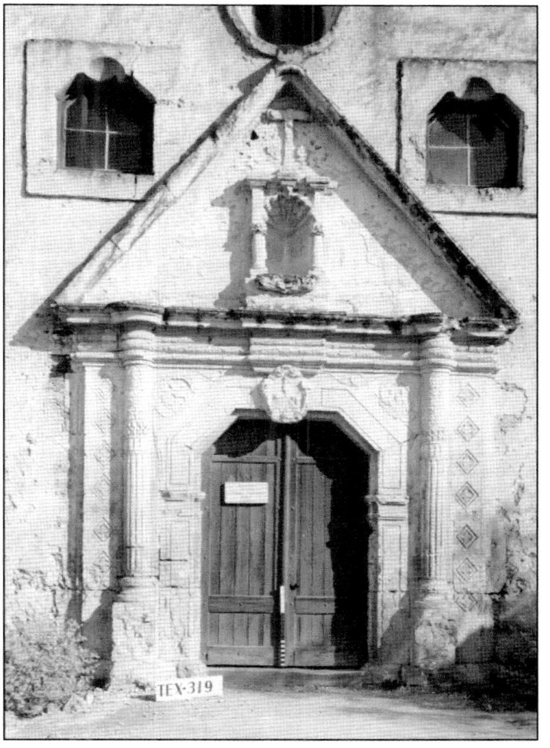

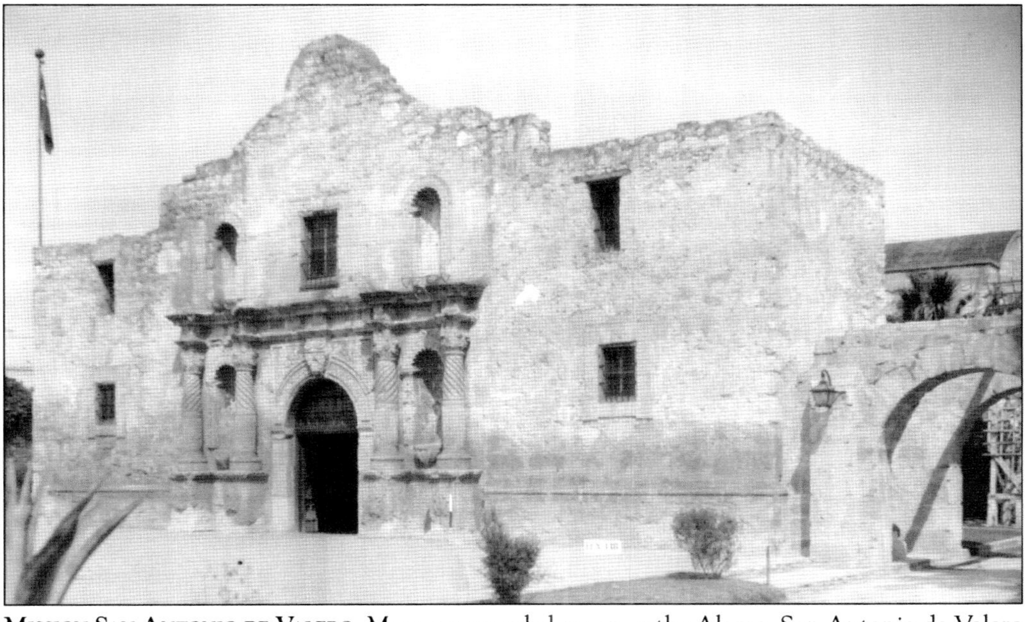

MISSION SAN ANTONIO DE VALERO. More commonly known as the Alamo, San Antonio de Valero includes four highly decorative columns that surround the church's entrance. Combining both fluted and spiral details, each carved column is fully round within the entrance ornamentation. The structure seen today was begun in the 1750s but was never fully completed, as the mission's population declined. (HABS.)

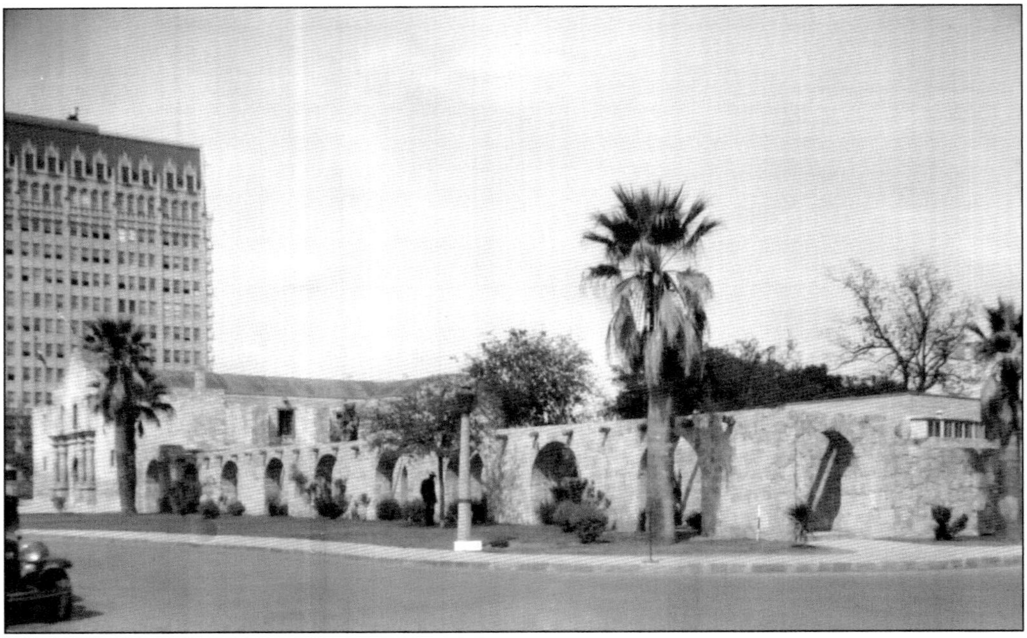

Mission San Antonio de Valero Arcade. As seen in this view looking northeast from Alamo Plaza, the church entrance is to the left of the arcade. Just behind the entrance is the neo-Gothic Medical Arts Building. This 1930s photograph shows the concrete barrel-vaulted roof, newly completed by the Works Progress Administration. The Alamo is the only mission of the five to be cared for by the Daughters of the Republic of Texas. (HABS.)

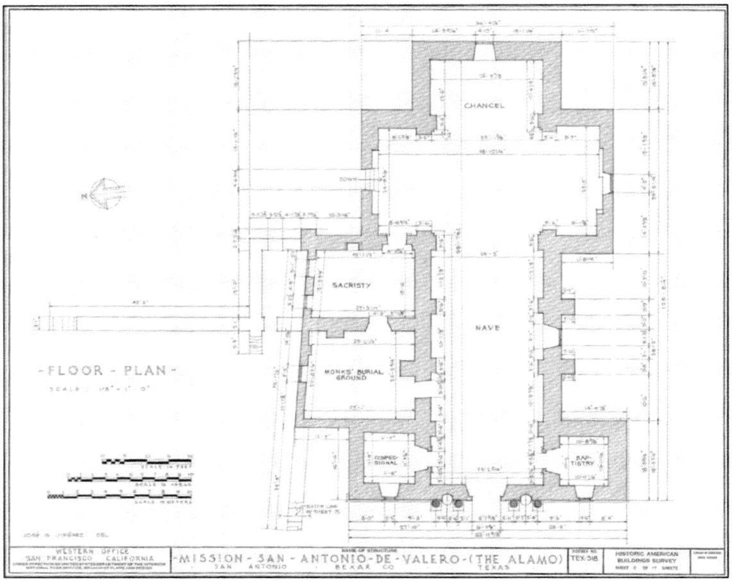

Mission San Antonio de Valero Floor Plan. Drawn by Jose G. Jimenez for the Historic American Buildings Survey, the floor plan depicts the church organization and the wall thickness at four feet. Not only is the drawing scaled in feet and meters, but it also shows varas, a common unit of measure during the Spanish Colonial era. (HABS.)

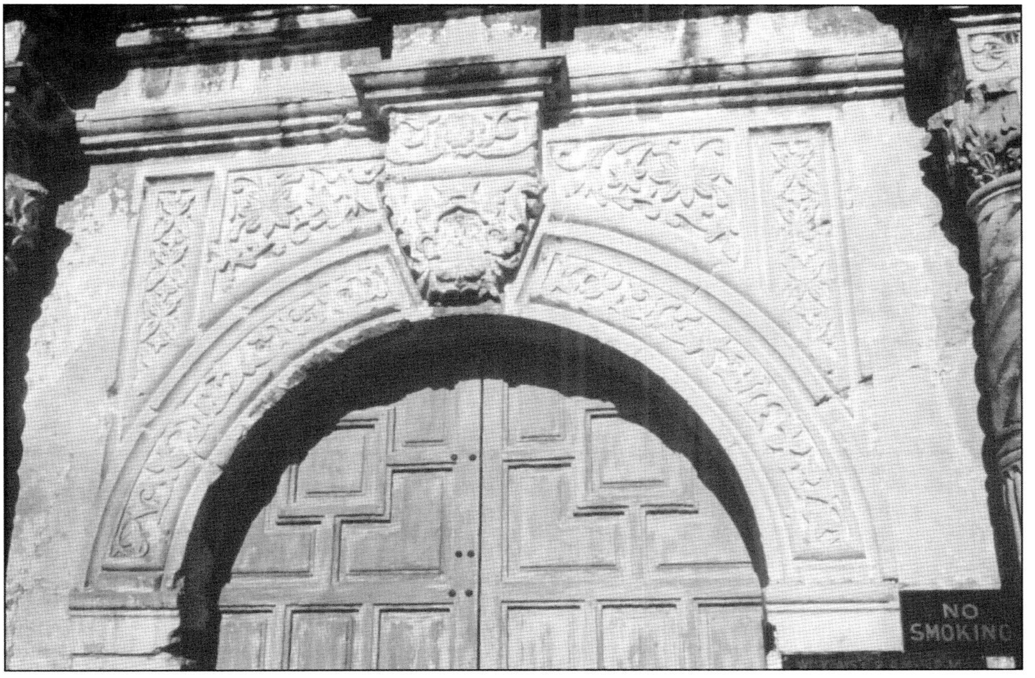

DETAIL OF DOOR AT MISSION SAN ANTONIO DE VALERO. Delicate floral designs surround the doorway arch, keystone, and tympanum of the front entrance to the church. There are several conflicting opinions as to what is actually carved into the keystone; the meaning remains unclear. (HABS.)

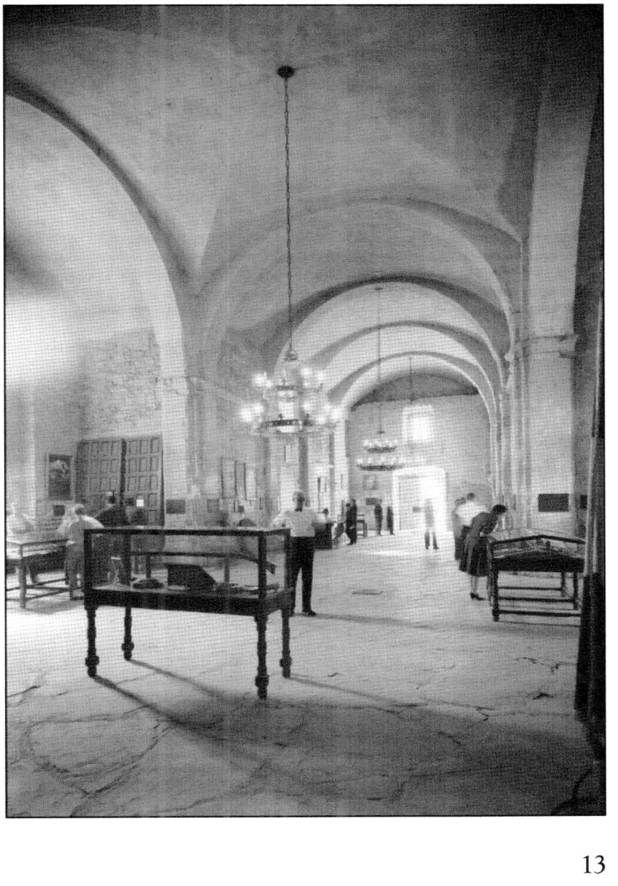

INTERIOR VIEW OF MISSION SAN ANTONIO DE VALERO. The church's nave provides a clear testament to the impressive structure that the missionaries intended to build but were unable to complete. Finished in concrete, the top of the original stone wall can be seen just above the pilasters, most visible above the doors on display in the corner at left. (HABS.)

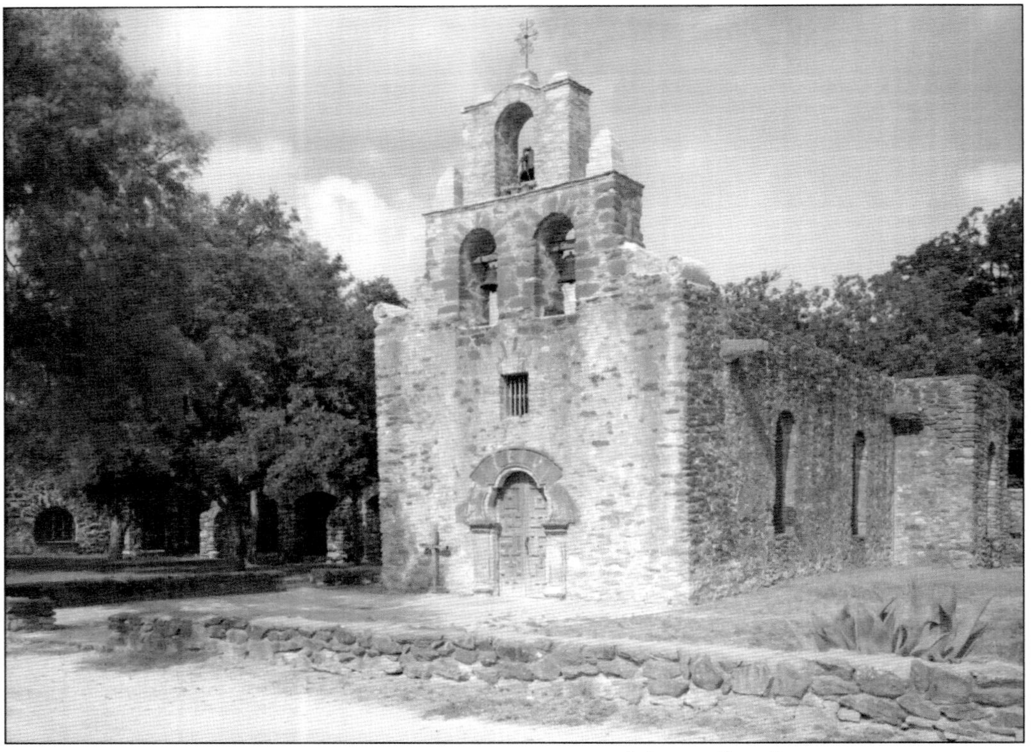

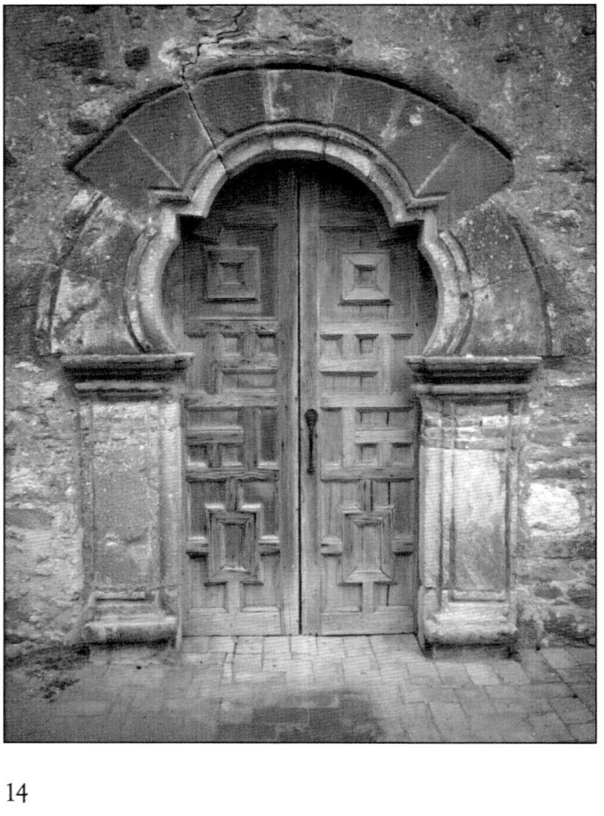

Mission San Francisco de la Espada. The chapel structure was originally built as the sacristy for a larger church that was never completed. The bell tower was added in the 1780s, when the structure was converted for use as the main church. Mission Espada's bell tower houses three alcoves within two tiers and decorative scrollwork at the base of the parapet. Moved to this location in 1731 from East Texas, Mission Espada had over 50 families and 200 individuals that called this community home. (HABS.)

Mission San Francisco de la Espada Chapel Main Entry Detail. The horseshoe arch is visually supported by carved pilasters but lacks the floral motifs and ornamentation present on the other church entrances. This is likely due to the building's former use as a sacristy. (HABS.)

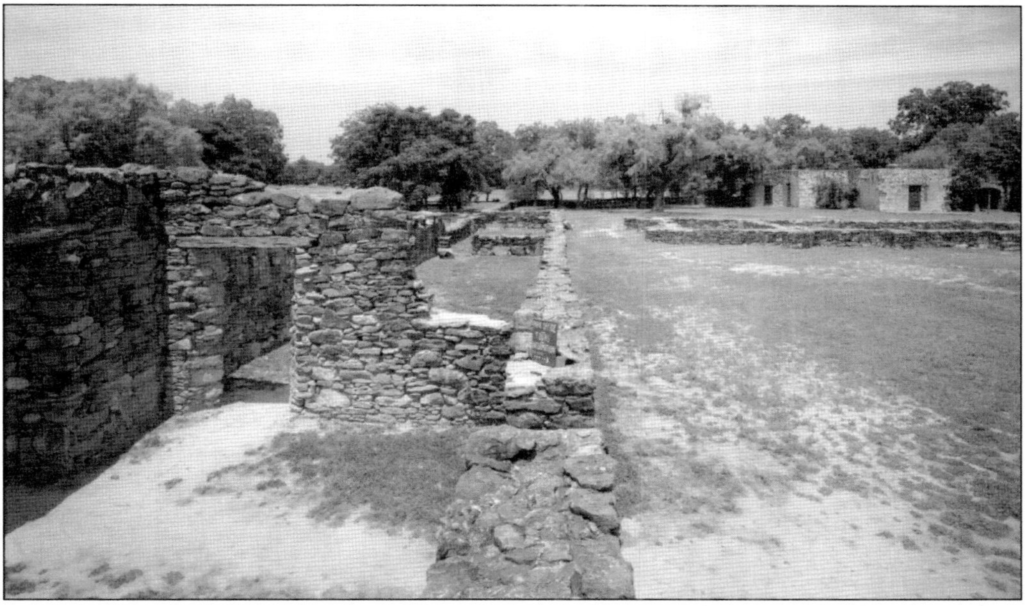

SOUTH WALL RUINS AT MISSION SAN FRANCISCO DE LA ESPADA. Near the entrance and museum along the south wall, these ruins were once residential quarters for the indigenous converts. Perpendicular to the residences, the remains of the granary can be seen to the right. Constructed during the mid-18th century, the granary was converted to a church from 1773 until 1776. Beyond the granary, at far right, is the rectory. (HABS.)

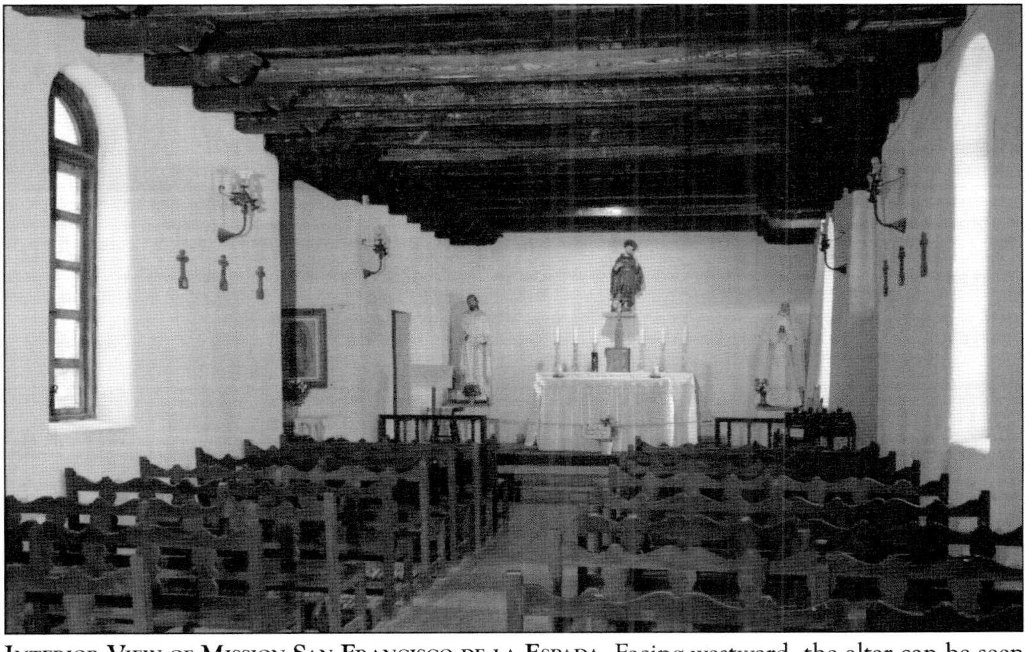

INTERIOR VIEW OF MISSION SAN FRANCISCO DE LA ESPADA. Facing westward, the altar can be seen at the end of the sanctuary on an elevated platform just beyond the transept. Founded in 1690, Mission Espada was relocated to this site in 1731. Diocesan priest Fr. Francis Bouchu converted the chapel to the cruciform plan by adding the transept in the 19th century. (HABS.)

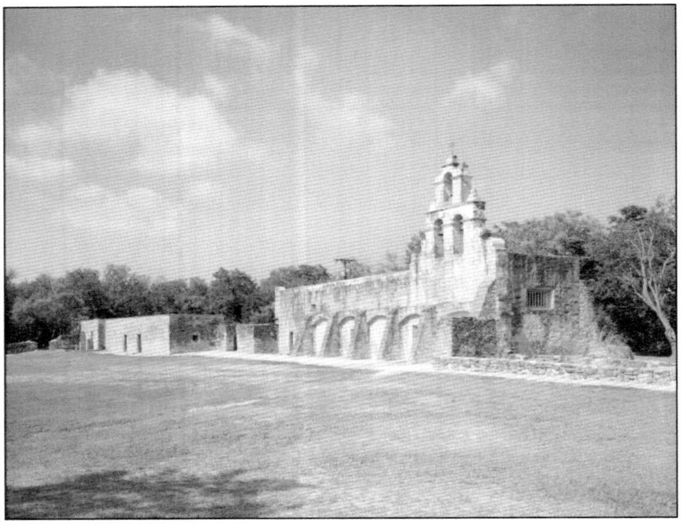

Mission San Juan de Capistrano. This general view of the chapel, as seen from the east during the mid-20th century, demonstrates the need for substantial buttressing. Extensive investigations and stabilization projects have been completed, revealing continuous rebuilding of structures on this site, substantiated by the discovery of earlier foundations. The chapel seen today is possibly the final of three prior structures. (HABS.)

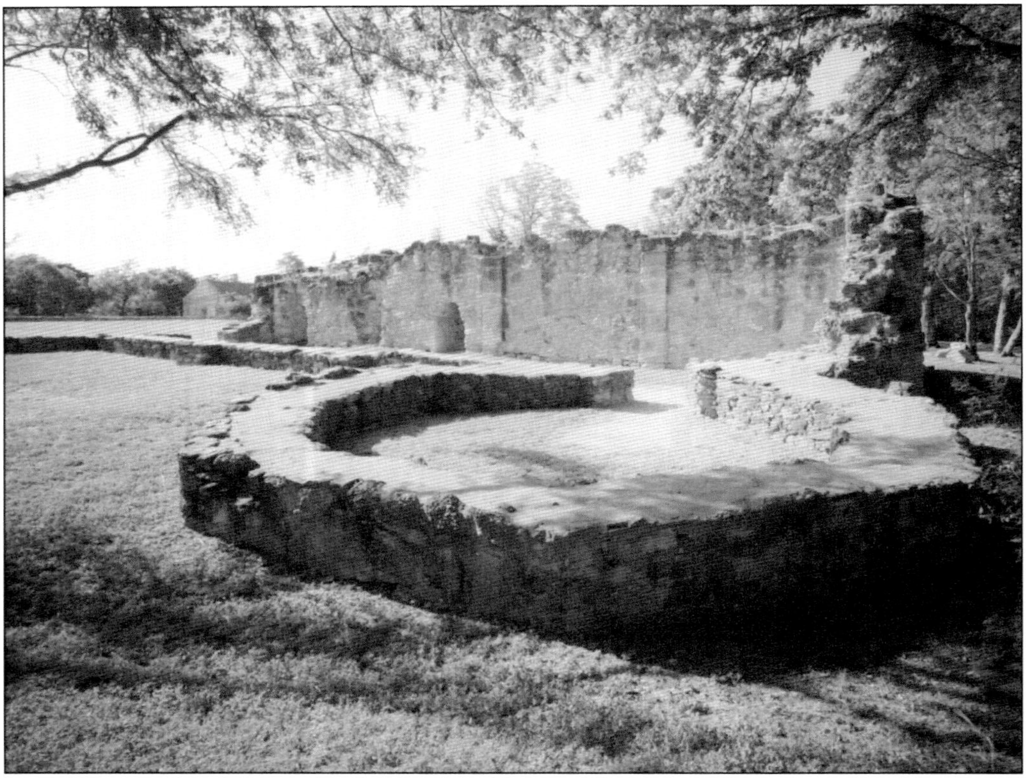

Old Church at Mission San Juan de Capistrano. With the builders having difficulty finding properly skilled labor to complete the vaults, the larger church shown here was never completed. Antonio Salazar, the third and final architect for the project that began in 1772, abandoned the undertaking. The prior architect, Joseph Padron, wished to be buried in the church, and upon his death in 1779, the cemetery was consecrated. The circular foundation in the foreground is believed to have housed the sacristy. (HABS.)

Mission San Juan de Capistrano Interior. The chapel decor is simple wall relief, distinguishing the inset doorways with pilasters. Capped with an arch, the doorway on the left is the main entry point situated below the bell tower. Near the altar, the other door is flanked by two pilasters but does not carry the arch detail. This chapel has undergone extensive renovation work of the interior and was completed in 2012. (HABS.)

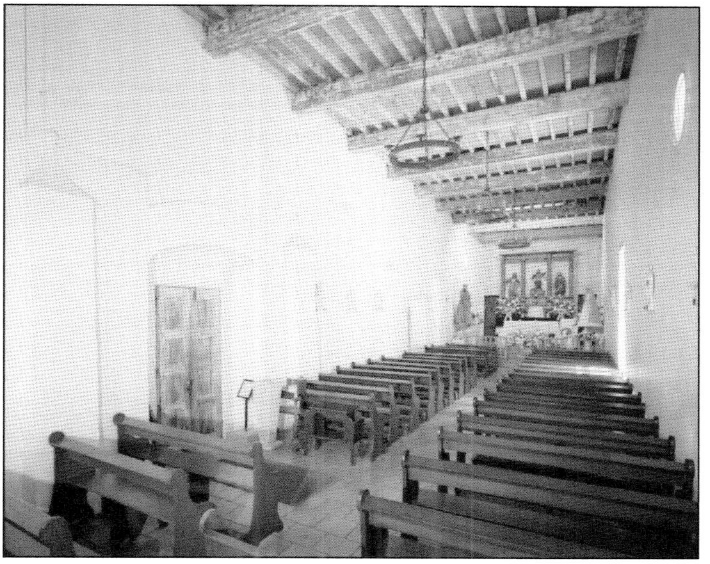

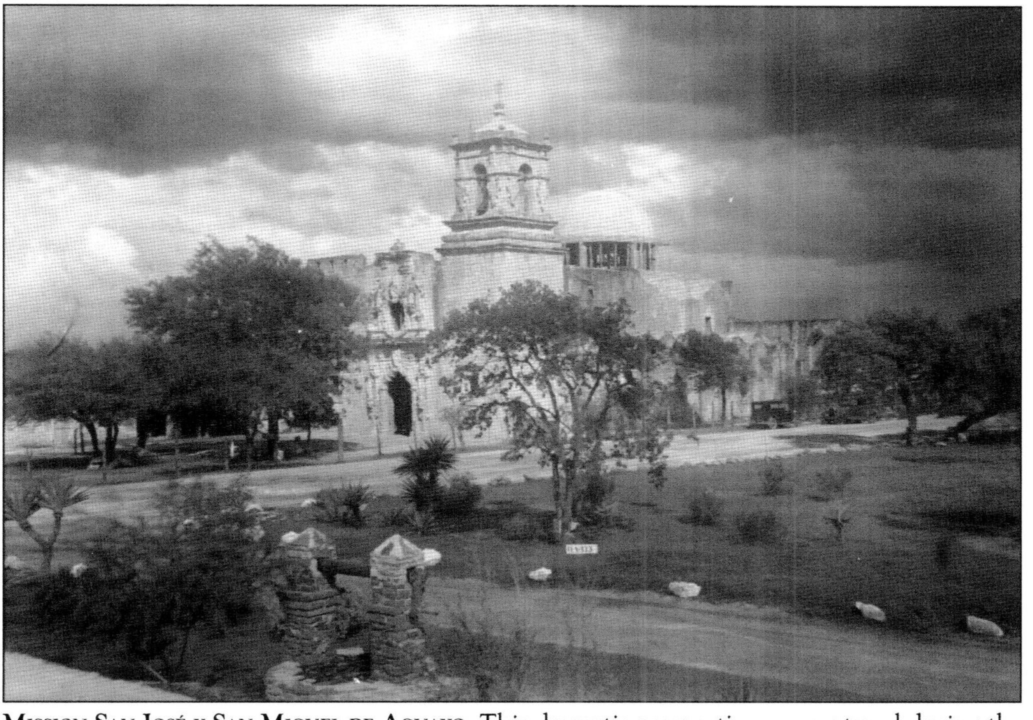

Mission San José y San Miguel de Aguayo. This dramatic perspective was captured during the restoration work on the central dome. The original dome collapsed around 1870. In this view looking northeast at the church entrance, the artistry of the stonework is carried to the full height of the structure. Referred to as the "Queen of the Missions," this church is the largest and most elaborate example of Spanish Colonial architecture in San Antonio. (HABS.)

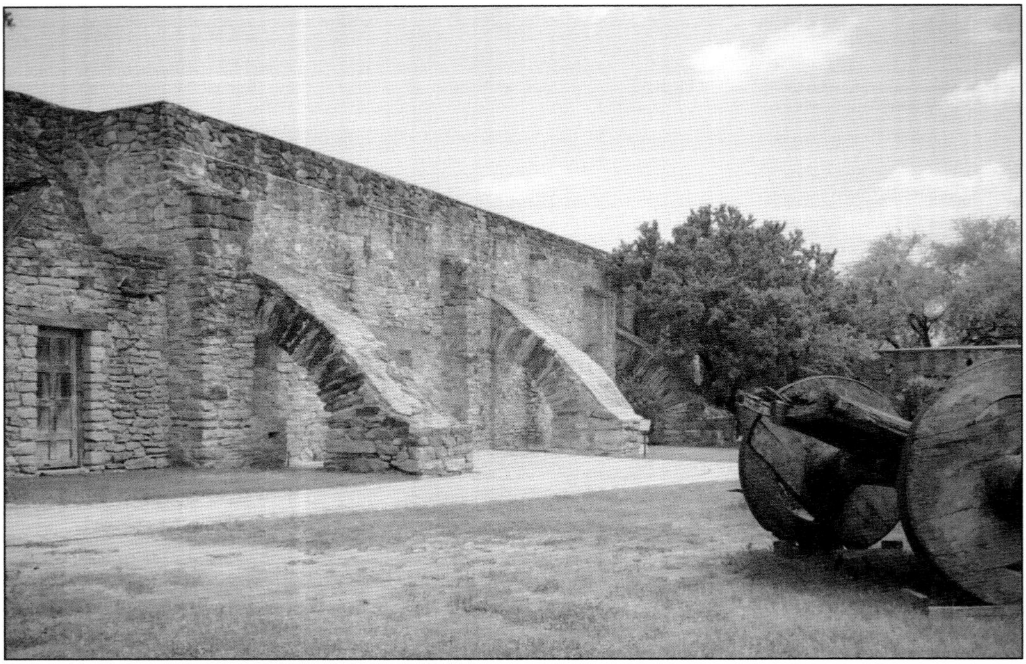

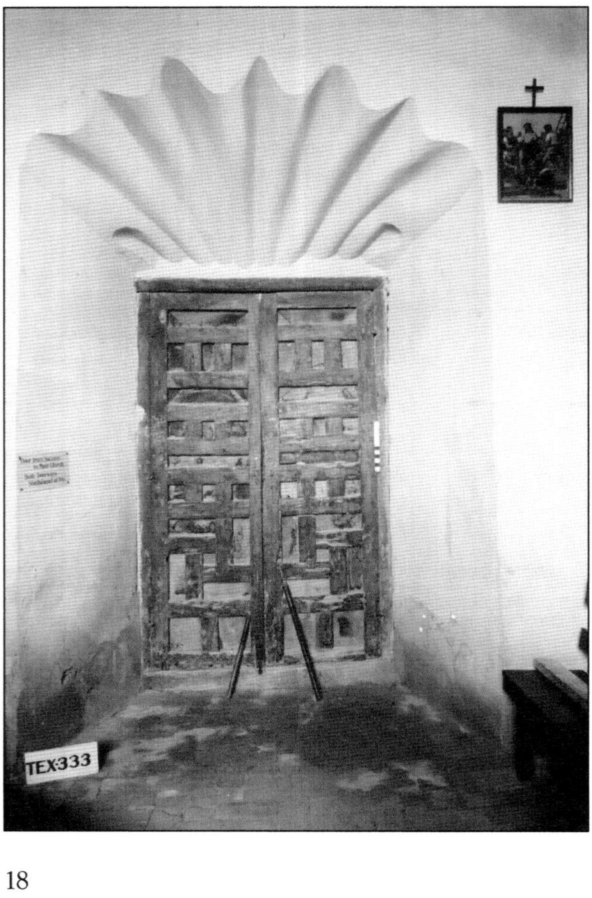

Granary at Mission San José y San Miguel de Aguayo. The granary was originally a storehouse for the farming community at Mission San José. Later converted to housing, the barrel-vaulted structure was largely in ruin until the San Antonio Conservation Society intervened by purchasing it in 1926. The flying buttresses are an excellent example of the engineering required to support the lateral forces within the structure. (HABS.)

Detail of Interior Door at Mission San José y San Miguel de Aguayo. Simple yet elegant, this doorway decoration is integrated into the massive structure, revealing the thickness required for stone construction. Skillful plasterwork on this doorway situated between the small and main chapels mirrors the smooth, undulating parapet on the small chapel's south exterior facade. (HABS.)

Two

National Historic Landmarks

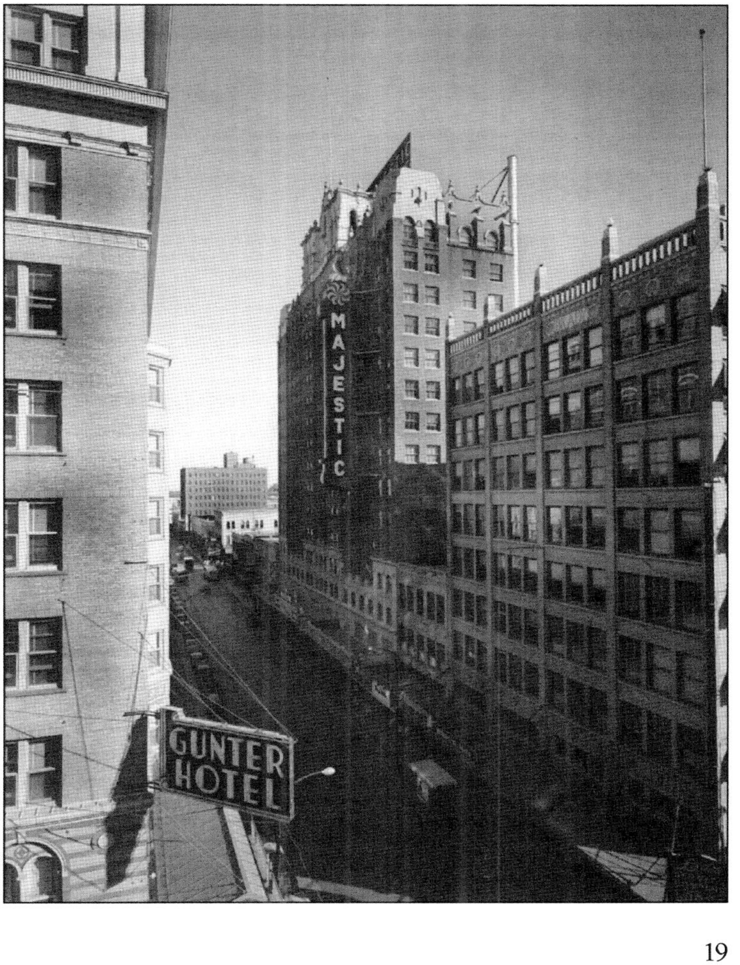

MAJESTIC THEATER. Constructed in 1929, the Majestic Theater is San Antonio's oldest and largest atmospheric movie palace, with seating for over 2,300 people. Designed by architect John Adolph Emil Eberson, the elaborate Spanish Courtyard–style theater features a simple dome ceiling that utilizes a Brenograph Junior projector to simulate passing clouds. After a major restoration, the Majestic Theater became a National Historic Landmark in 1993. (UTSA, Zintgraff Studio Collection.)

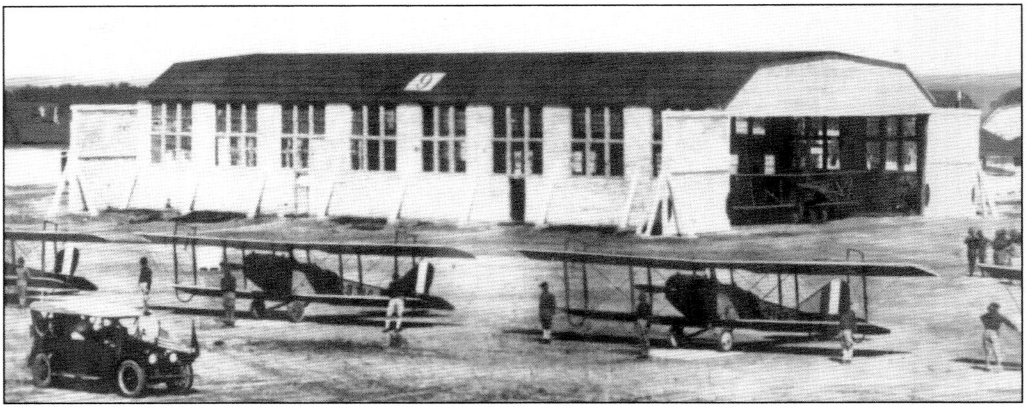

Hangar 9 at Brooks Air Force Base. Also known as the Edward H. White II Museum, Hangar 9 is the nation's oldest surviving aircraft hangar from World War I. Listed in the National Register of Historic Places in 1970, this structure is the sole survivor of 30 similar aircraft storage and repair facilities temporarily constructed at Brooks and Kelly Fields in 1918. Established for aviation training, the hangar at Brooks was designed by Albert Kahn to house the Curtiss JN-4 "Jenny" biplane. (LOC.)

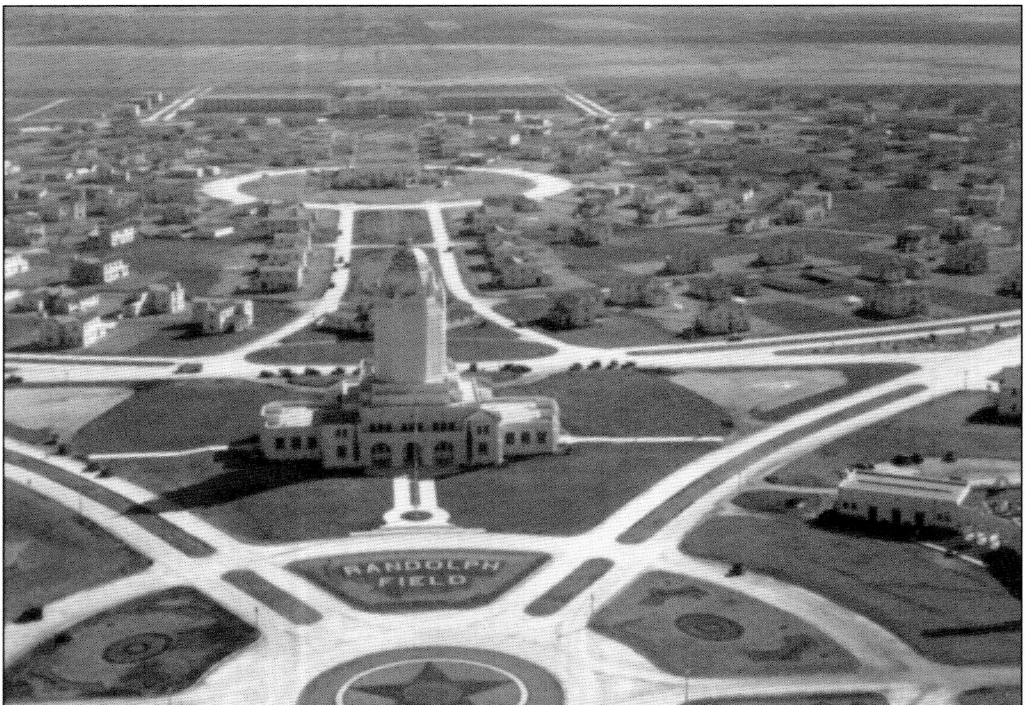

Randolph Field Historic District. Named in honor of Capt. William M. Randolph, the Air Corps Primary Flying School opened northeast of downtown in 1931. A radical new concept in airfield design and flight training, Randolph Field was also the headquarters for the Air Corps Training Center. The unique military installation utilized Mission Revival, Spanish Colonial Revival, and Art Deco styles throughout the base's 350 contributing buildings. Randolph Field became a National Historic Landmark in 2001 and is an active military station. (PTH/North Texas.)

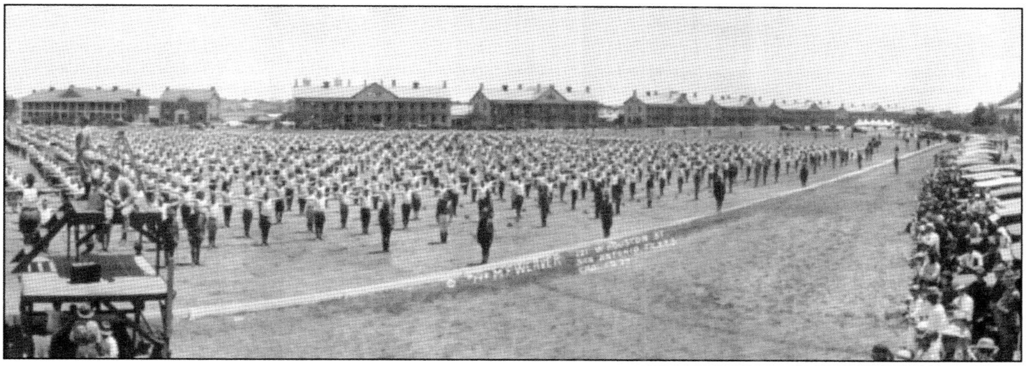

Fort Sam Houston. One of the Army's oldest installations, this post was constructed in 1876. Designated as Fort Sam Houston in 1890, the base continued to expand through the 1930s. With over 800 historic buildings, Fort Sam Houston is the largest collection of historically significant structures in the Department of Defense. National Historic Landmark status was awarded in 1975, and the fort still continues to operate as an active military base. Flag Day preparations take place on the parade grounds of Fort Sam Houston in this 1918 photograph taken by M.F. Weaver. (LOC.)

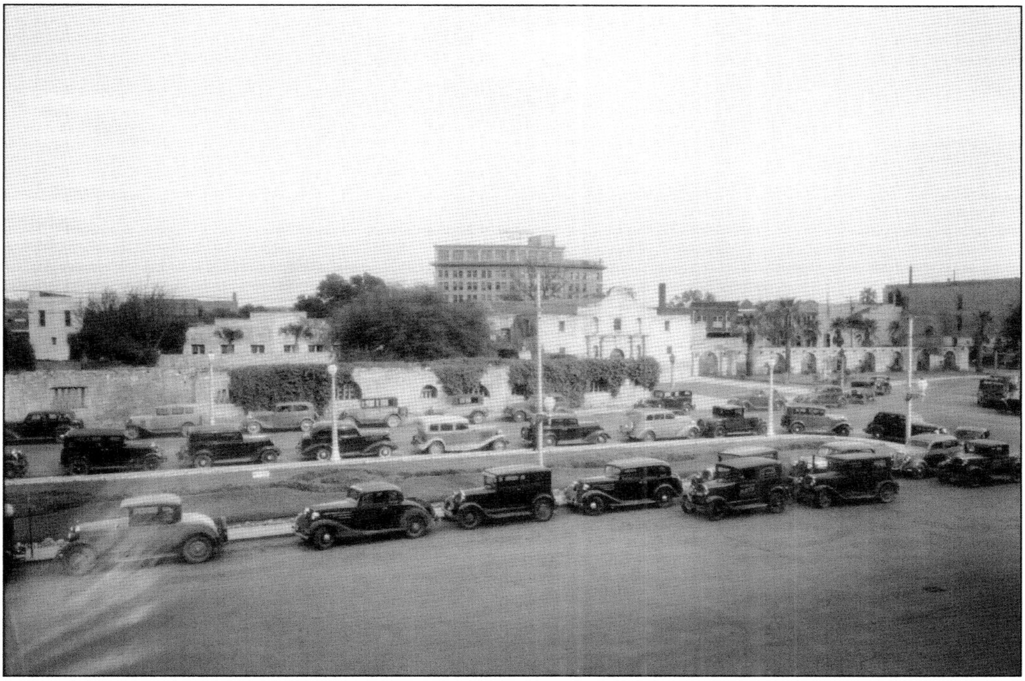

The Alamo in 1936. Alamo Plaza is transformed during the early 20th century, as photographed by Arthur W. Stewart from the balcony of the Crockett Block buildings. One hundred years after the pivotal battle of the Texas Revolution, the Crockett Hotel is visible directly behind the Alamo. National Historic Landmark status for the Alamo was achieved in 1960. (HABS.)

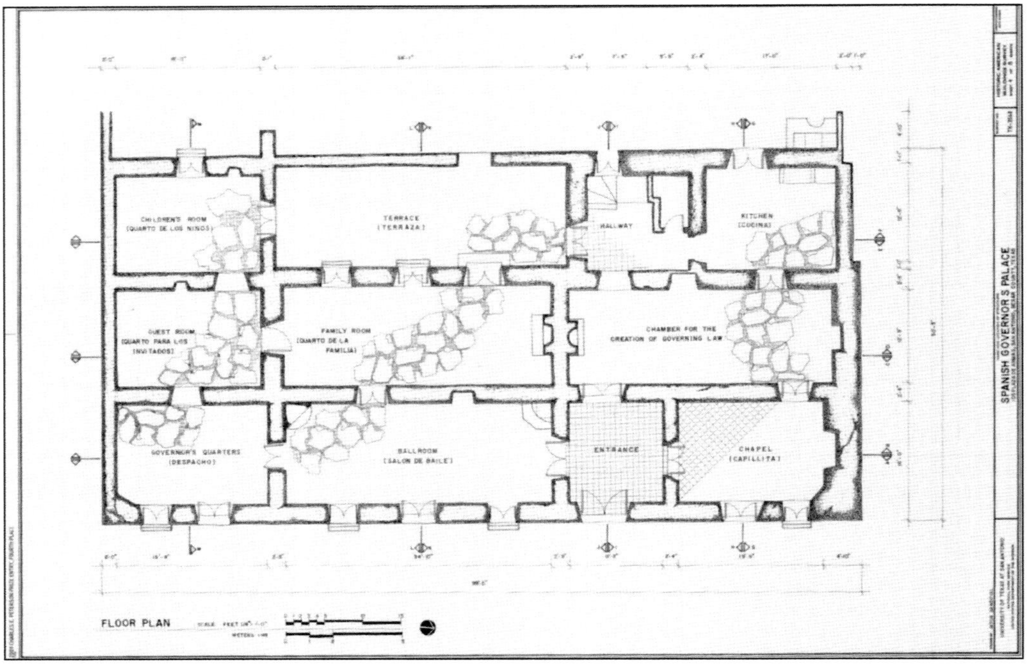

Spanish Governor's Palace. At the center of Military Plaza lies the Presidio San Antonio de Bexar, the remains of the home built by the Spanish governor of Coahuila and Texas. His title was the Marquis de San Miguel de Aguayo, ruling from 1719 to 1722. Renamed by Adina Emilia DeZavala in 1915 during a 15-year preservation campaign, the Spanish Governor's Palace was finally purchased by the City of San Antonio and restored in 1930. Woodwork restoration was competed by local carpenters Johannes Scholze and John Hall. Above is the elaborated floor plan of the 1930s restoration, as drawn by Charles E. Peterson. Below is a view of the fully restored interior of the Spanish Governor's Palace dining quarters, photographed by Carol M. Highsmith. (Both, HABS.)

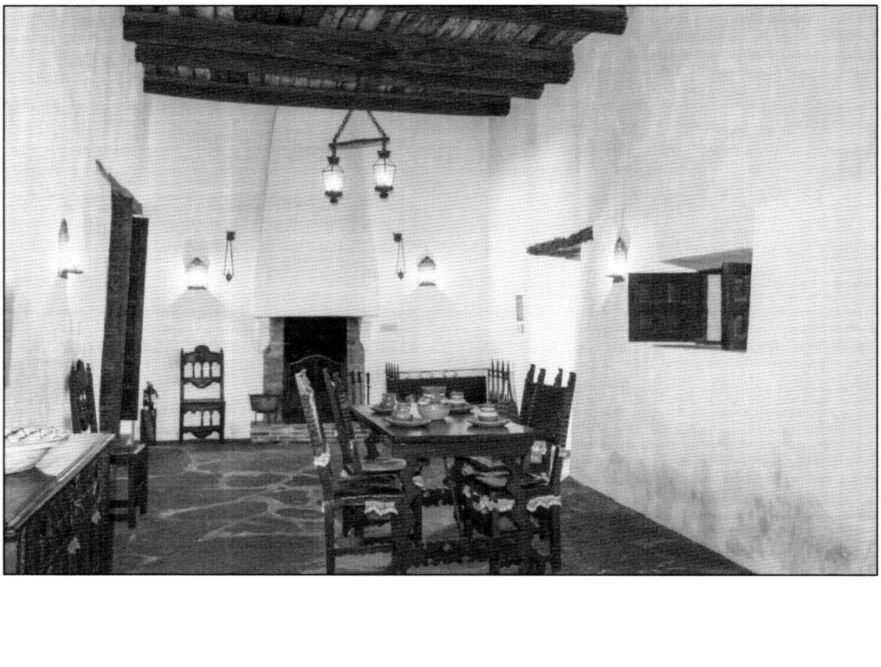

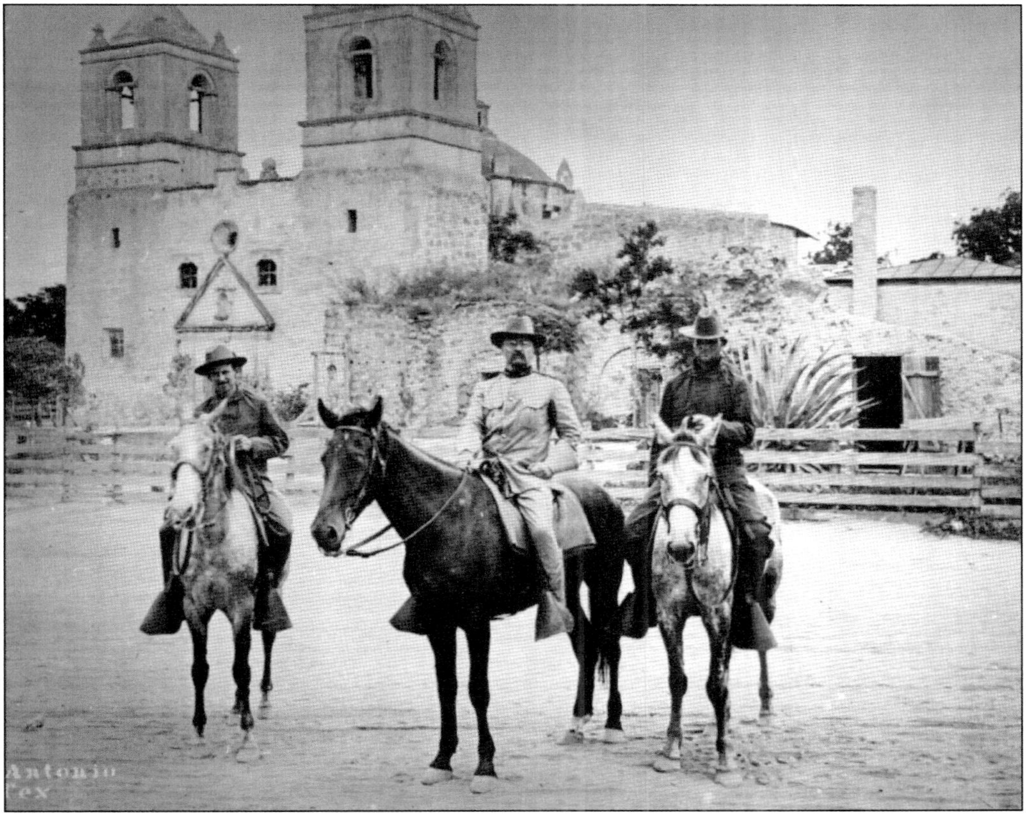

Mission Concepción. Standing as the oldest unrestored stone church in the United States, this mission church was named a National Historic Landmark in 1970. Above, posing with two companions, Theodore Roosevelt (center) is in San Antonio recruiting for the Rough Riders Volunteer Calvary in 1898. The intact roof dome can be seen just behind the bell tower on the right. On the right is the church interior as seen in the mid-20th century. (Above, LOC; right, HABS.)

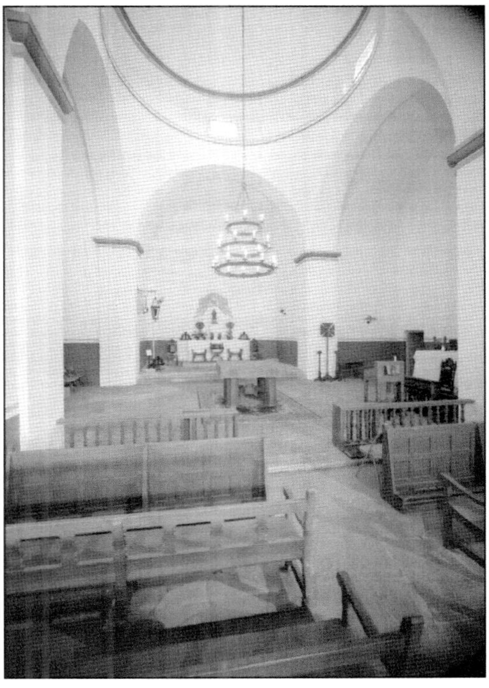

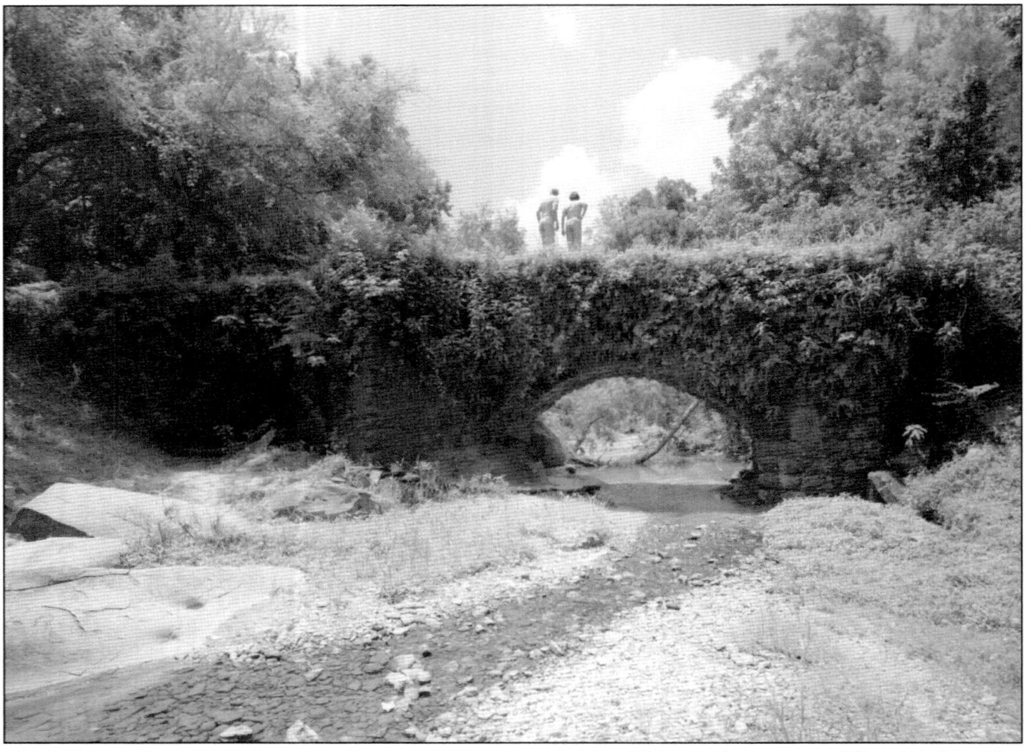

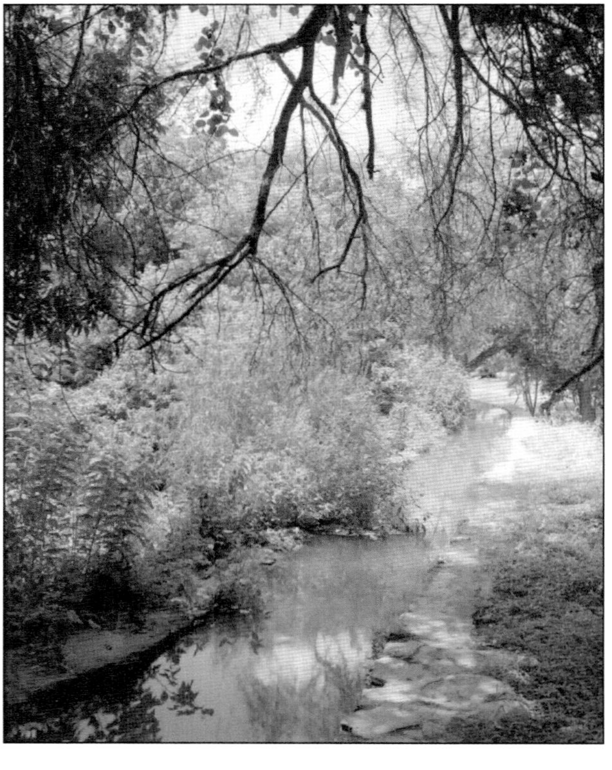

ESPADA AQUEDUCT. The simple arch, constructed of local limestone, forms the span across Piedras Creek. Lying east of Espada Road, the aqueduct utilizes a massive stone support structure. Built in 1731 by Franciscan missionaries, the gravity flow system provided a reliable source of water where rainfall was intermittent; it has continuously run since 1745. A National Historic Landmark since 1964, the Espada Aqueduct is also a Historic Civil Engineering Landmark. Above, a couple examines the aqueduct that is largely obscured by overgrowth sometime during the mid-20th century. At left, a small section of the Espada Aqueduct is shown running through level terrain. (Both, HAER.)

Three

THE NATIONAL TRUST, KING WILLIAM DISTRICT, AND WALTER MATHIS

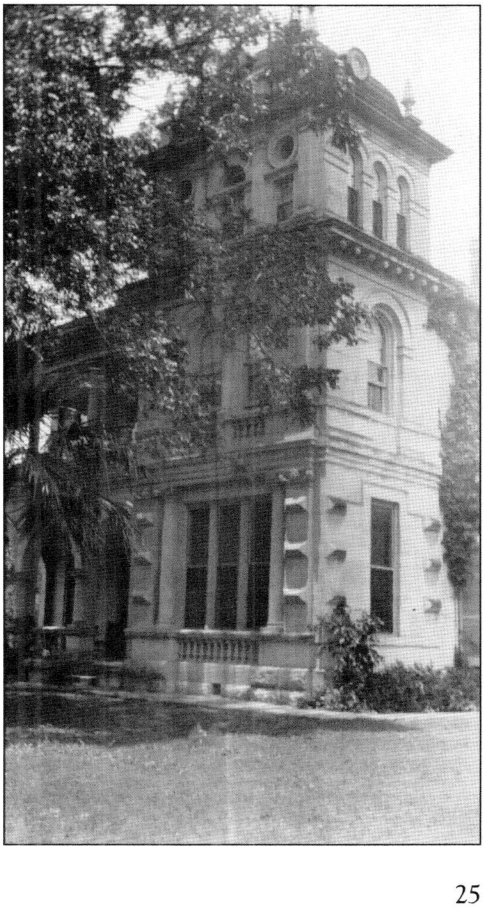

NORTON-POLK-MATHIS HOUSE. Russell C. Norton, a local hardware merchant, built this home at 401 King William Street in 1876. Designed by architect Francis Crider, the original residence was a one-story, four-room structure built of locally quarried limestone. The second level was added in 1879, but the extensive changes came after the home was sold in 1882. The Italianate-style tower addition and other improvements were completed during cattleman Edwin Polk's ownership during the 1890s. (VFMG.)

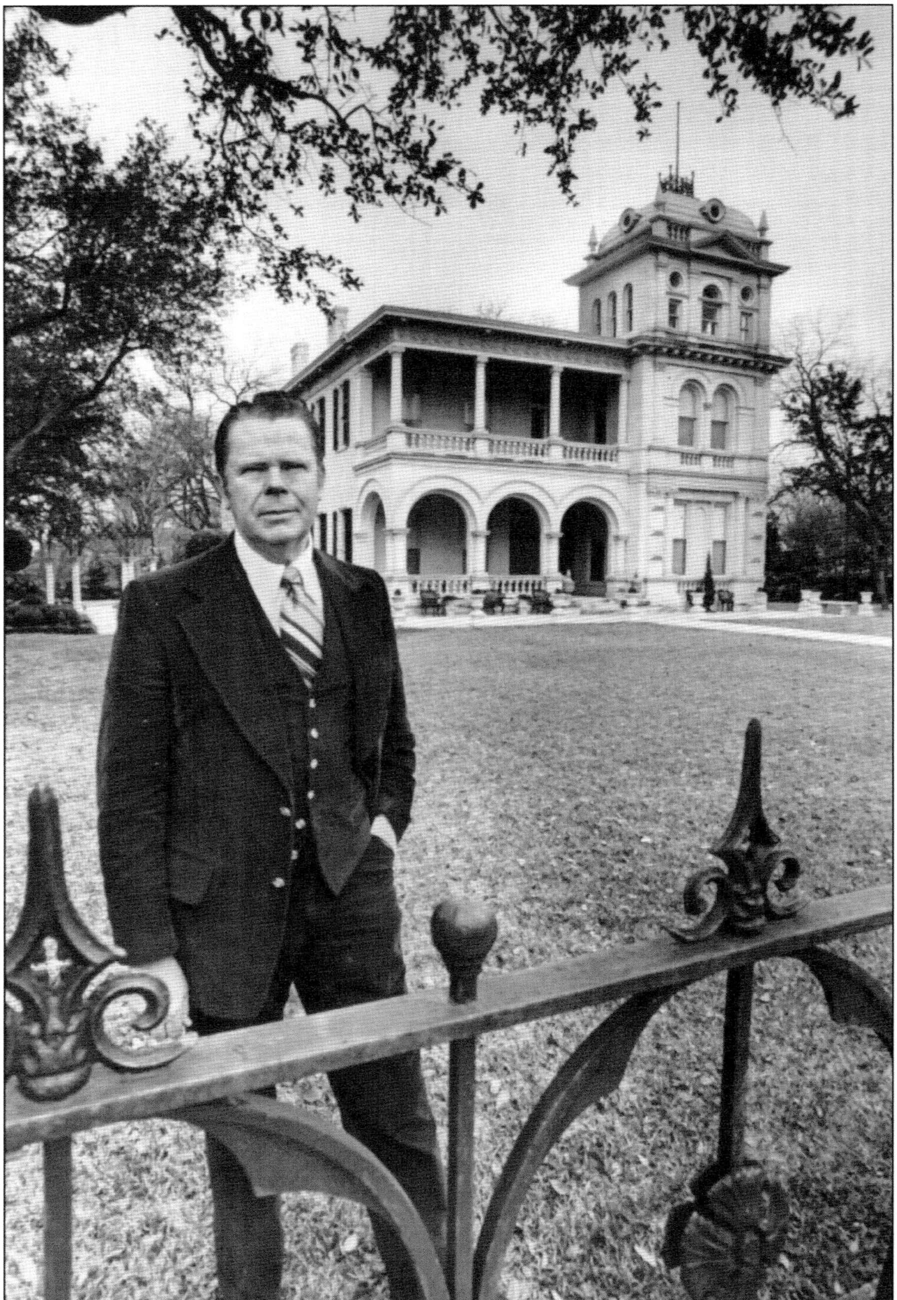

VILLA FINALE. Walter Mathis stands proudly before his final home on King William Street. Mathis was convinced by architect and friend O'Neil Ford to purchase the property in 1967 from James and Irene Campbell. This restoration project compelled Mathis to acquire 14 properties while residing in the King William area to encourage historic preservation among homeowners and neighbors. He then donated Villa Finale, with its entire fine art collection and furnishings, to the National Trust for Historic Preservation in 2004. (VFMG.)

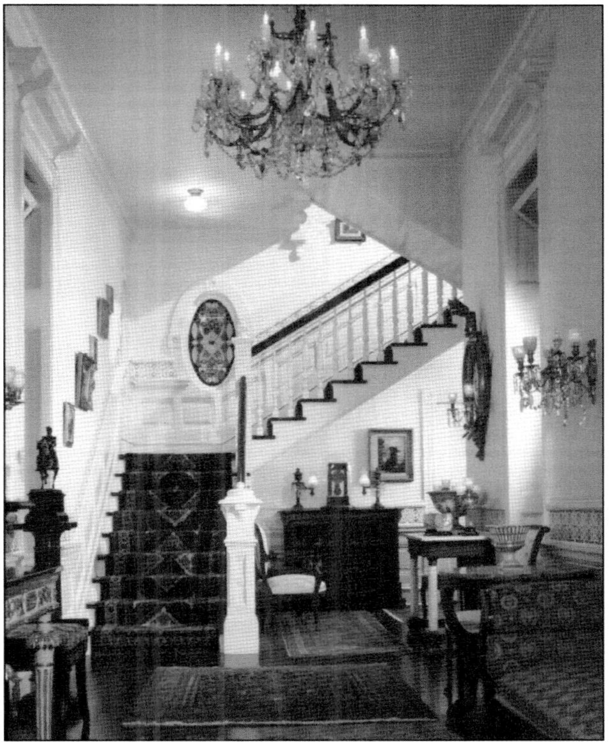

VILLA FINALE ENTRANCE HALL. The entrance hall of the home, which was divided into multi-residential apartments during the post–World War II era, is seen here meticulously restored under the direction of Walter Mathis and the guidance of architect O'Neil Ford. Temporarily living at the Plaza Hotel and utilizing a makeshift apartment in an upstairs chamber of the home during construction, Mathis took a year and a half to accomplish the restoration, with carpenter Basilio Gonzalez as the crew master. (VFMG.)

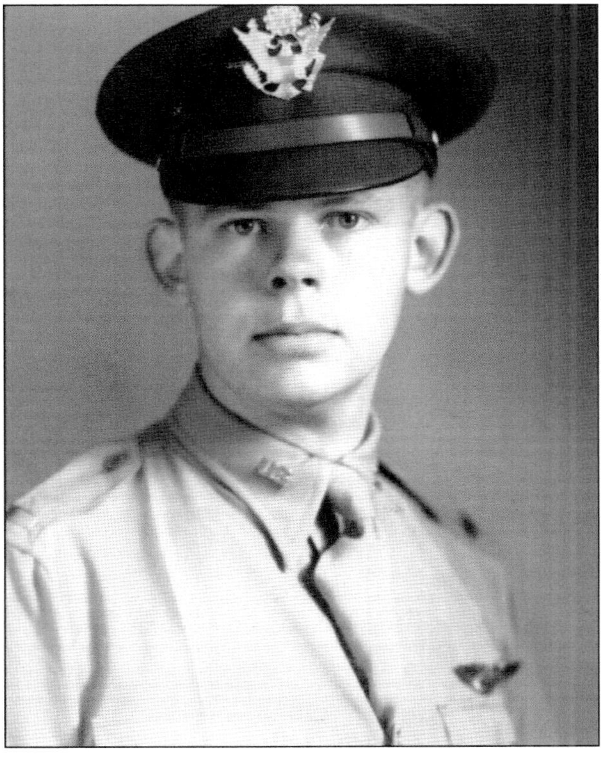

WALTER NOLD MATHIS. Born the youngest of four children to Arthur Mathis and Mary Jane Nold, Walter Nold Mathis was a graduate of Jefferson High School in San Antonio. He later served as a captain in the US Army Air Forces during World War II as a Pathfinder Squadron pilot over Europe. Of the 27 pilots chosen for their final missions over Germany, Mathis was one of only three that returned. Receiving an Air Medal for meritorious achievement, Mathis was also a three-time recipient of the Distinguished Flying Cross. (VFMG.)

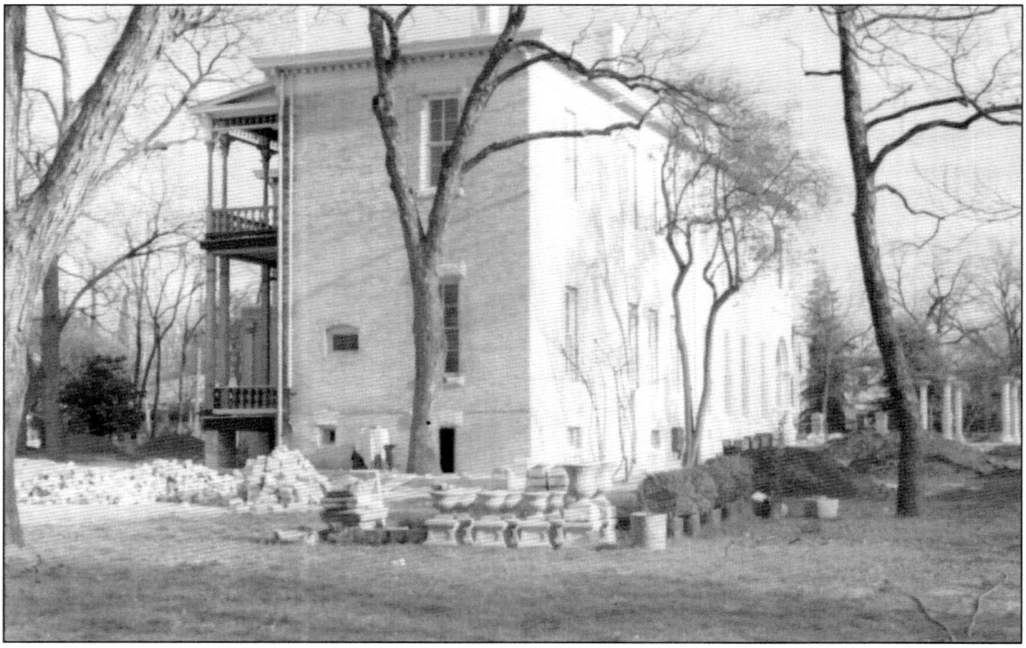

Preparing the Villa Finale Garden. Stacks of bricks and stone pavers await placement on the Villa Finale grounds. To the right, the base of the gazebo has been installed but is still under construction. Concrete planters, trees, and shrubs will complete the formal garden designed by Walter Mathis. The design was inspired by early 19th-century patterned gardens, the Mathis family home in Rockport, and other historic homes in Texas. (VFMG.)

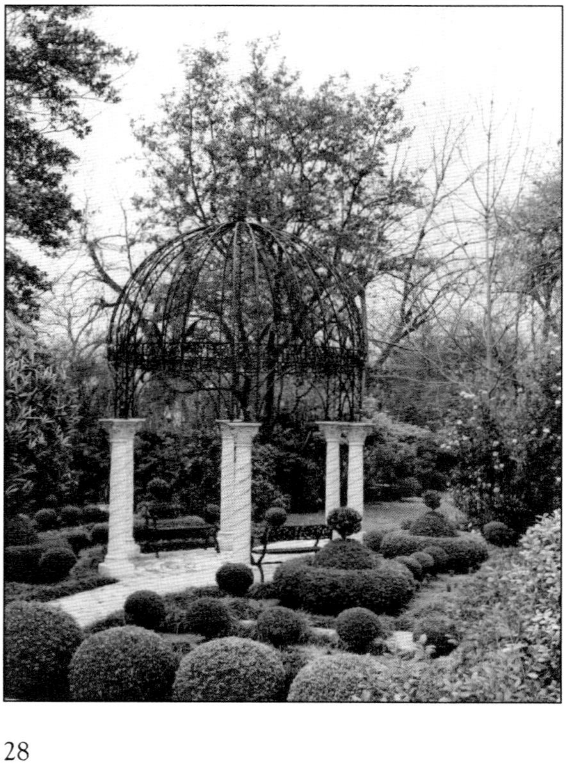

Villa Finale Garden Gazebo. The decorative columns at the base of the gazebo were preserved from Walter Mathis's former home in Monte Vista, which was demolished for highway construction near East Mulberry Street and Stadium Drive. The iron dome was added a few years later, finally completing the garden by the mid-1980s. (VFMG.)

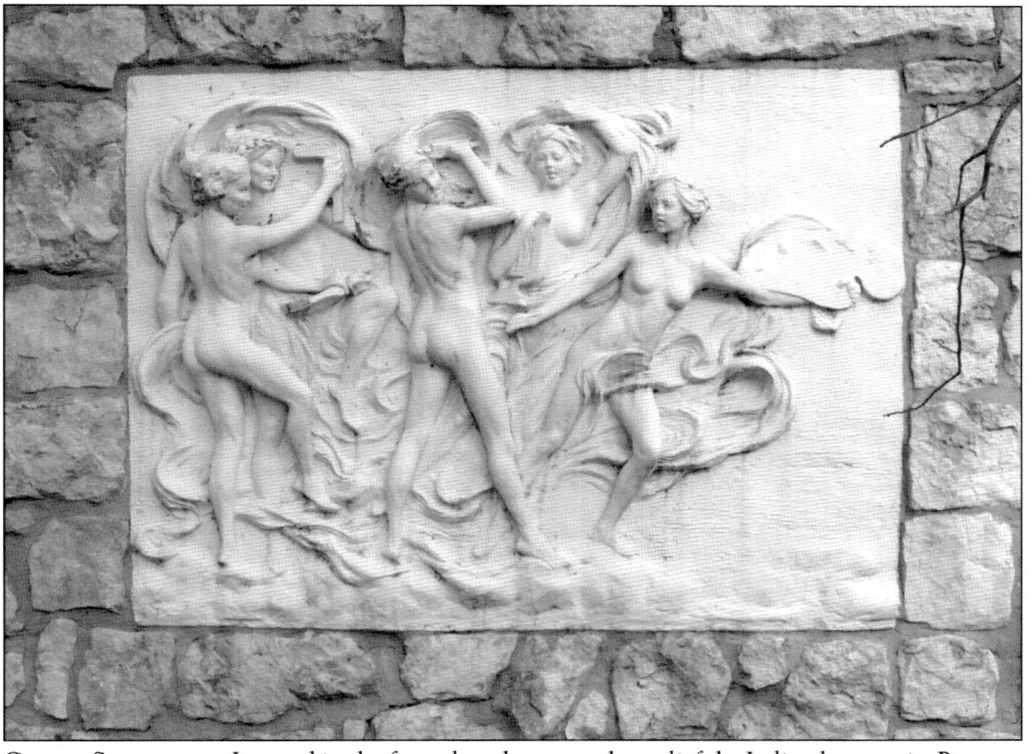

COPPINI SCULPTURES. Located in the formal garden, stone bas-reliefs by Italian-born artist Pompeo Coppini portray the *Triumph of the Arts*. Coppini's work can be found locally and throughout Texas, including the *Spirit of Sacrifice* cenotaph in Alamo Plaza. (HABS.)

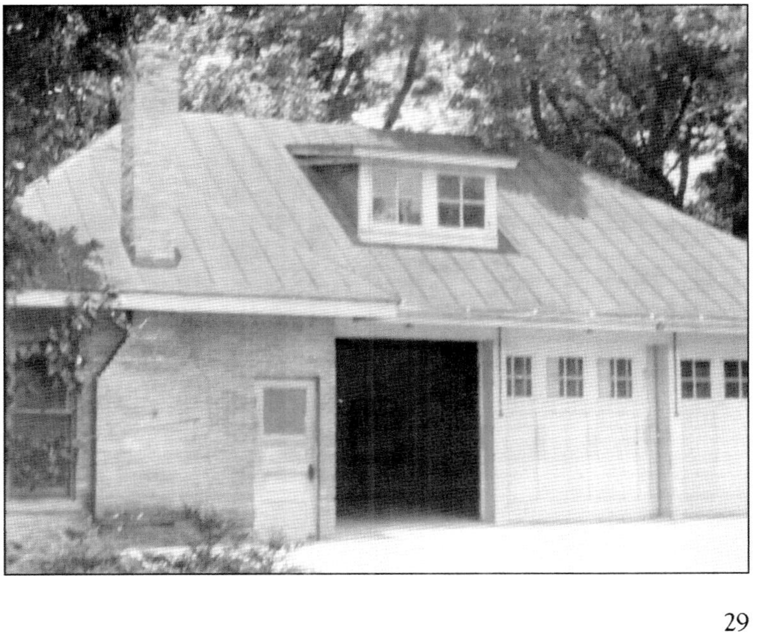

CARRIAGE HOUSE. At the rear of the property, the brick carriage house is adjacent to the San Antonio River at the end of East Sheridan Street. The outbuilding was utilized as an apartment prior to Walter Mathis's ownership, and is equipped with a kitchen, bathroom, and upstairs chamber. (VFMG.)

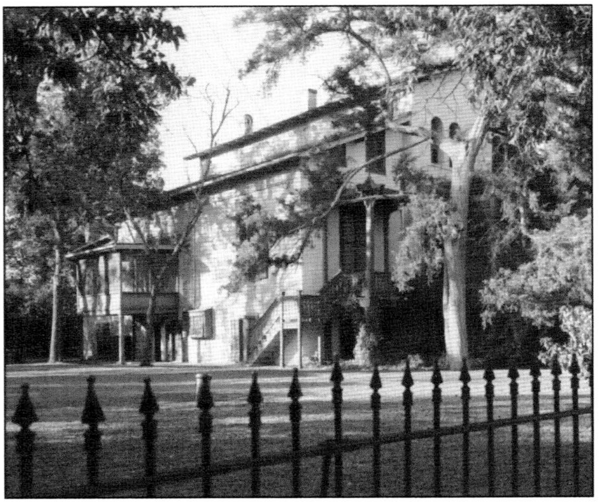

Wulff House. Situated at 107 King William Street, the limestone residence was built by Anton Wulff. A German immigrant and the first commissioner for city parks, Wulff was a prominent local merchant who settled in San Antonio in the mid-19th century. In 1974, the San Antonio Conservation Society purchased the home, receiving federal and private funding to restore the structure with the cooperative fundraising efforts of Walter Mathis. The property also includes the Stuemke Barn, relocated by master stonemason Curtis Hunt in 1982. (HABS.)

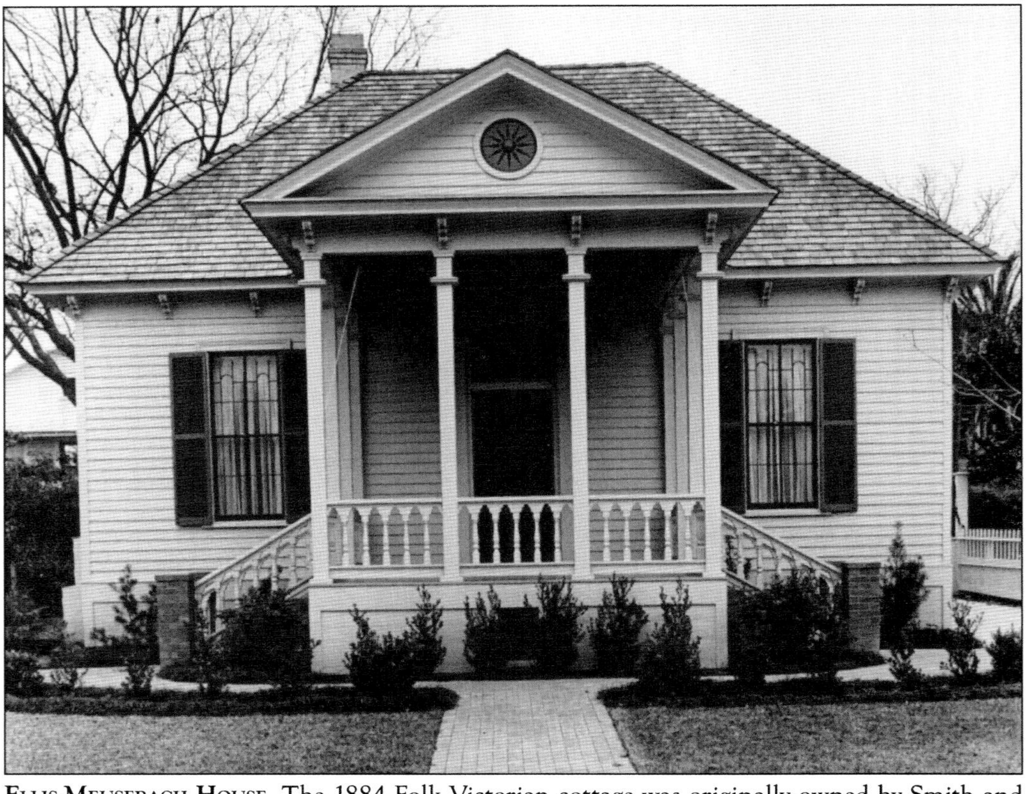

Ellis-Meusebach House. The 1884 Folk Victorian cottage was originally owned by Smith and Josie Ellis. Purchased by Otto Meusebach in 1889, the cottage was home to his family until 1902. Walter Mathis acquired the cottage at 414 King William Street for restoration and donated it to the National Trust for Historic Preservation in 2004 as part of the Villa Finale estate. (VFMG.)

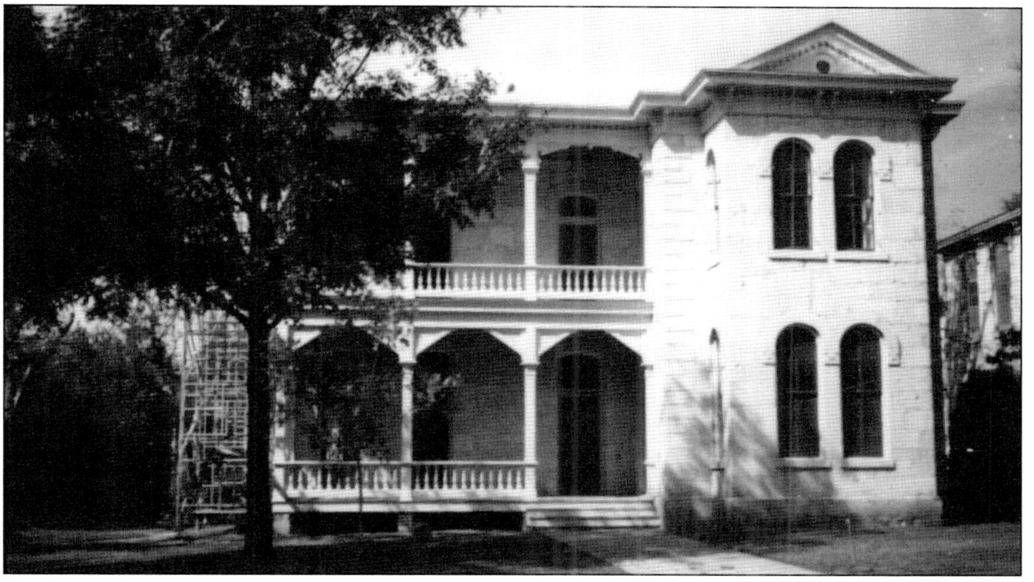

HUMMEL HOUSE. The Italianate limestone house constructed in 1884 was commissioned by local gunsmith Charles Hummel. Designed by local architects James Wahrenberger and Albert Beckman, the home became the preservation undertaking of Walter Mathis, and it was divided into five apartments prior to his purchase. Scaffolding can be seen on the south facade in this snapshot taken during exterior restorative work. (VFMG.)

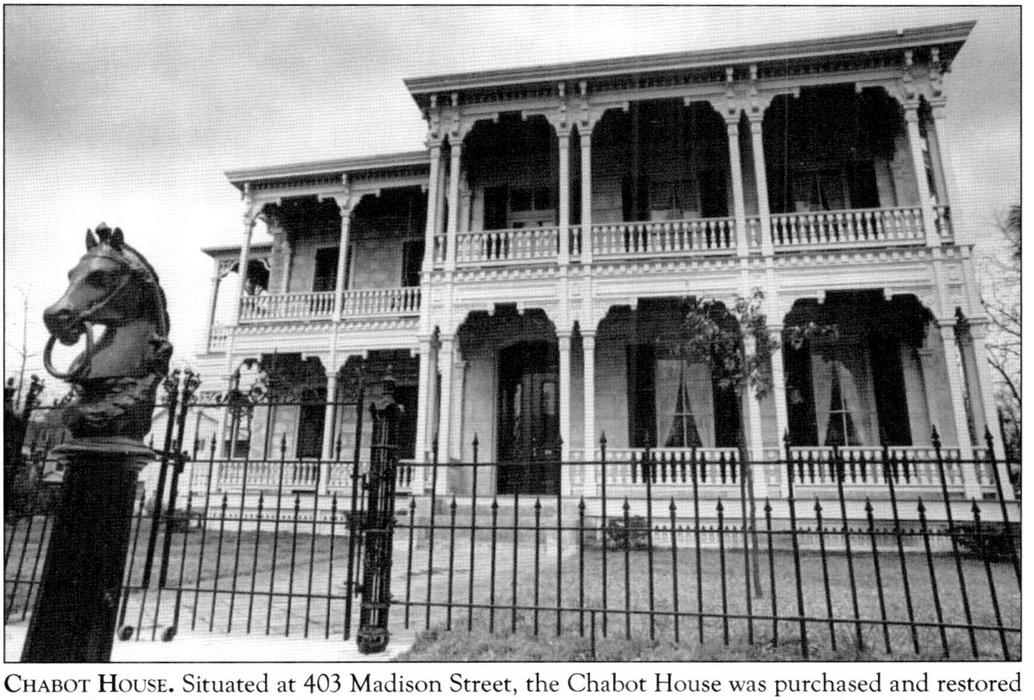

CHABOT HOUSE. Situated at 403 Madison Street, the Chabot House was purchased and restored in 1976 by Walter Mathis, who gave attentiveness to original architectural details. Built 100 years earlier by George S. Chabot and his wife, Mary Van Derlip, the stone structure has extensive exterior woodwork along the two-story, full-facade galleries. (VFMG.)

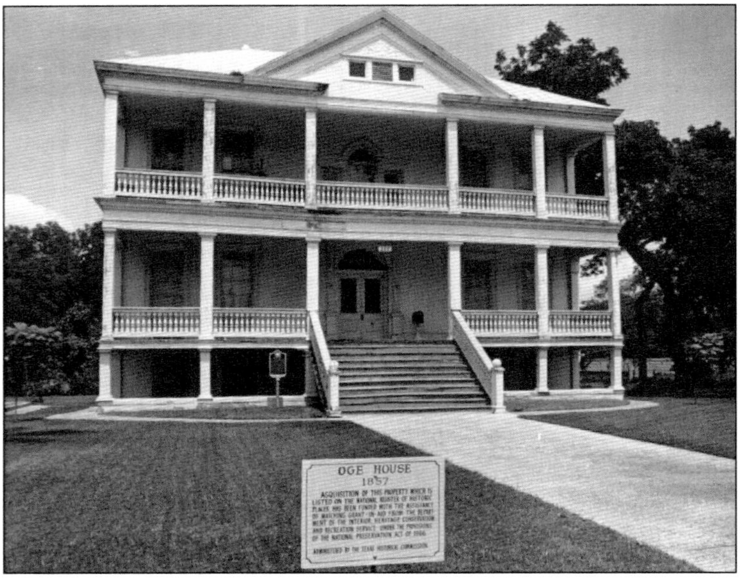

Oge House. Redesigned by architect Alfred Giles in the 1880s for Louis Oge, this home was originally built in 1857 by attorney Newton Mitchell and wife, Catherine Elder, as a one-story cottage with a basement. Mitchell was a Texas Ranger, successful rancher, and business leader. The home was recorded as a Texas Historic Landmark in 1971; the project was spearheaded by Walter Mathis. (VFMG.)

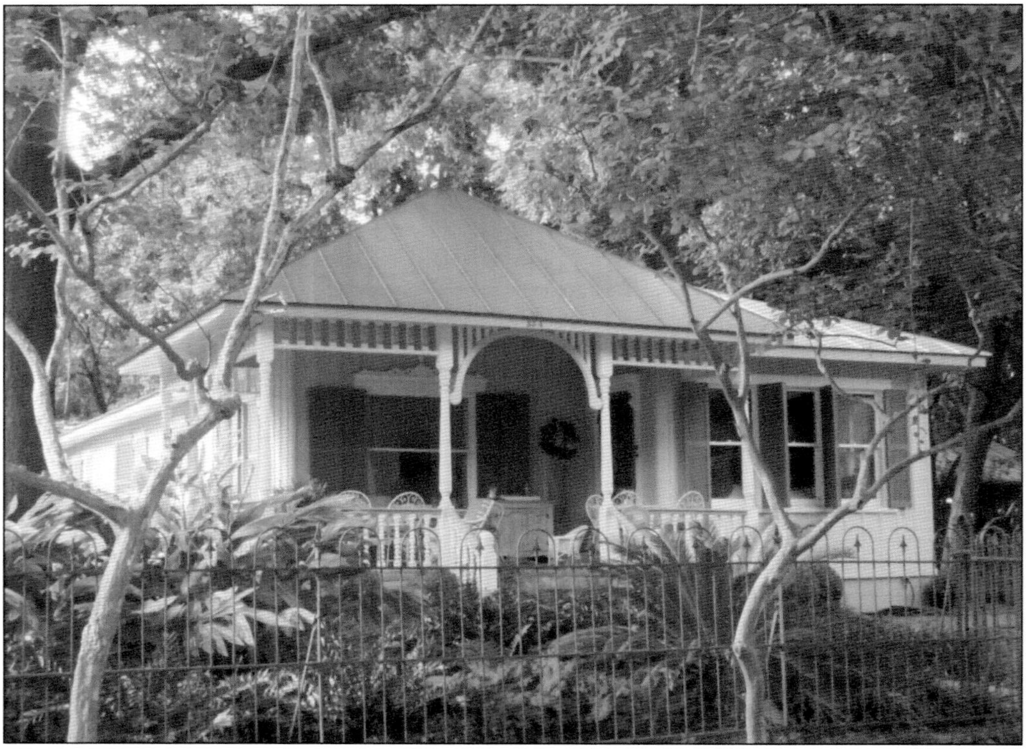

La Trinidad Parsonage. The cottage built in 1921 utilized reclaimed building materials from an 1886 church. Originally located at the intersection of what are today San Fernando and South Pecos Streets, the parsonage was relocated to 334 King William Street in 1950. La Trinidad Templo Methodista Mexicano Church continued to use the parsonage until 1975, when it was sold to Walter Mathis. After a renovation, new owners purchased the home the following year. (SAPA.)

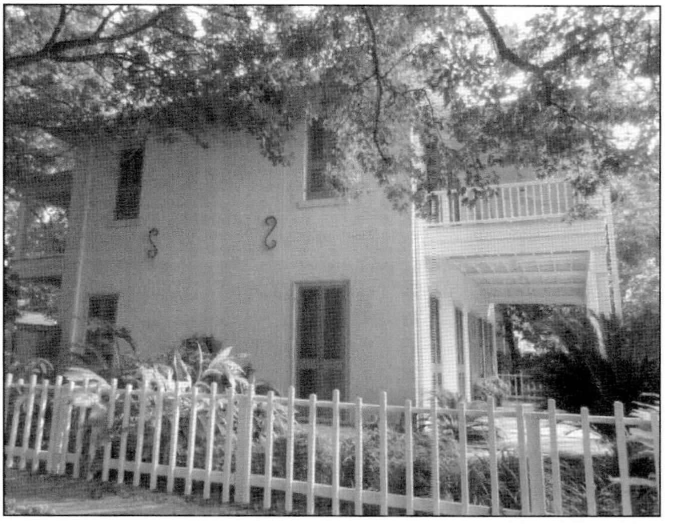

VAN DERLIP HOUSE. The former home of Juliana Van Derlip is located at 337 Madison Street. Widow of local attorney David Van Derlip, Juliana purchased the one-story stone residence from J.D. and Carrie B. Martin in 1875. Built around 1871, the home was expanded in 1890, similar to the original vernacular style, creating the second-level living spaces and front and rear open porches. Purchased by Walter Mathis, the residence was a preservation project in the 1980s. (SAPA.)

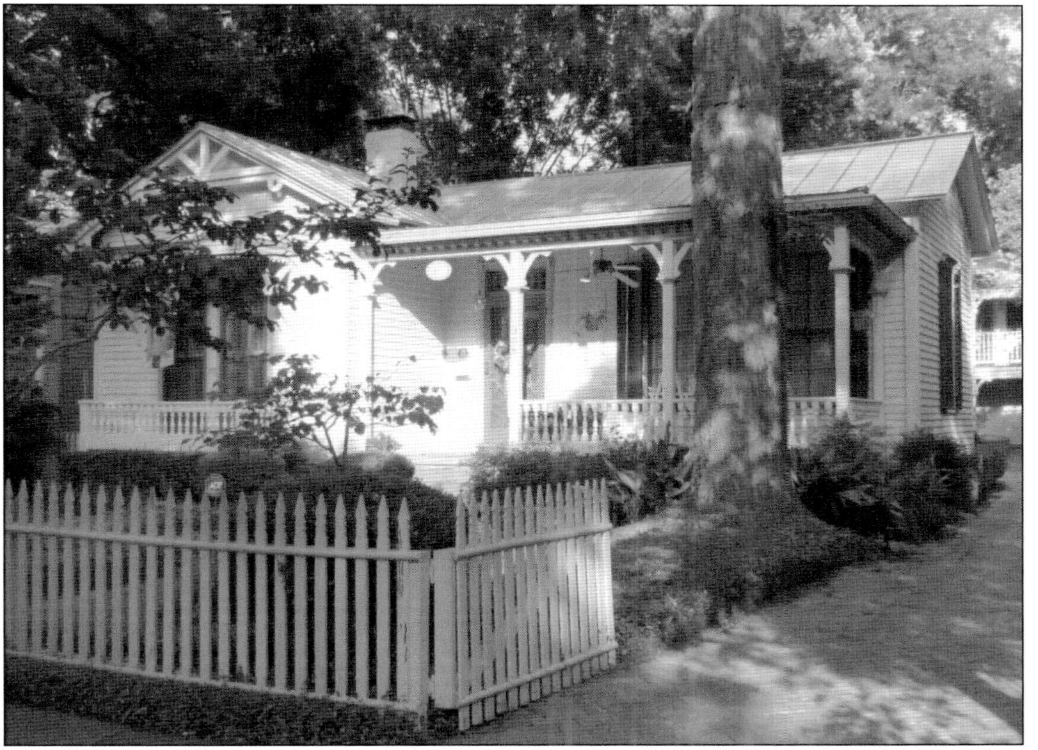

ALFRED GILES HOUSE. British architect Alfred Giles moved to San Antonio from New York City in the 1870s. Giles became a prominent architect in San Antonio, and his finest residential examples include the Groos House and the Steves Homestead, both located on King William Street. The 1883 Folk Victorian cottage was designed by Giles for his young family. After he purchased it from Roma Hafermann in 1988, Walter Mathis took on the residence as another preservation project. (SAPA.)

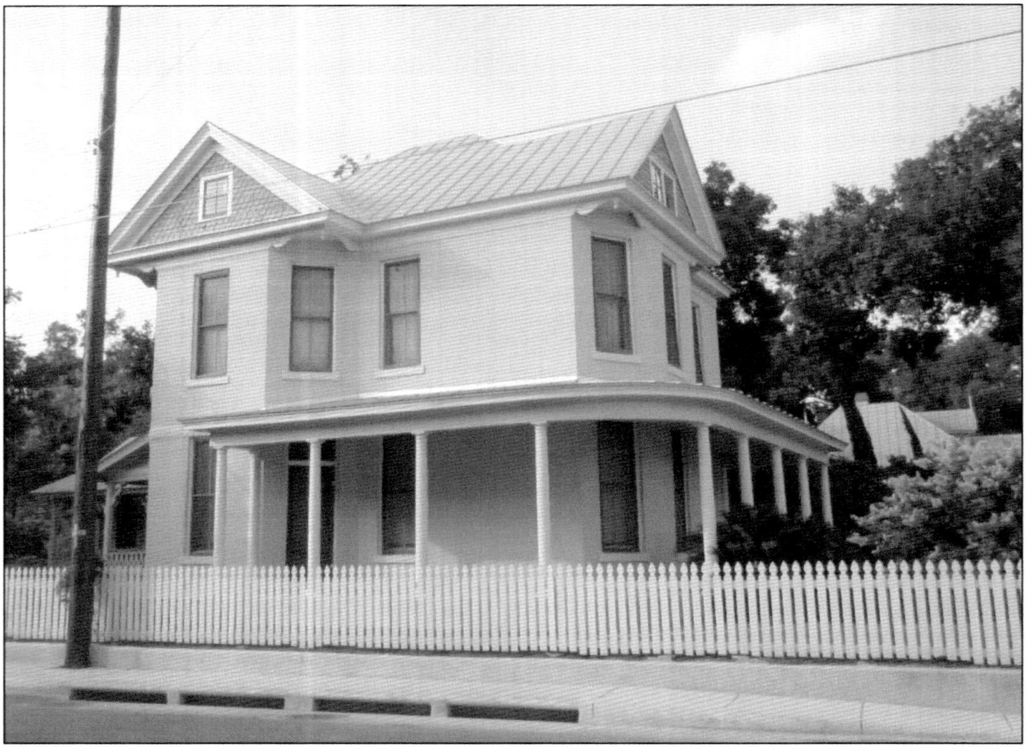

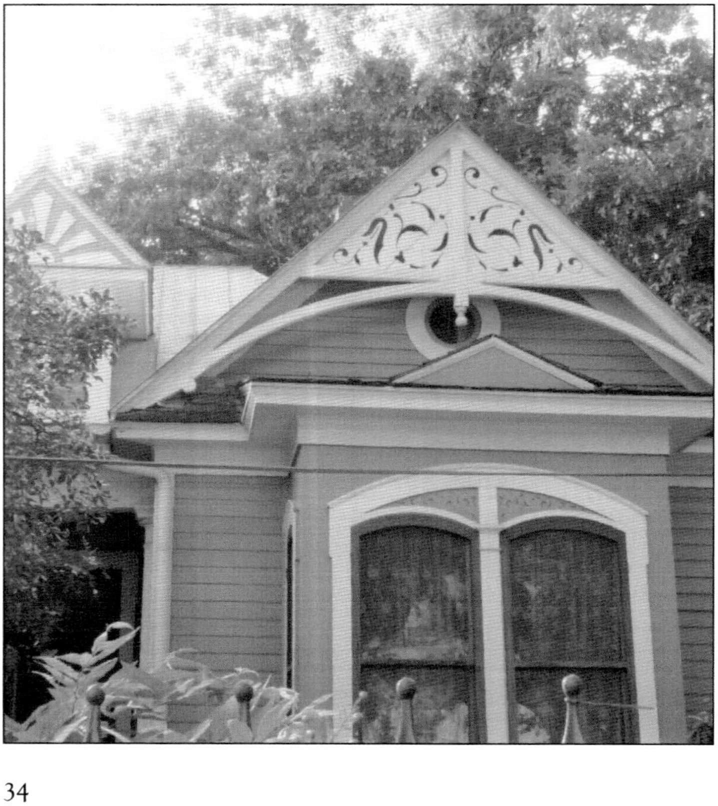

S.M. Martin House and Bertrand-Lawson Cottage. Both residences were candidates in the preservation campaign of Walter Mathis. Constructed in 1889 at the corner of Guenther and South Alamo Streets, the two-story brick home above belonged to the wife of S.M. Martin. The Bertrand-Lawson Cottage, left, was constructed in 1905 for Charles H. Bertrand and Annie Oge Bertrand. Harry and Eva Lawson purchased the home in 1925 from Annie's sister, Josephine Oge Flannery, and lived there for 42 years. (Both, SAPA.)

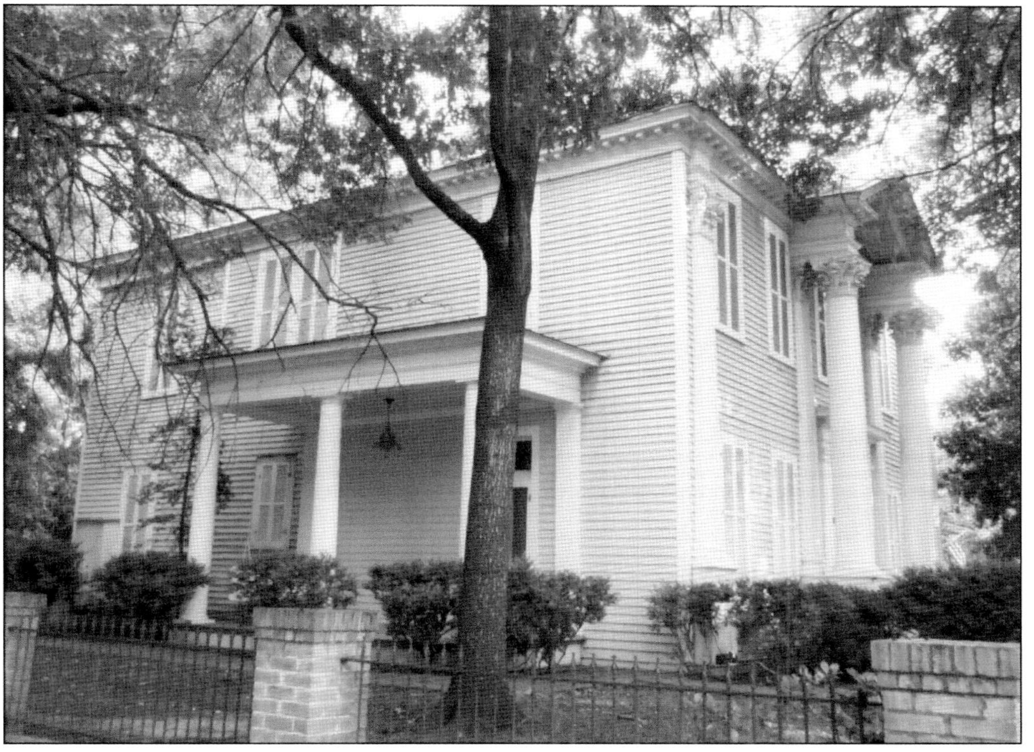

Pancoast House and Cottage. The home of Josiah and Sally Pancoast was originally built in 1878, and was expanded to two stories in 1886. Surviving today as an independent residence, the cottage was constructed on the same property in 1900. Across the street from Villa Finale, both the cottage and main residence were restored by Walter Mathis. Above is the northwest elevation of the Pancoast House as seen from Sheridan Street. Below is the Pancoast Cottage, photographed by W.G. Goodspeed sometime after completion of the restoration. (Above, SAPA; below, VFMG.)

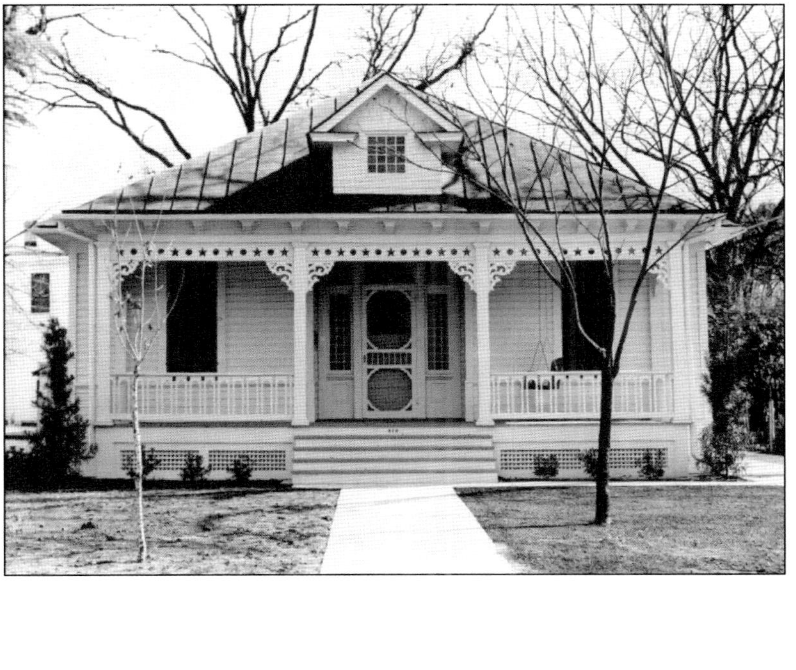

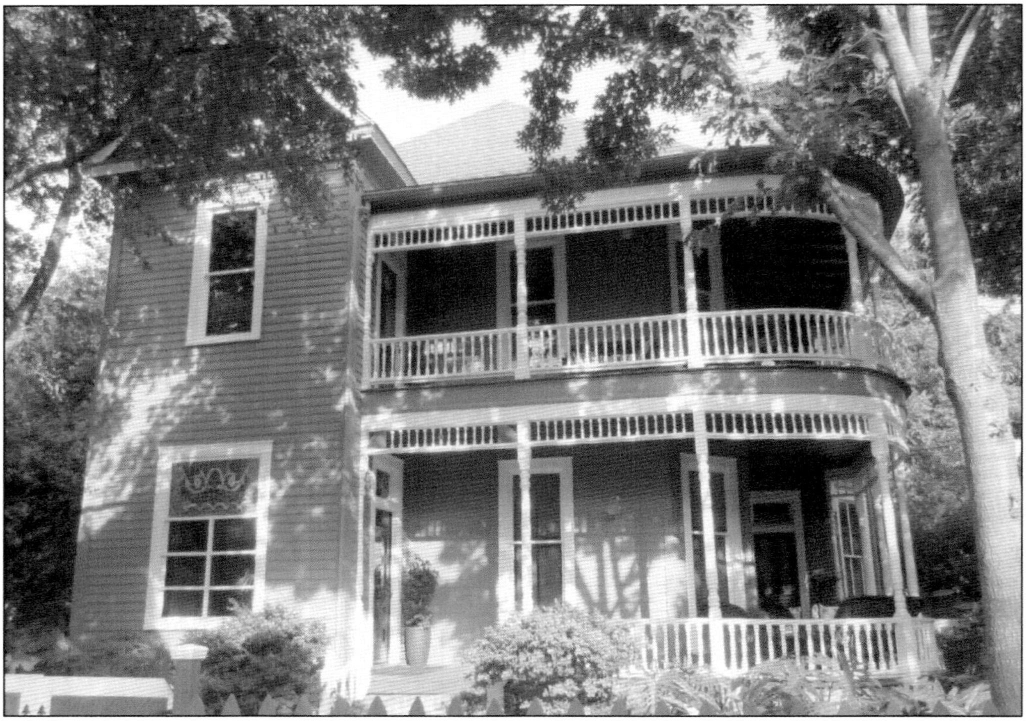

KALTEYER HOUSE. The wood-frame home of William and Olga Kalteyer was originally constructed in 1895 facing South Alamo Street. The two-story residence features a full double-deck gallery, more commonly found on Texas Queen Anne homes and those in the Gulf Coast states. Interestingly, the home was picked up and turned around to face Madison Street during restoration efforts by Walter Mathis in the 1970s. (SAPA.)

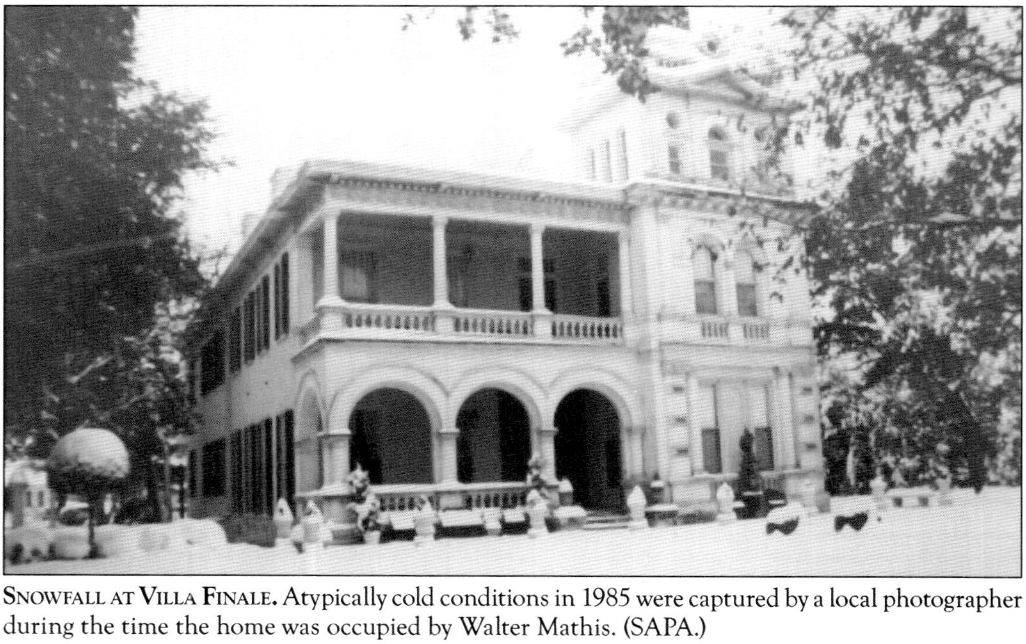

SNOWFALL AT VILLA FINALE. Atypically cold conditions in 1985 were captured by a local photographer during the time the home was occupied by Walter Mathis. (SAPA.)

Four

HOUSE MUSEUMS AND HISTORIC RESTAURANTS

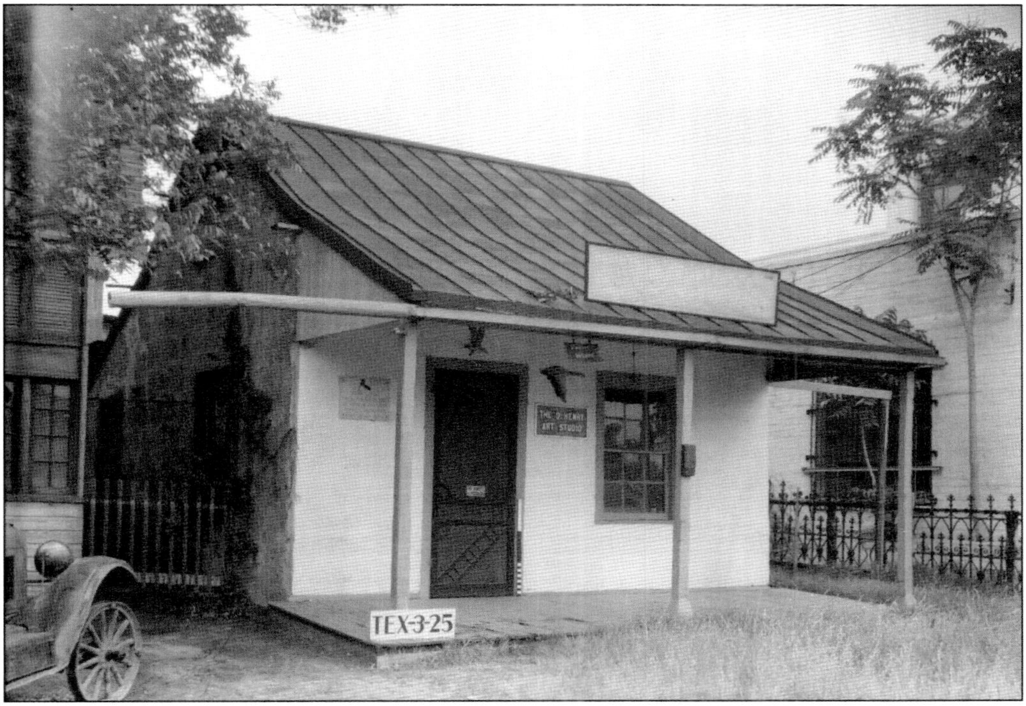

O. HENRY HOUSE. American author William Sidney Porter lived in the home during the late 1890s, issuing a weekly newspaper while residing in San Antonio under the pseudonym O. Henry. The two-room residence, built by John Kush around 1855, originally stood on South Presa Street. Moved to the Lone Star Brewery grounds in 1960, the small residence was relocated again in the late 1990s to 601 Dolorosa Street, where it sits today as a museum. (HABS.)

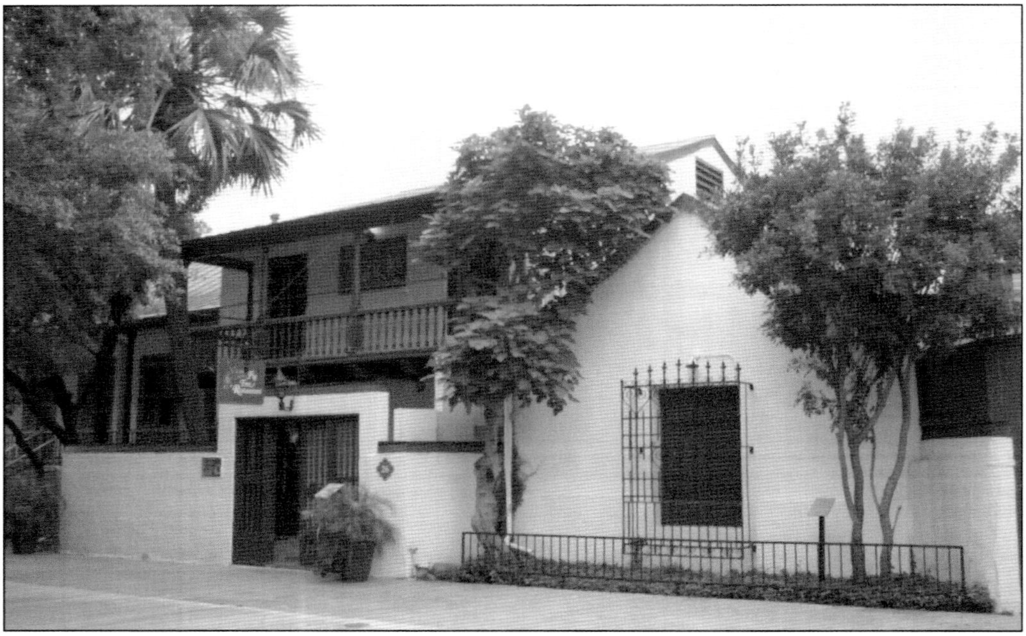

Gray-Guilbeau House. Constructed by James Gray in the mid-19th century, the adobe home was sold to French consul Francois Guilbeau in 1853. Located in La Villita Historic Arts Village, one of the oldest neighborhoods in San Antonio, the structure has operated as the Fig Tree Restaurant since 1971. (SAPA.)

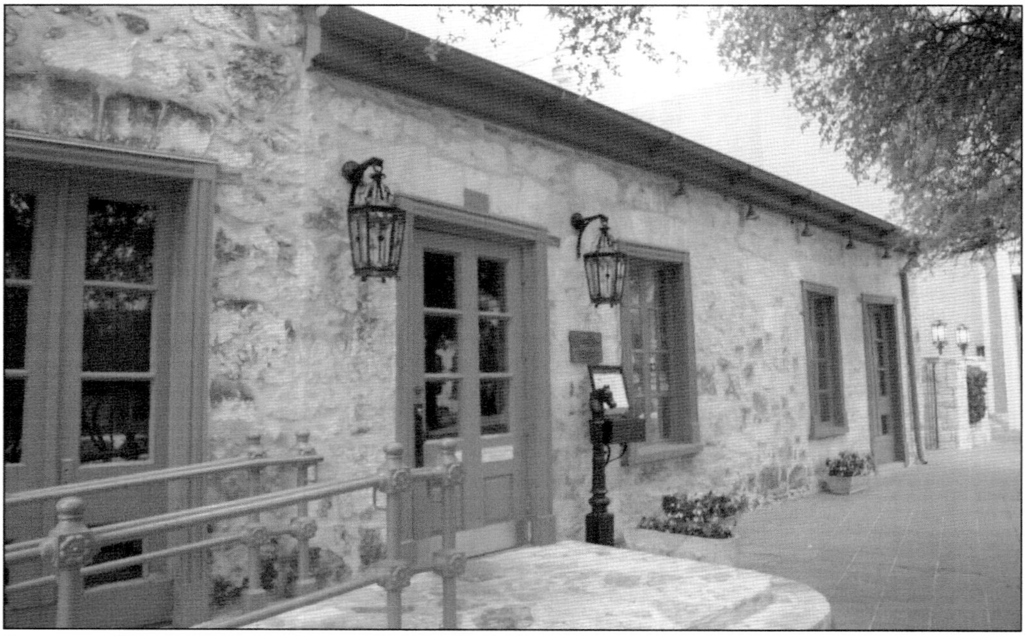

Bombach House. Carpenter Otto Bombach built the two-story limestone residence and store around 1850. The San Antonio Conservation Society purchased the property in 1950 and discovered a basement during restoration. Located in La Villita Historic Arts Village, the structure has operated as the Little Rhein Steak House since 1967. (SAPA.)

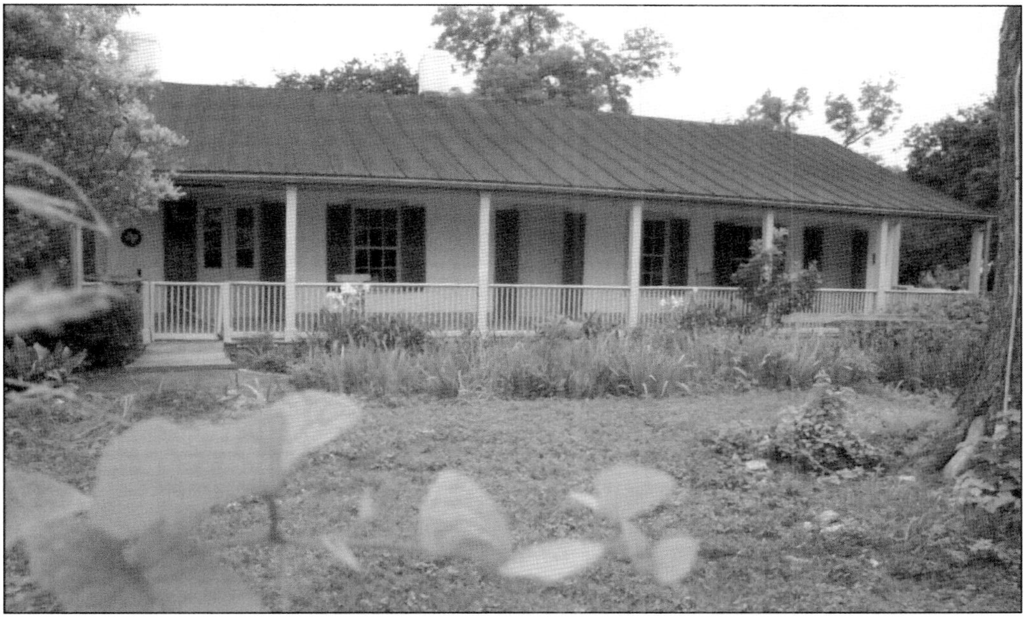

YTURRI-EDMUNDS HISTORIC SITE. Home to several historic structures, the property has been owned by the San Antonio Conservation Society since 1961. Pictured above, the Yturri-Edmunds House Museum was built around 1850 and is constructed of adobe bricks. The property was a land grant to Manuel Yturri Castillo from the Mexican government in 1824. Largely a reconstruction, the mill below features stone steps and an adobe brick wall—all that remain from the original structure. Reconstruction work in 1972 was overseen by millwright A.A. Kozielski and millstone craftsman R. Borrego Jr. The 1881 Oge Carriage House and the Postert House, built around 1855, also moved on-site. (Both, SAPA.)

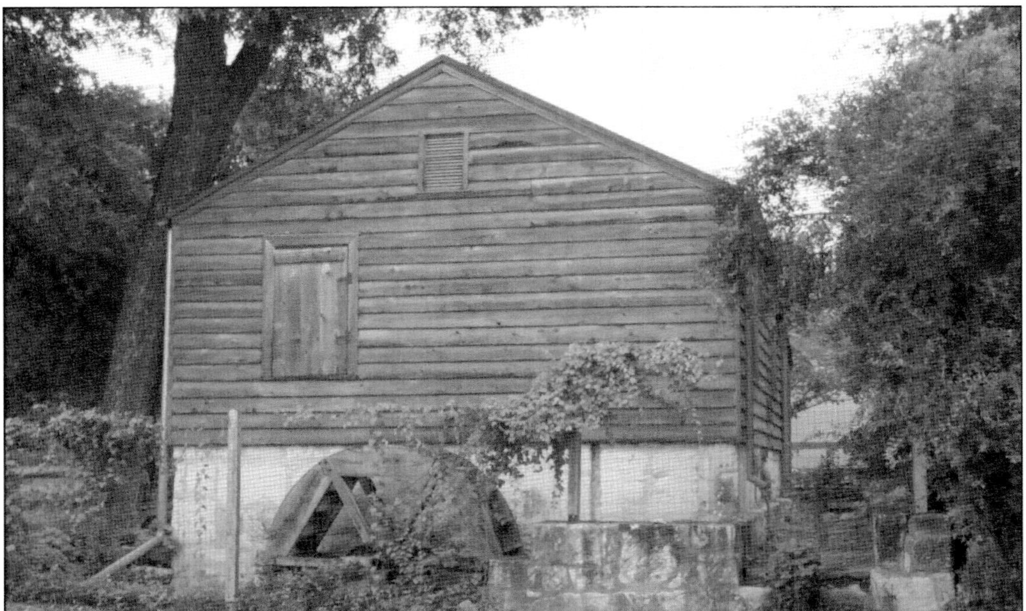

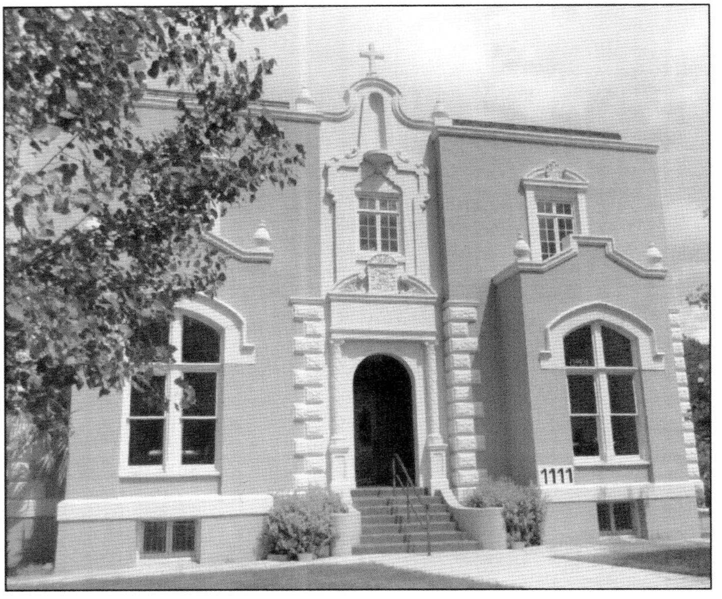

St. Scholastica Convent. Founded in the early 1900s by the Benedictine Sisters, relocating from Cuba, this convent mainly focused on elderly care in the King William neighborhood. Constructed in 1939, the convent served as the motherhouse for the sisters and continued at this location until the Bendictines sold the property in 1985. The former convent is now home to the well-established Liberty Bar. (SAPA.)

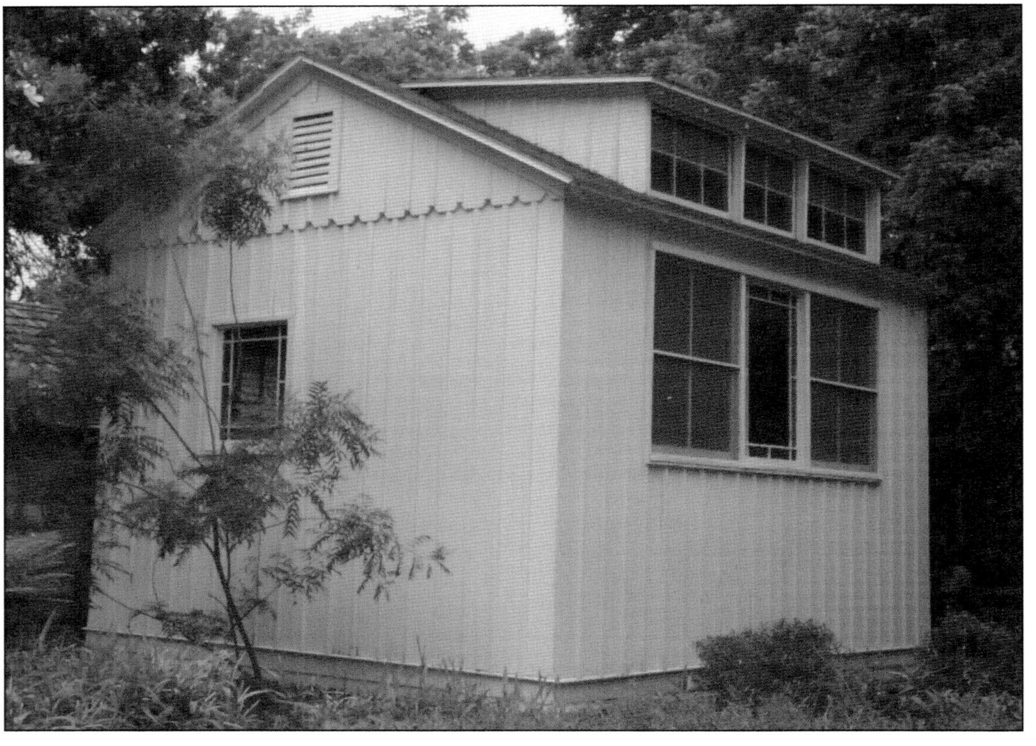

Onderdonk Studio. Gifted to the Witte Museum by the Onderdonk family, the studio of Texas landscape artist Julian Onderdonk was originally constructed at 128 West French Place in the Monte Vista neighborhood in 1915. The board-and-batten structure utilizes large north-facing windows and has basic shed-style roof dormers to facilitate proper lighting for the artist and his students. Onderdonk's sister, Eleanor, was the first curator of art for the Witte Museum collection. (SAPA.)

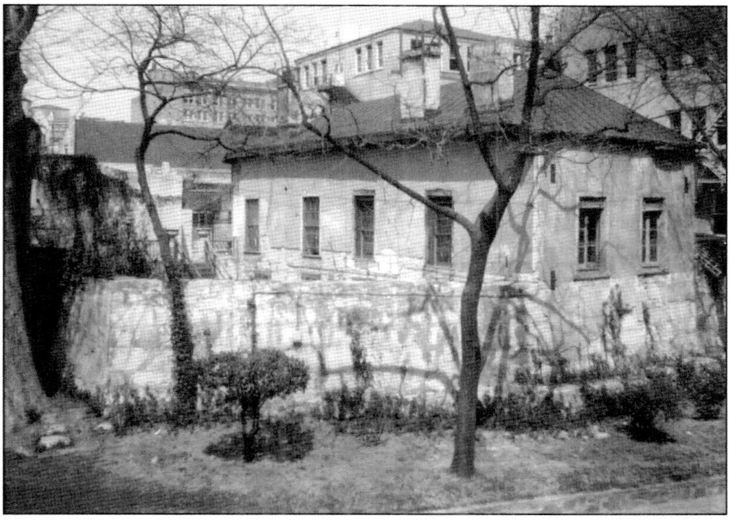

Twohig House. Irish immigrant John Twohig was a local merchant, banker, and Texas patriot. His downtown home, along the San Antonio River, was originally located at St. Mary's and Commerce Streets. When acquired by the City Public Service Company in 1941, the two-story limestone structure, built in the 1840s, was moved the Witte Museum grounds. (HABS.)

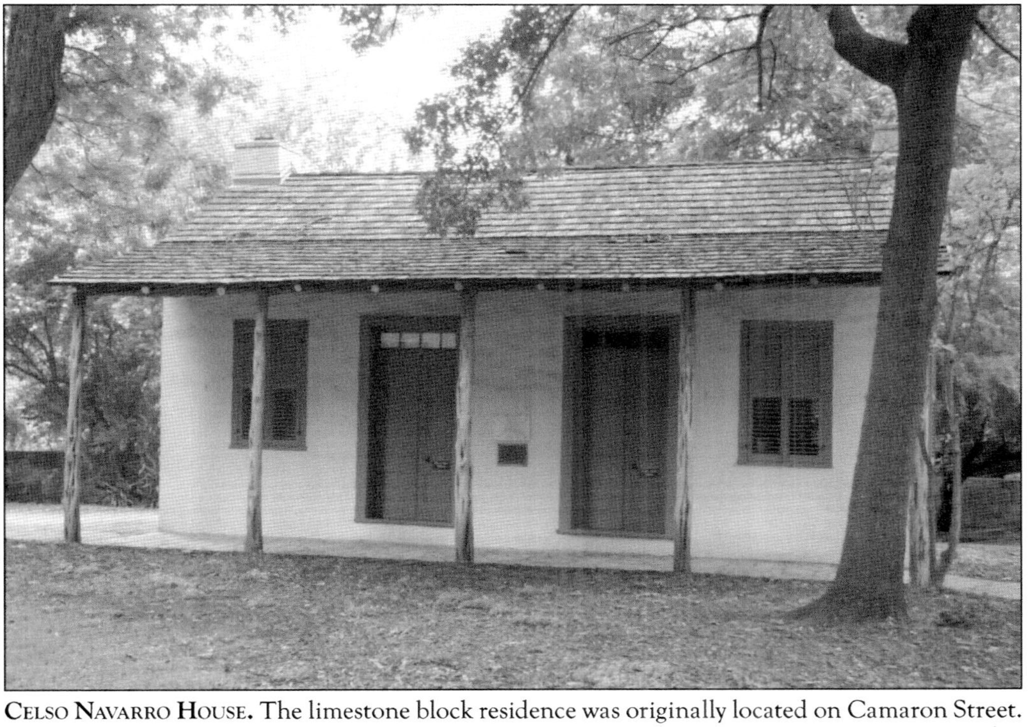

Celso Navarro House. The limestone block residence was originally located on Camaron Street. Moved to the Witte Museum in 1948, the residence was constructed in 1835. Adjacent to this structure is the Dog-Trot Cabin, constructed by President Roosevelt's National Youth Administration Program in 1939. (SAPA.)

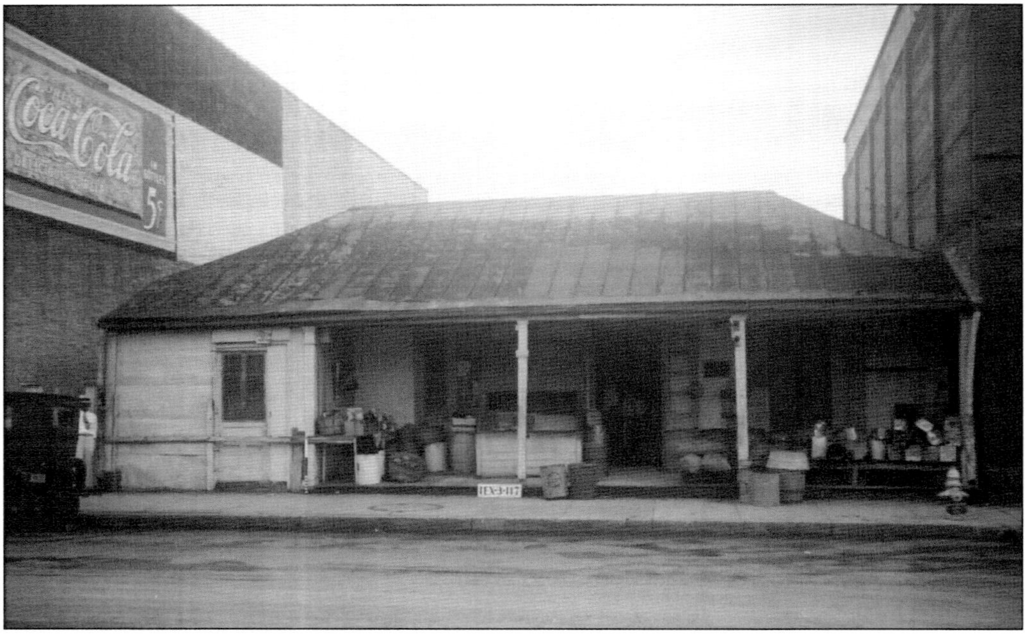

JOSE FRANCISCO RUIZ HOUSE. Utilized by the Witte as its museum store, the plastered rock residence was relocated to Witte grounds in 1943. Believed to have been the first public schoolhouse in the city, the home belonged to one of only two native Texans to sign the Texas Declaration of Independence. (HABS.)

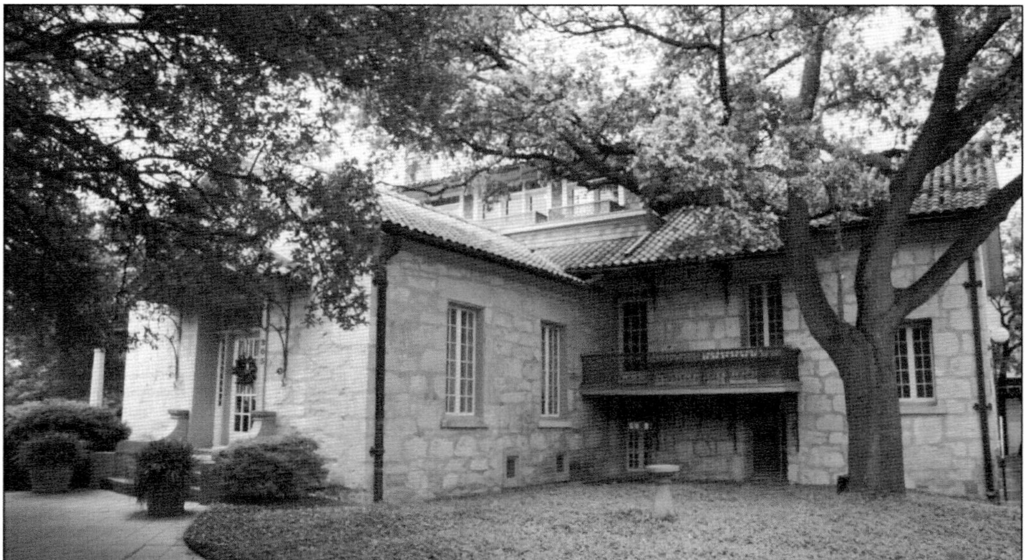

GUENTHER HOUSE. Constructed in 1860 utilizing locally quarried limestone, the original one-story home was built by Carl H. Guenther and his wife, Henrietta. Here, they raised seven children. It was not until 1902 that their youngest son, Erhard, took over as the mill's president. He later made extensive modifications to the residence, which include the east-facing veranda and green tile roof. Today, the home operates as a house museum and restaurant, adjacent to the Pioneer Flour Mill in the King William Historic District. (SAPA.)

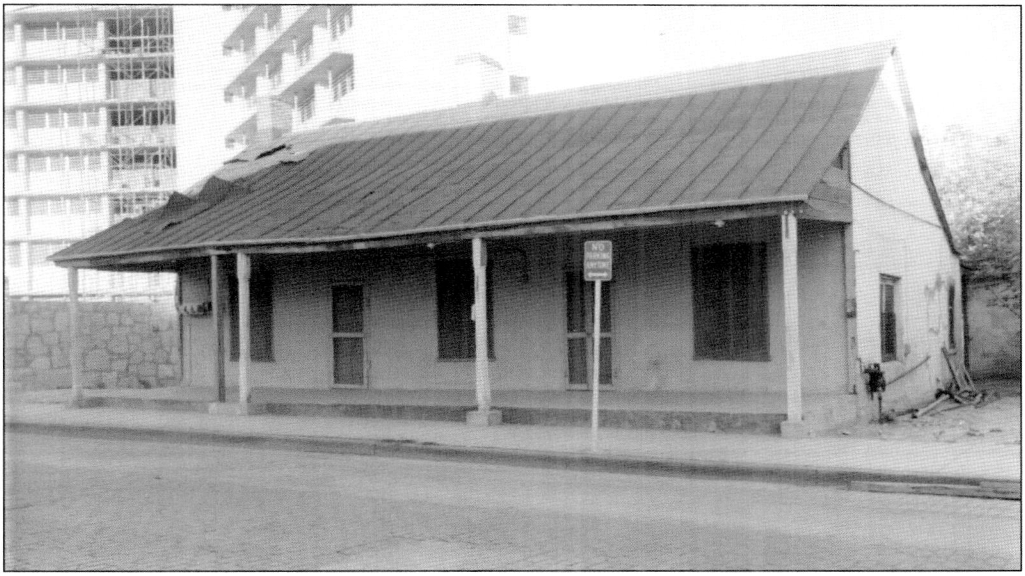

CASA NAVARRO STATE HISTORIC SITE. The adobe and caliche block home of Texas native Jose Antonio Navarro was constructed at this location around 1830–1850 in what was called the "Laredito" neighborhood. The site contains the Navarro residence and a two-story office and store. Navarro was a native merchant and statesman who signed the Texas Declaration of Independence. Purchased and restored by the San Antonio Conservation Society in the early 1960s, the property was deeded to the State of Texas in 1975. (HABS.)

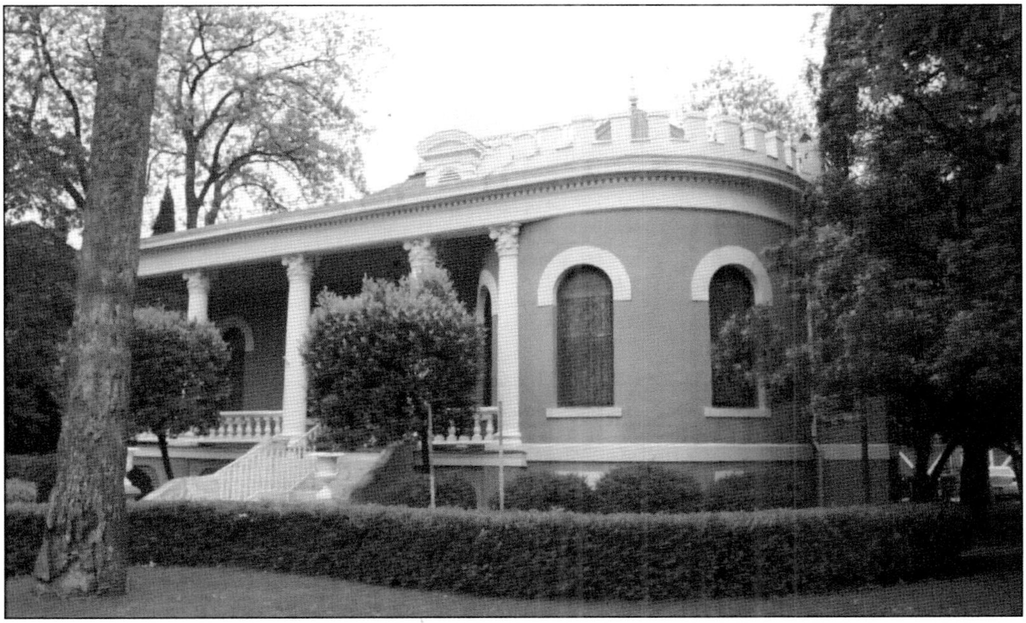

GETHING HOUSE. Built in 1891, the late 19th-century cottage has unusual castellation trimming along the roof edge of the rotunda. Located at 409 Guenther Street in the King William Historic District, the museum is only open to the public during the few weeks of the San Antonio Fiesta each spring as "Miss Margaret's Victorian House Tour." (SAPA.)

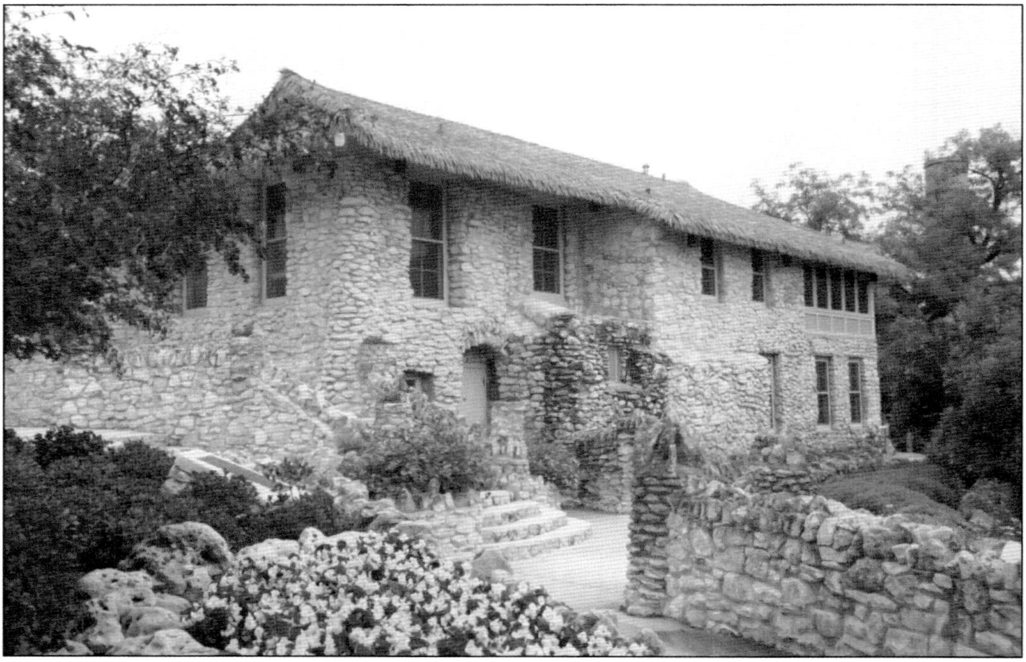

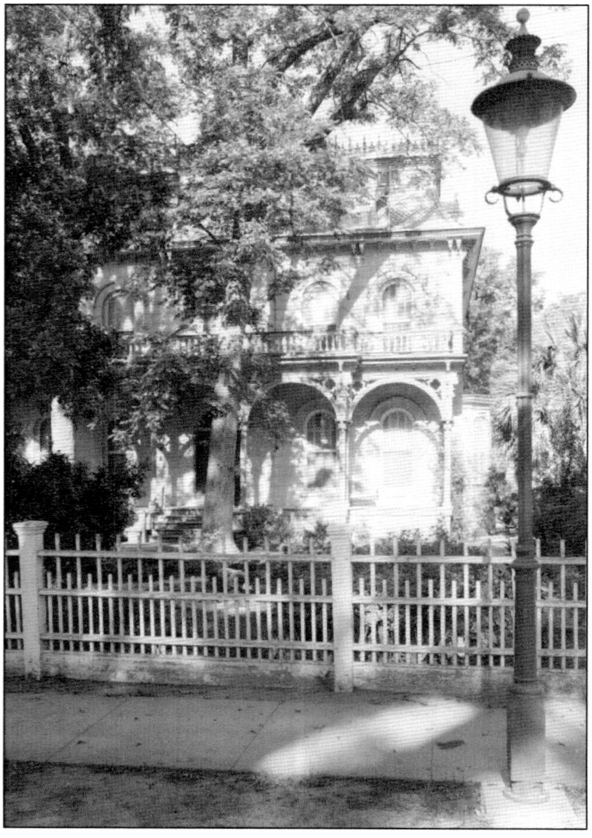

Jingu House and Sunken Gardens. As part of an agreement between city parks commissioner Ray Lambert and Japanese American artist Kimi Eizo Jingu in 1919, the Japanese Garden and two-story residence was created in Brackenridge Park on the grounds of a former quarry. Combining local materials with Japanese traditions, the limestone house also contained the Bamboo Room, which opened in 1926. A major restoration of the home and café was completed in 2012, and it is once again open to the public for light dining. (SAPA.)

Steves Homestead. The 1876 Second Empire home, located at 509 King William Street, was built for lumber company owner Edward Steves. Donated to the San Antonio Conservation Society by Steves's granddaughter, the home has been a museum since 1954. The homestead grounds also include servant quarters, a natatorium, and a carriage house dating to 1875. (HABS.)

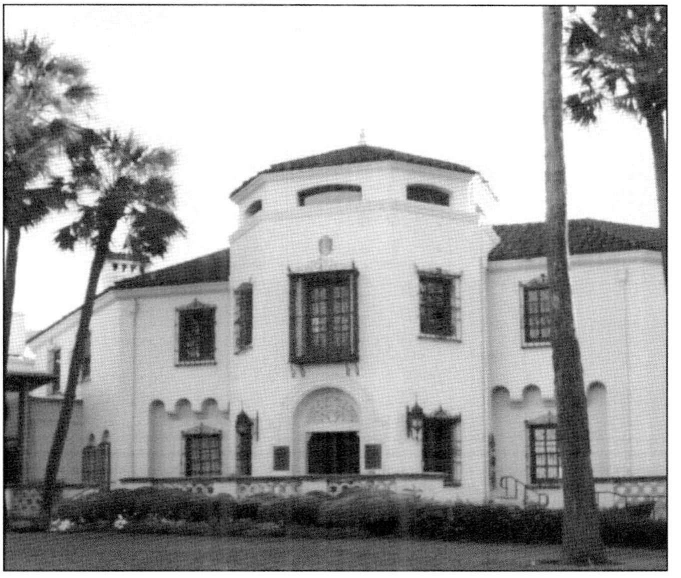

McNay Art Museum. Designed by local architects Atlee B. Ayres and Robert Ayres for oil heiress Marion Koogler McNay, the Spanish Eclectic–style, 24-room residence was built in 1927. In 1954, the McNay was established as the first museum of modern art in the state of Texas. An addition was designed in 2008 by French architect Jean-Paul Viguier, adding 45,000 square feet. The museum is home to over 20,000 works of art, including Marion Koogler McNay's original collection. (SAPA.)

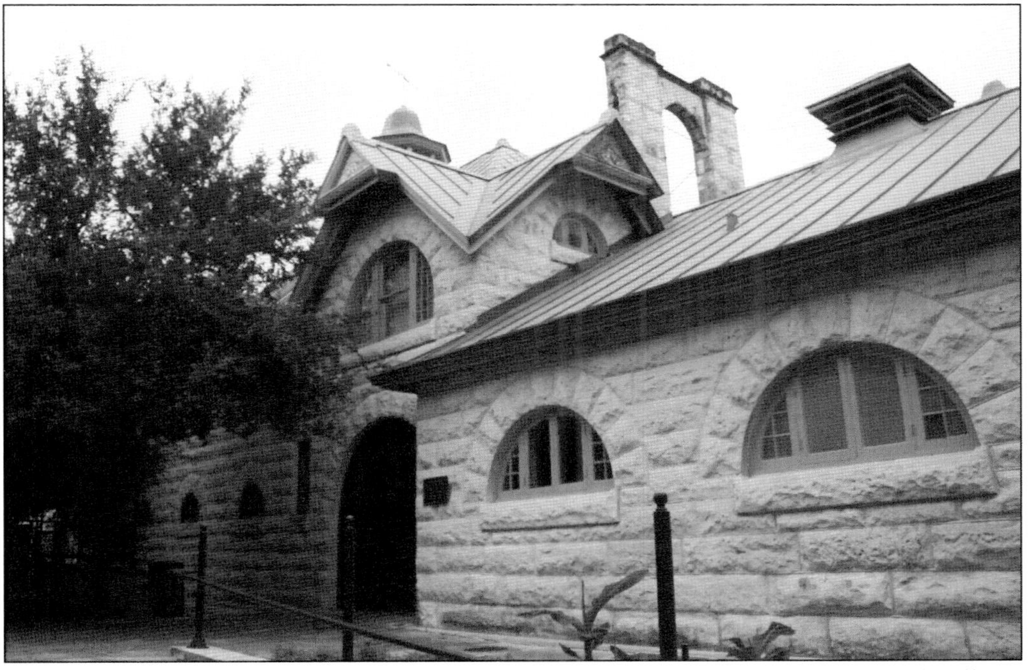

Sullivan Carriage House. Originally constructed in 1896 for Irish immigrant Daniel Sullivan at Fourth and Broadway Streets, the Richardsonian Romanesque carriage house and stable was designed by British architect Alfred Giles. Relocated in 1988 under the direction of third-generation master stonemason Curtis Hunt, the carriage house now serves as the San Antonio Botanical Gardens restaurant and gift shop. The gardens are also home to several other historic structures, including an 1880s log cabin of the Alexander Kennedy Auld family and a limestone and *fachwerk* structure known as the Schumacher House, among others. (SAPA.)

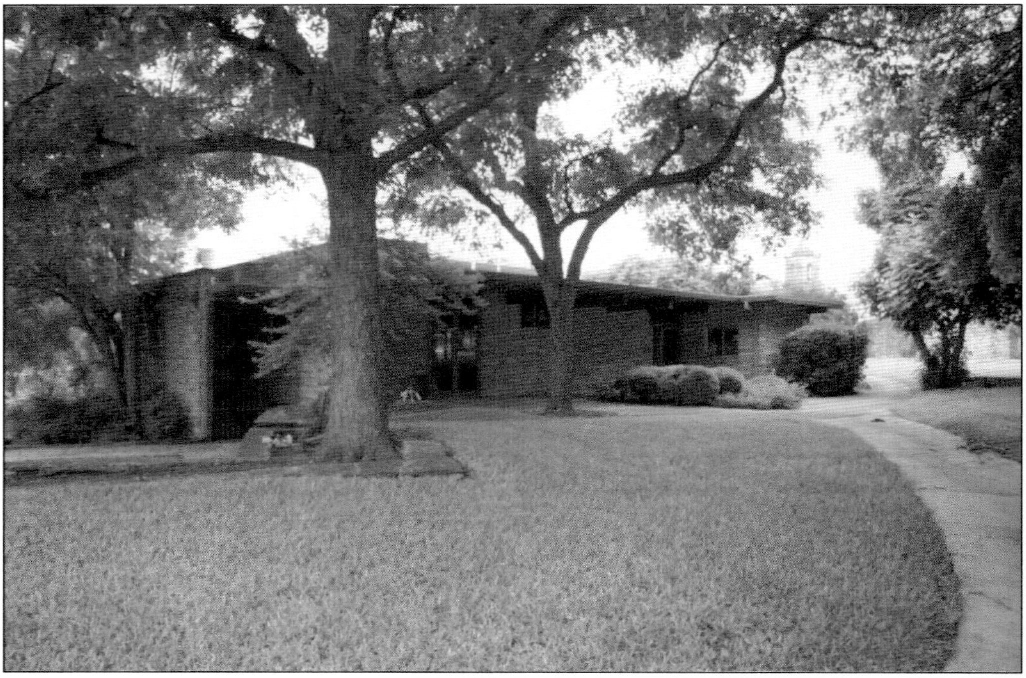

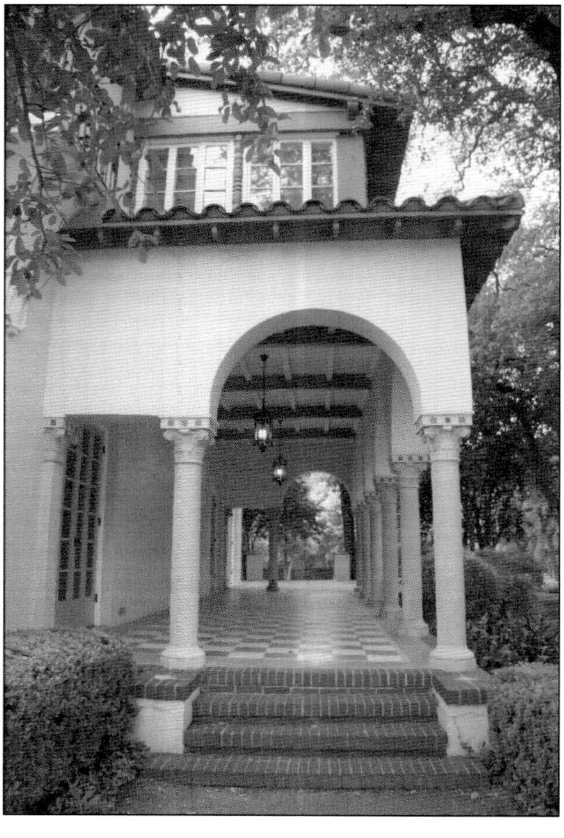

Ethel Wilson Harris House. Known as the caretaker's residence at Mission San José y San Miguel de Aguayo, the Mid-Century Modern home is now an educational facility utilized for group activities within the San Antonio Missions National Historical Park. The mission's bell tower can be seen just over the roofline to the right. (SAPA.)

Harry and Hannah Landa Residence. Locally known as the Landa Branch Library and Gardens, the former residence was designed by architect Robert B. Kelly in 1929. The Italian Renaissance Revival home contains a chandelier and marble fireplace mantel that were purchased by the Landas while traveling in Italy. The detail depicts the decorative columns and tile on the east terrace. (SAPA.)

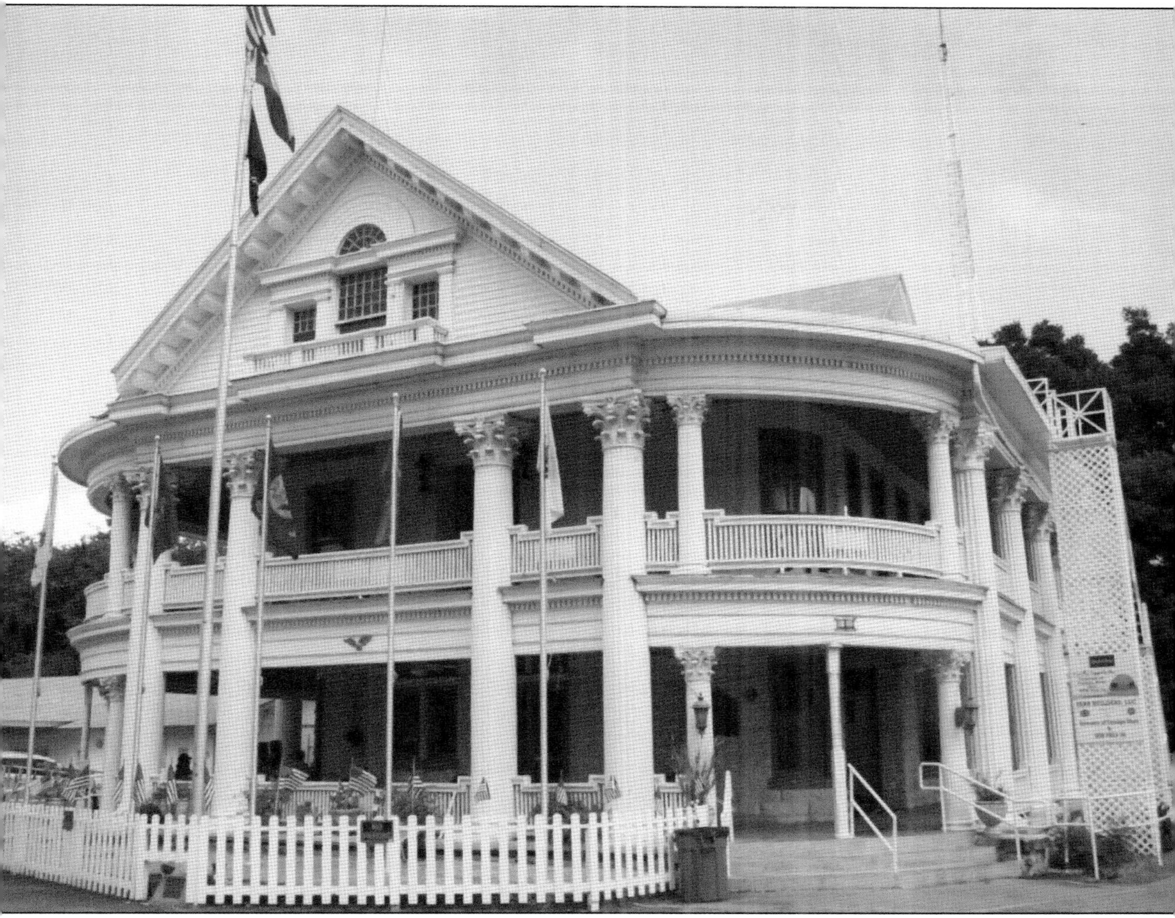

Van Alvin Petty House. Designed by local architect Atlee B. Ayres in 1904 for lumber company owner Van Petty and his wife, Cordelia Dabney Petty, the Neoclassical residence was home to the couple and their three sons. Noted for advancements in seismography and geophone instrumentation, their sons developed the Petty Geophysical Engineering Company. The home was donated by Van Petty to the Veterans of Foreign Wars Post 76 for membership use in 1946 but is also open to the general public. (SAPA.)

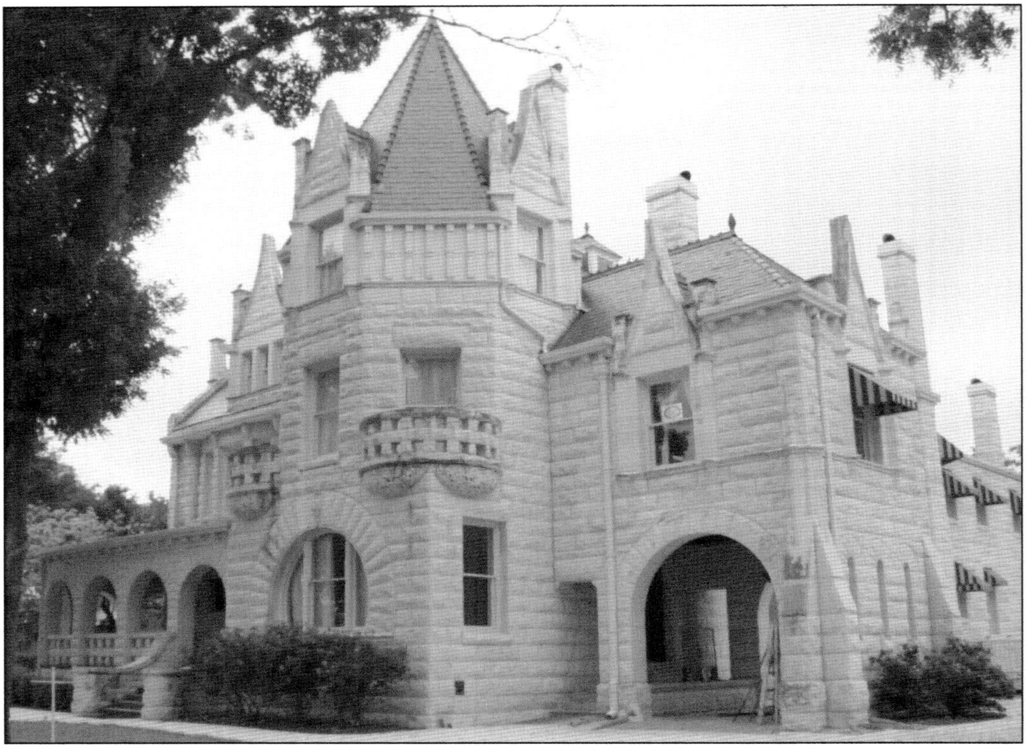

TERRELL CASTLE. Situated in San Antonio's Government Hill Historic District, the home of lawyer and statesman Edwin Holland Terrell was built in 1894. Serving as the US envoy to Belgium between 1889 and 1893, Terrell was heavily influenced by the Châteauesque architecture in Brussels. Also known as Lambermont, the residence was designed by British architect Alfred Giles and is unique in style in San Antonio. (Both, SAPA.)

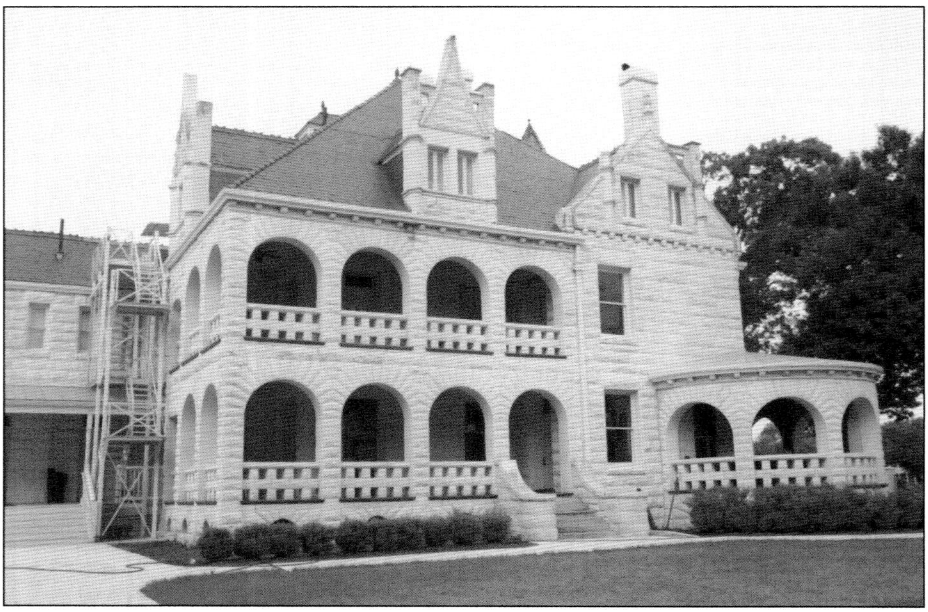

Five

Civic Architecture, Schools, and Universities

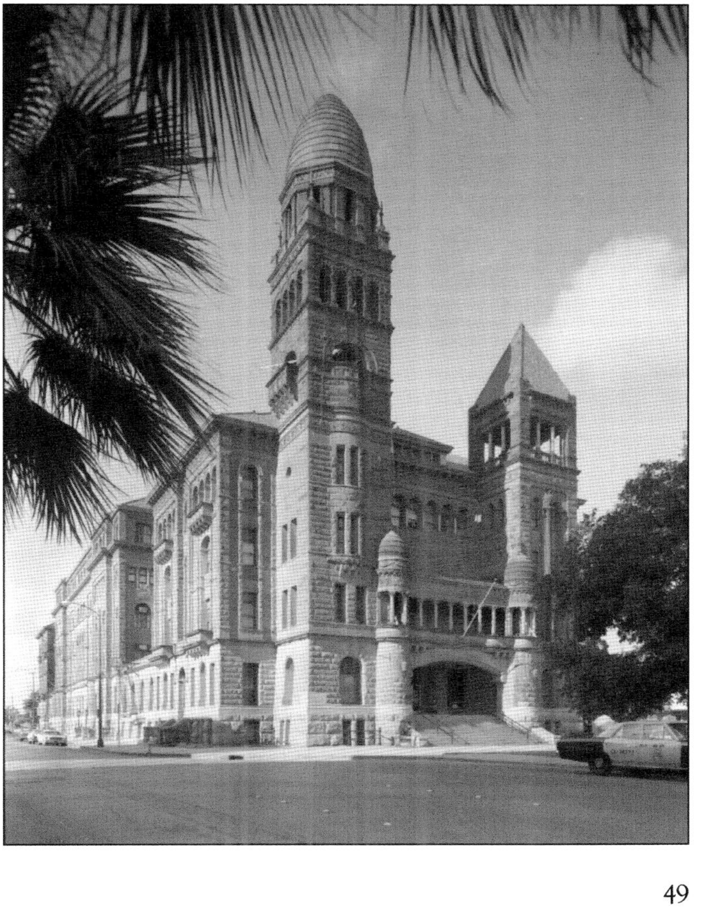

Bexar County Courthouse. Constructed of red sandstone and capped with a contrasting green tile roof, the courthouse was fully completed by 1896. The structure was designed by Virginia-born architect James Riely Gordon, who is well known throughout Texas and the United States for his landmark courthouse designs. Bexar County Courthouse is an excellent example of Gordon's mastery of the Richardsonian Romanesque style. (HABS.)

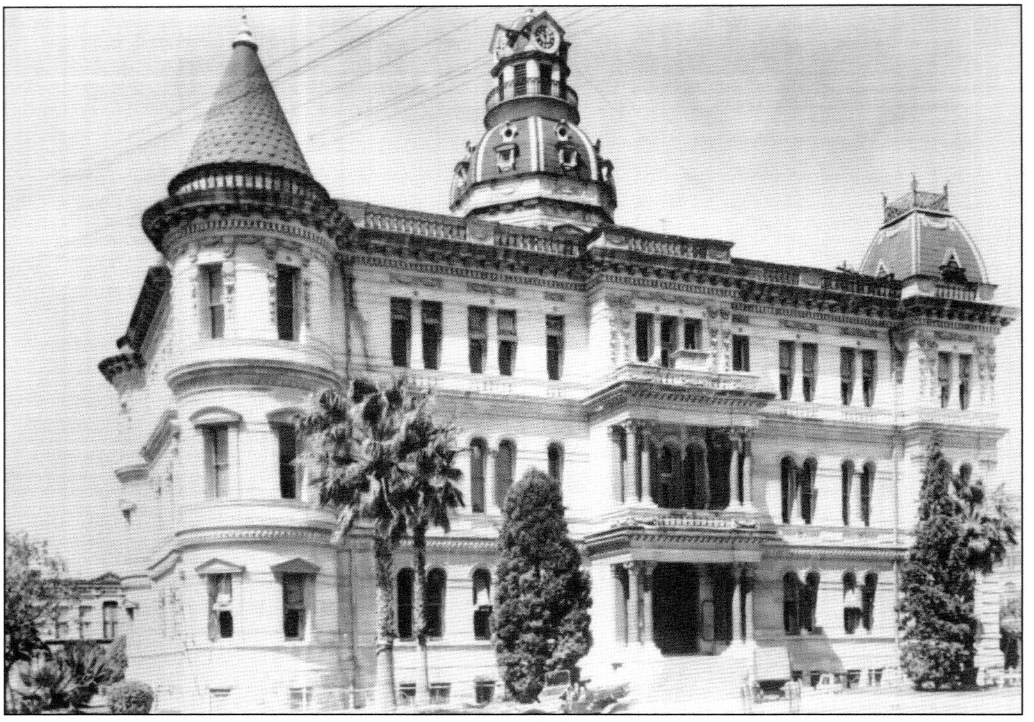

CITY HALL. Originally constructed in 1891, city hall (above) featured corner turrets and a central dome designed by local architect Otto Kramer. The highly decorative roof treatments and facade ornamentation reflect the Second Empire style. Expansion of the city offices required a major change to the roof structure when a fourth floor was added, which drastically changed the appearance of the building as seen below. The building was transformed into the Spanish Colonial Revival style (below) by Carleton W. Adams in 1927, and few of the original details remain. (Above, LOC; below, HABS.)

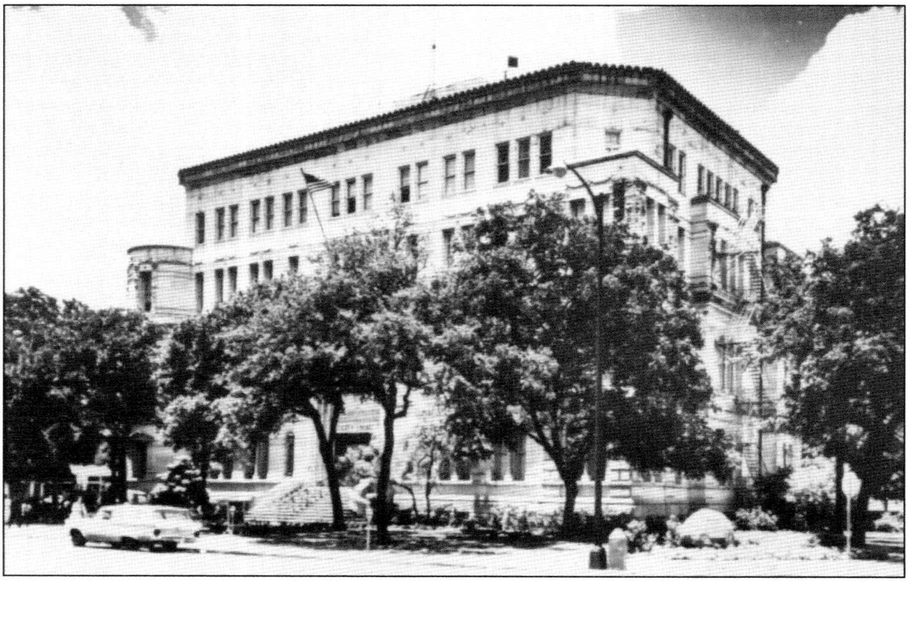

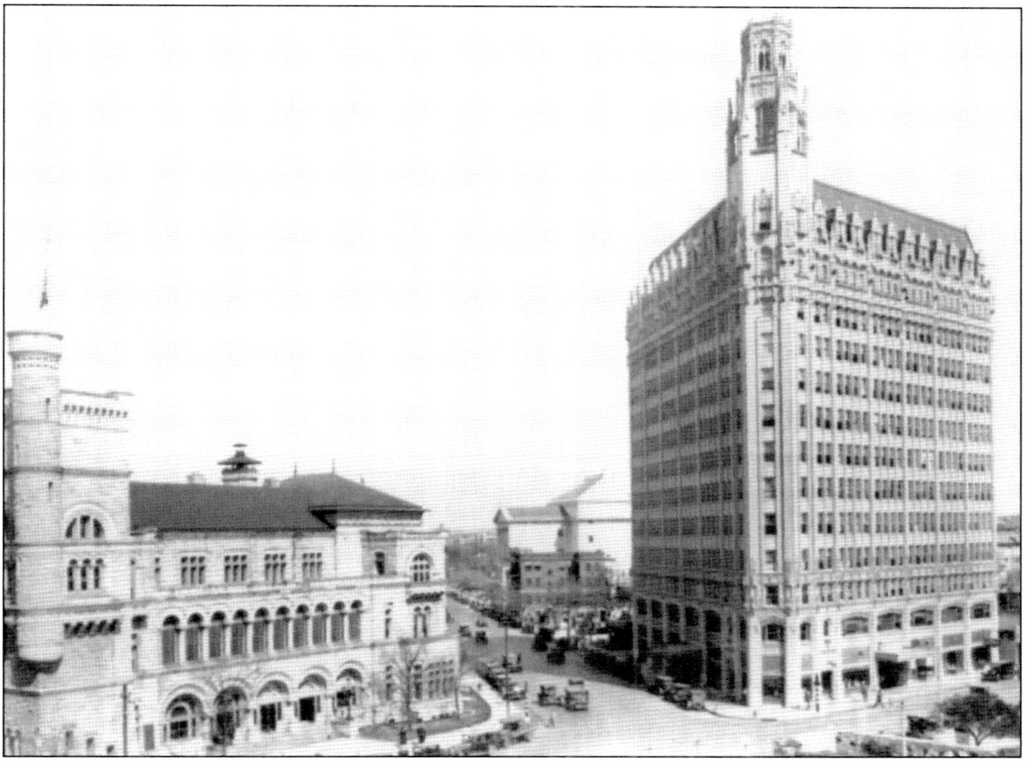

US Post Office and Courthouse. Constructed on the north perimeter of Alamo Plaza, the 19th-century former federal building, designed by architect James Riely Gordon, was located at 615 East Houston Street. Pictured above, to the left of the neo-Gothic 1923 Medical Arts Building, is the old post office and courthouse, built in 1877. Below, the Hipolito F. Garcia Federal Building replaced the old Richardsonian Romanesque structure in 1937. Both having studied at the École des Beaux-Arts in Paris, local architect Ralph H. Cameron and Philadelphia architect Paul P. Cret collaborated on the design, which exemplifies the Beaux-Arts style. (Above, UTSA; below, SAPA.)

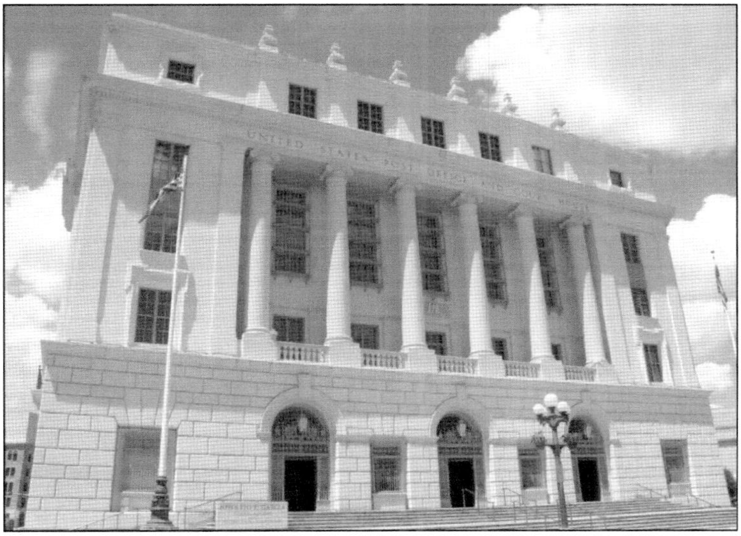

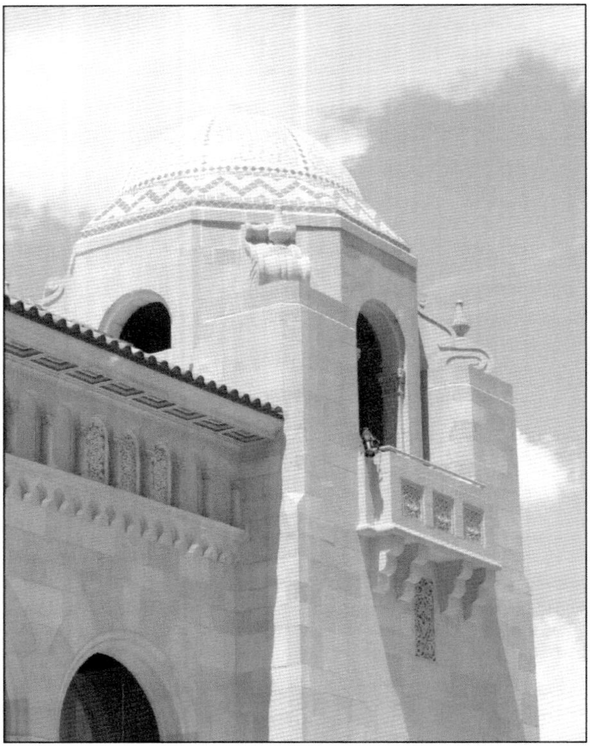

Municipal Auditorium. The design of the Spanish Colonial Revival public venue is credited to several local architects, including Emmett Jackson, George Willis, Atlee B. Ayers, and Robert Ayers. A state-of-the-art, world-class performance hall replaced the old auditorium and was completed in 2014, leaving only the original front facade intact. (SAPA.)

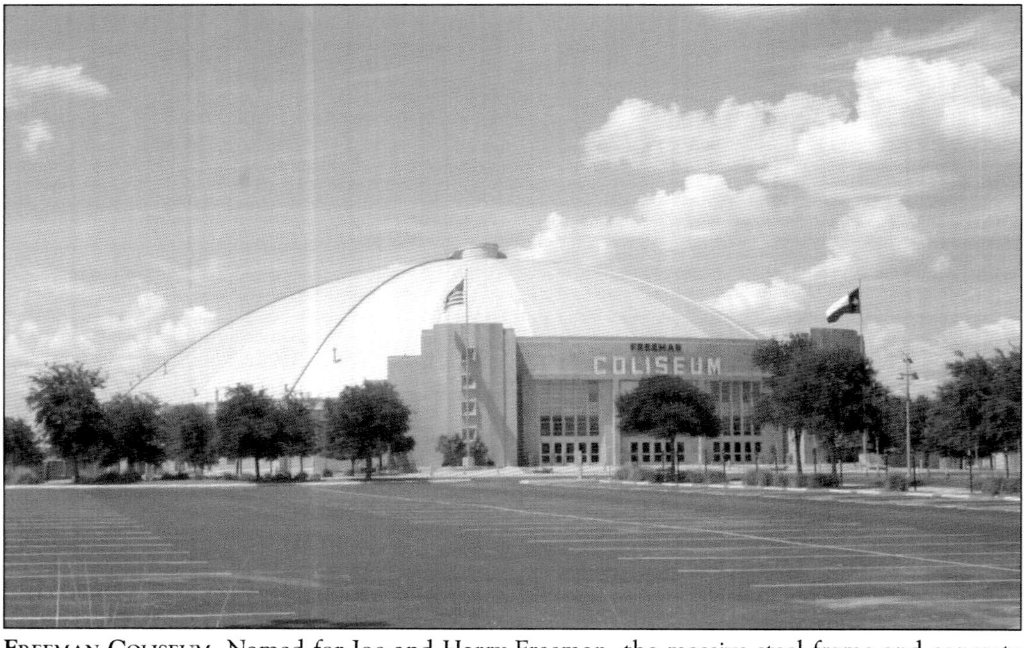

Freeman Coliseum. Named for Joe and Harry Freeman, the massive steel frame and concrete structure opened in 1949 on the city's east side. The versatile county-owned arena can seat between 9,000 and 11,000 spectators, depending on the event. Stylistically austere, the south-facing entrance features an Art Deco facade. A major renovation took place in 2007. (SAPA.)

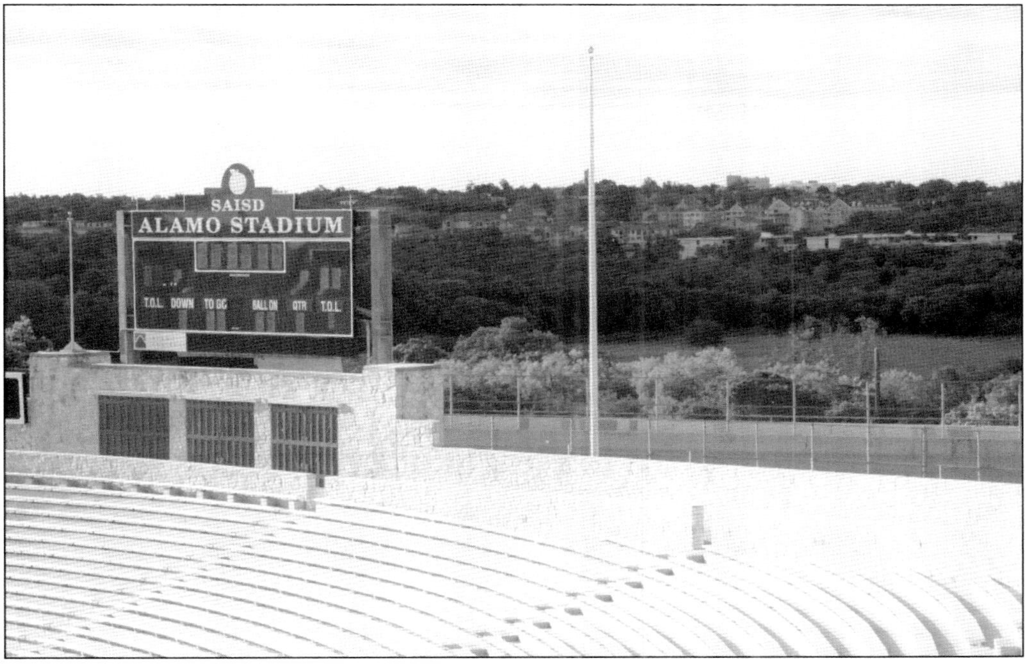

ALAMO STADIUM. A project undertaken by the Works Progress Administration around 1940, the stadium features local limestone surfacing over the entire structure. Continuing to serve the San Antonio Independent School District, the stadium can accommodate over 20,000 spectators. Alamo Stadium is adjacent to Trinity University, just east of the Monte Vista Historic District. (SAPA.)

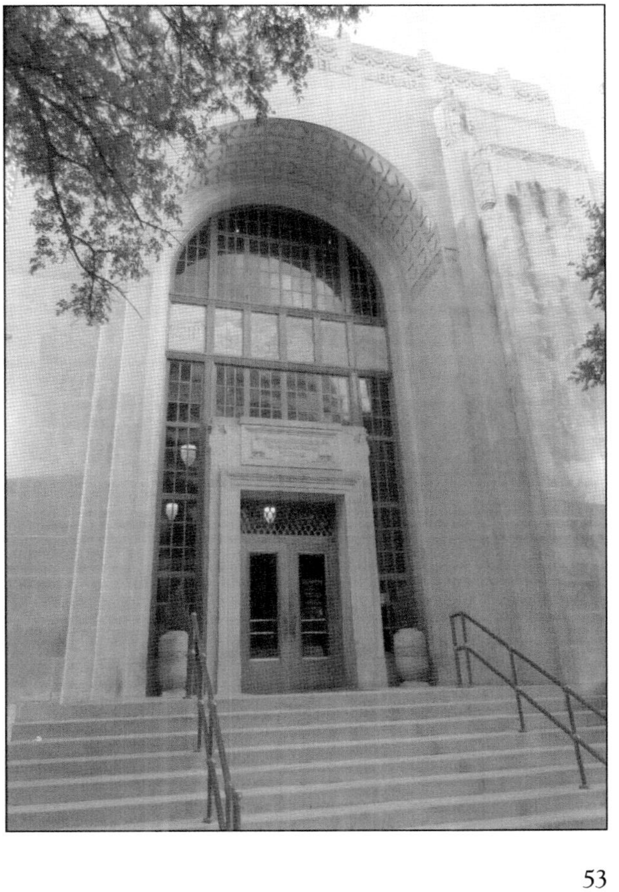

SAN ANTONIO PUBLIC LIBRARY. The original Carnegie library on this site opened in 1903. Massive flooding of the downtown area in the 1920s damaged the foundation, and this replacement, designed by local architect Herbert S. Green, was built in 1930. This facility served the public library system until 1968. Renovated in 2007, the former library is now home to the Briscoe Western Art Museum. (SAPA.)

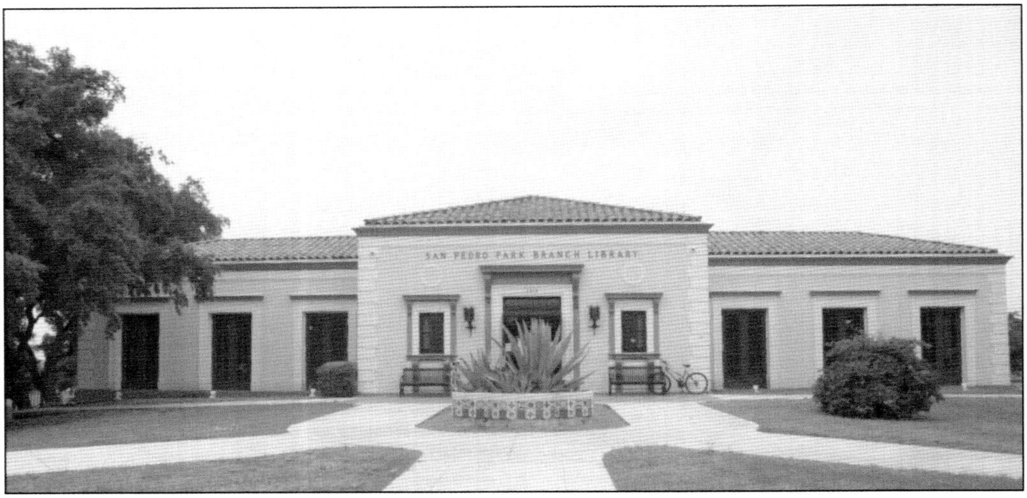

San Pedro Park Branch Library. Constructed in 1930 as the first branch library in the city, the Spanish Colonial Revival building was designed by local architects Atlee B. Ayres, Robert Ayres, and J.M. Marriott. The library sits within the confines of San Pedro Springs Park, near the Monte Vista Historic District and San Antonio College. (SAPA.)

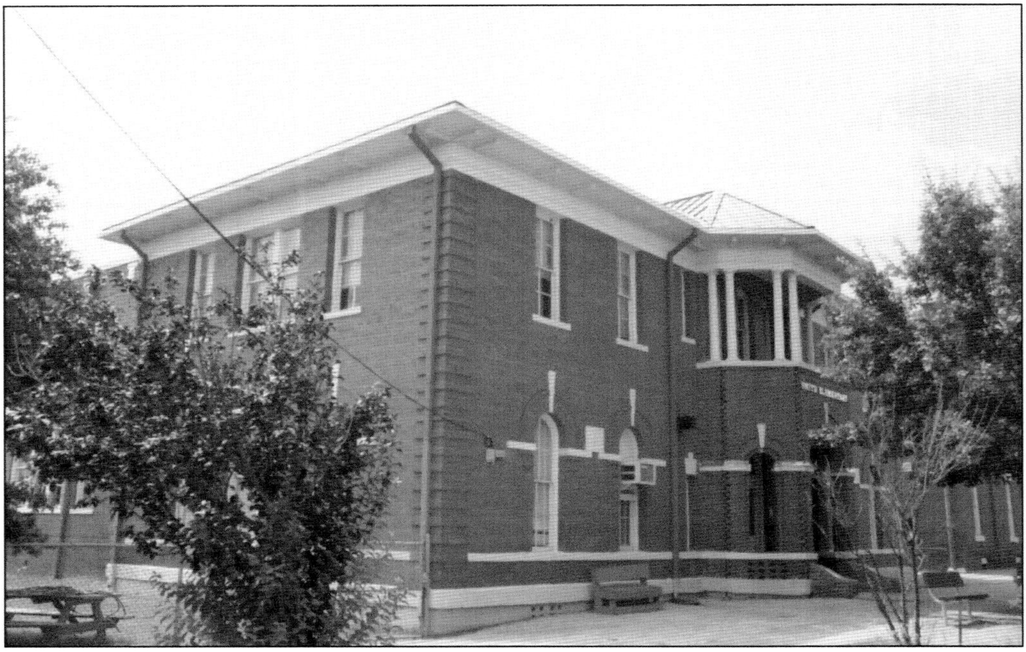

Smith School. Located at 823 South Gevers Street, the Smith School is named for two notable men from the Texas Revolution—Erastus Smith and John W. Smith. Built in 1903, the two-story, redbrick structure features a common symmetrical floor plan, although the recessed entry supports an atypical upper-story covered porch. (SAPA.)

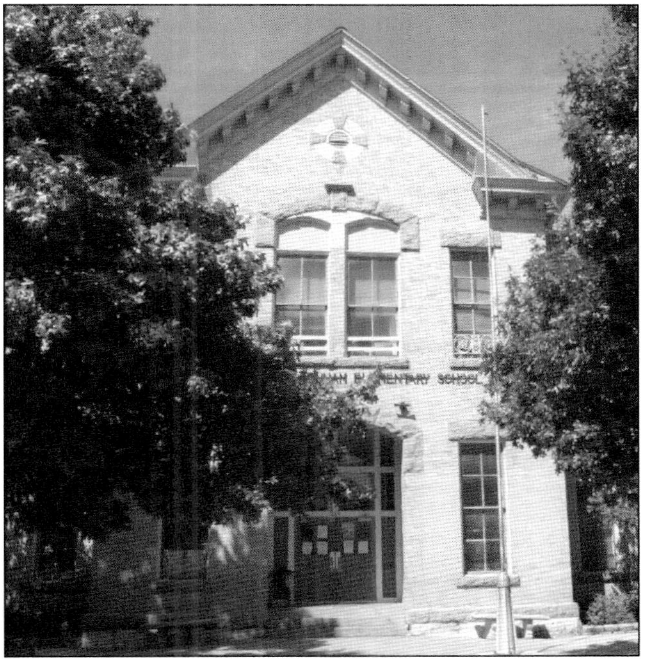

James Butler Bonham School. A permanent fixture in the King William neighborhood, this school has been in continuous operation since 1889. Constructed of stone, this basic schoolhouse model was utilized by many San Antonio area schools for several decades. (SAPA.)

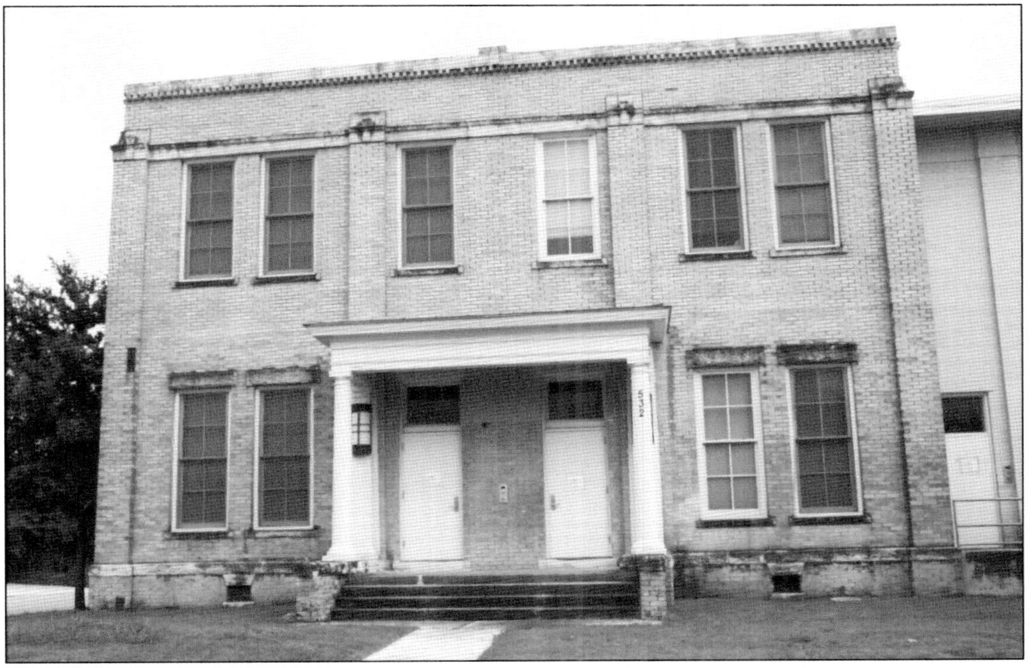

Brackenridge Colored School. Constructed in 1899 with funds donated by local businessman George W. Brackenridge, the school served east-side African American students. Assimilated into the San Antonio Independent School district in 1901, the facility was active until 1936. All that remains of the school is this basic brick structure known as Annex No. 2, which was completed in 1907. Members of the nearby St. Paul Methodist congregation purchased the building in the 1950s, and local historic landmark status was granted by the city in 1982. (SAPA.)

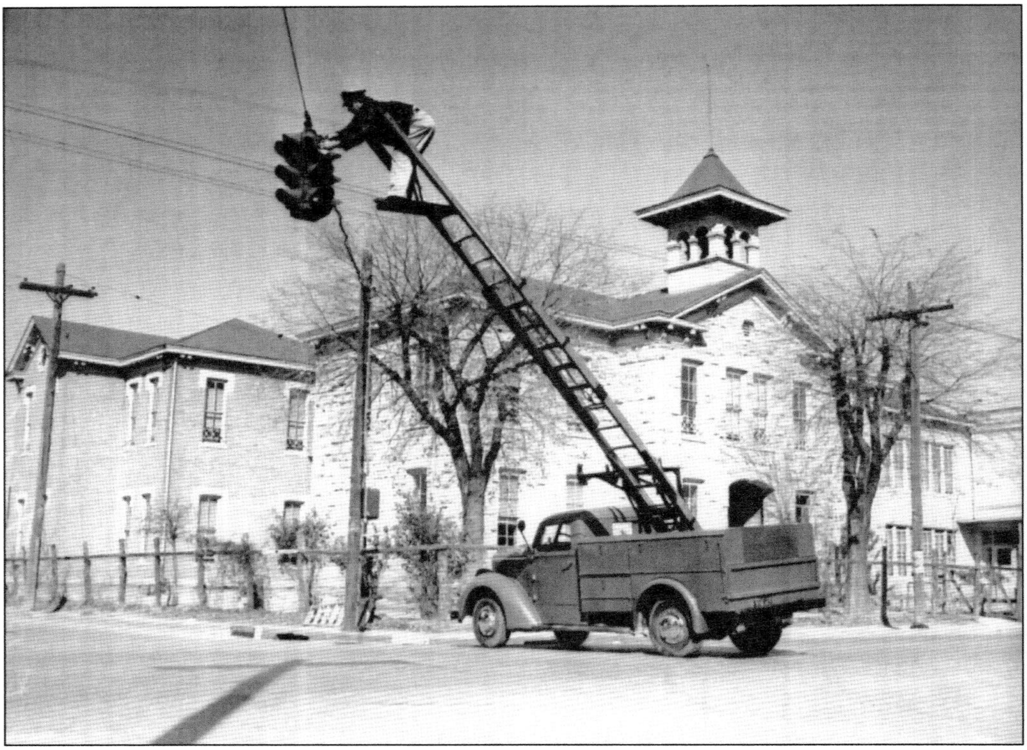

NAVARRO SCHOOL. Serving the educational needs of students since the late 19th century, Jose Antonio Navarro School opened as Public School No. 8. Renamed in 1902 for the Texas patriot, the school grounds include structures dating to 1886, 1892, 1902, and 1923. This photograph depicts Lineman P. Stowe changing the traffic light at the intersection of San Fernando and South Pecos Streets around 1940. Today, the school serves as a nontraditional high school under the banner of Navarro Academy. (UTSA.)

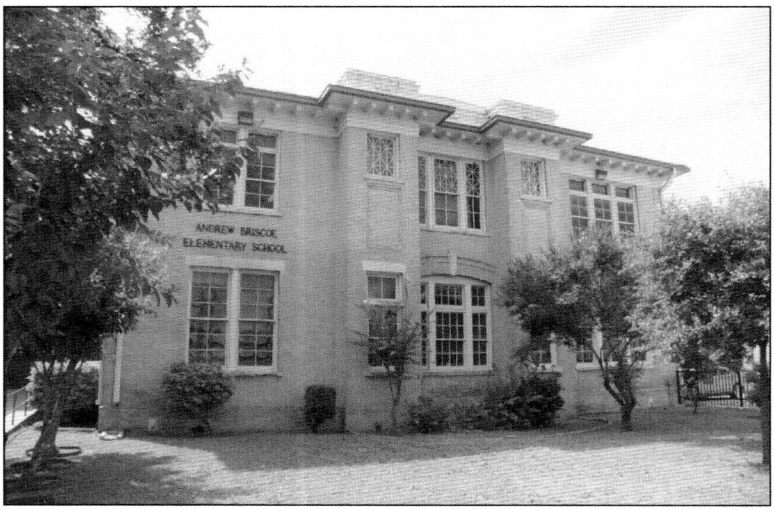

BRISCOE SCHOOL. Named for Texas Revolution patriot Andrew Briscoe, the original Public School No. 17, built in 1904, is located at 2015 South Flores Street. The unusual but highly decorative spoke-patterned windows are present on the school annex constructed around 1910. (SAPA.)

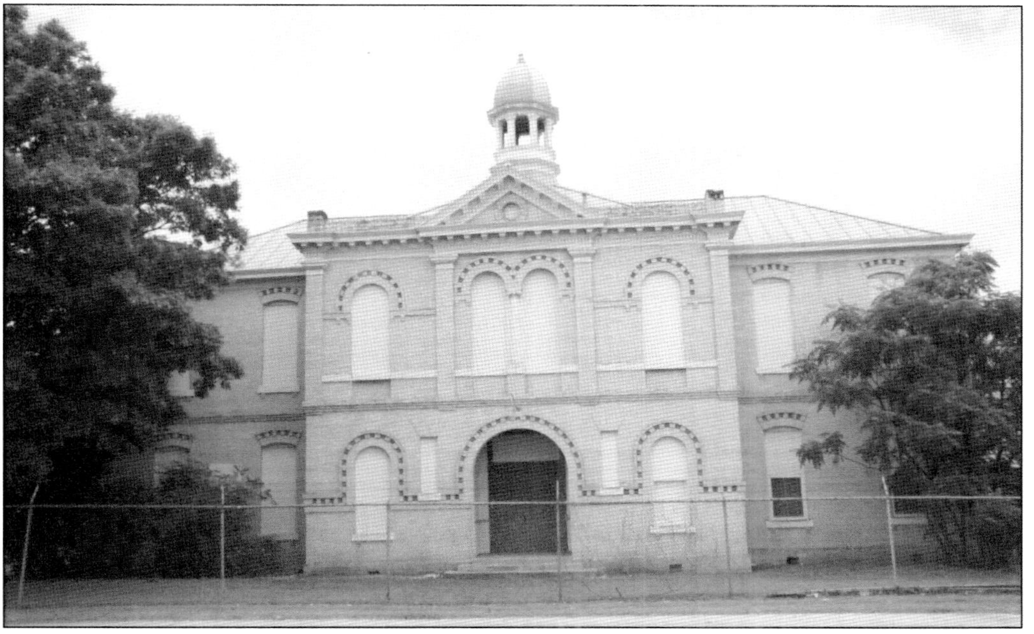

Government Hill Schoolhouse. Privately owned since 1959, the schoolhouse located in the historic Government Hill neighborhood was built around 1908 at the corner of Stafford and Calhoun Streets. Featuring round arch windows with alternating colored brickwork, the structure has decorative detailing that includes upper-story pilasters, an oculus in the pediment, and an original octagonal cupola. (SAPA.)

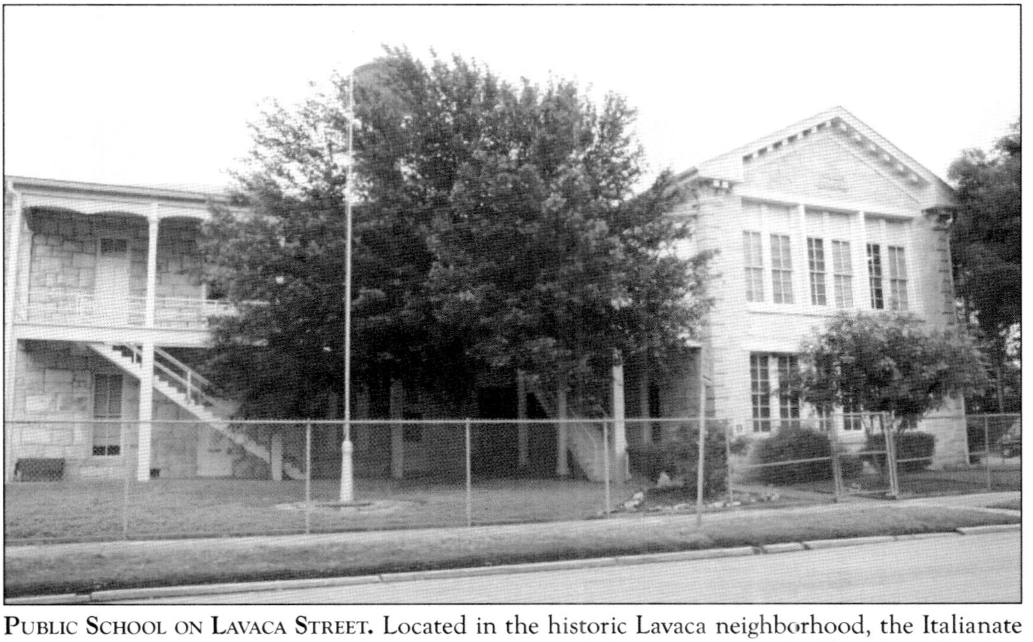

Public School on Lavaca Street. Located in the historic Lavaca neighborhood, the Italianate limestone structure opened to students in 1878. Formerly known as Lamar Public School No. 6, it now serves the San Antonio Independent School district as administrative offices. "Public School" is written in stone letters in the pediment facing Lavaca Street. (SAPA.)

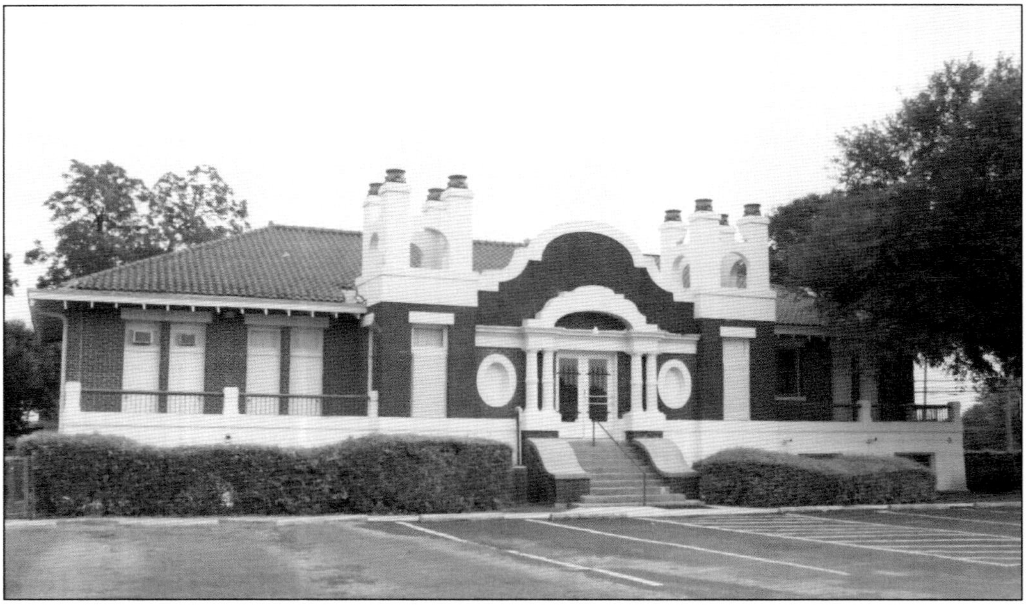

THOMAS SCHOOL. The Mission-style school is located at 5500 South Presa Street east of the old Hot Wells Hotel ruins. With the school having a history of relocating throughout San Antonio, this became the permanent location from 1918 until its closure in the late 1930s. The mimicked belfries are constructed of brick and the entry features unusual oval windows, unconventional of Mission architecture. (SAPA.)

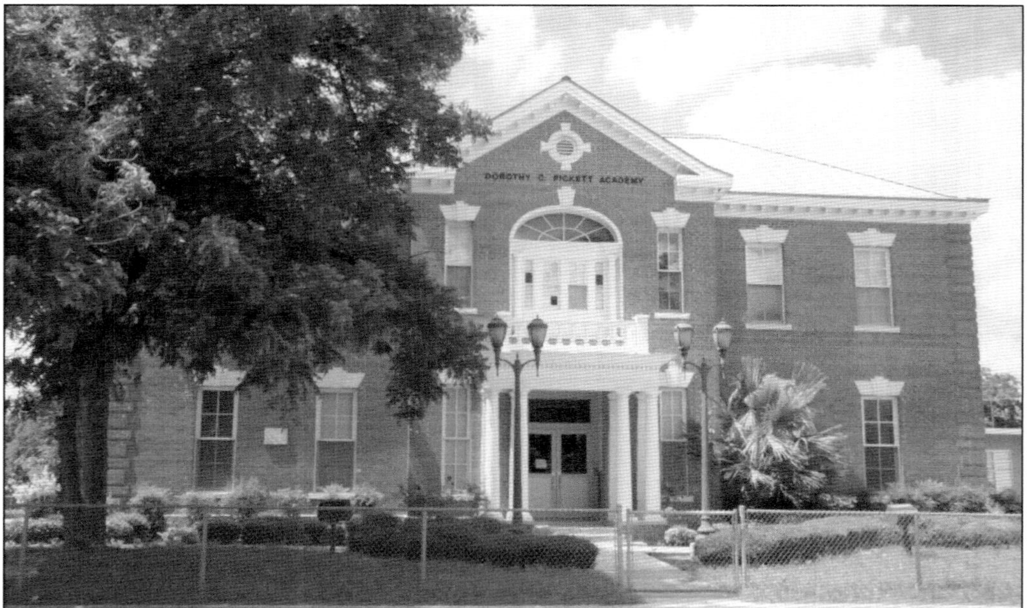

FANNIN SCHOOL. The 1907 redbrick structure was a replacement for the original 1894 schoolhouse. Also known as Public School No. 12, it was named for Texas War of Independence colonel James Walker Fannin Jr. Located at 1931 East Houston Street, the alternative high school is now known as the Pickett Academy. (SAPA.)

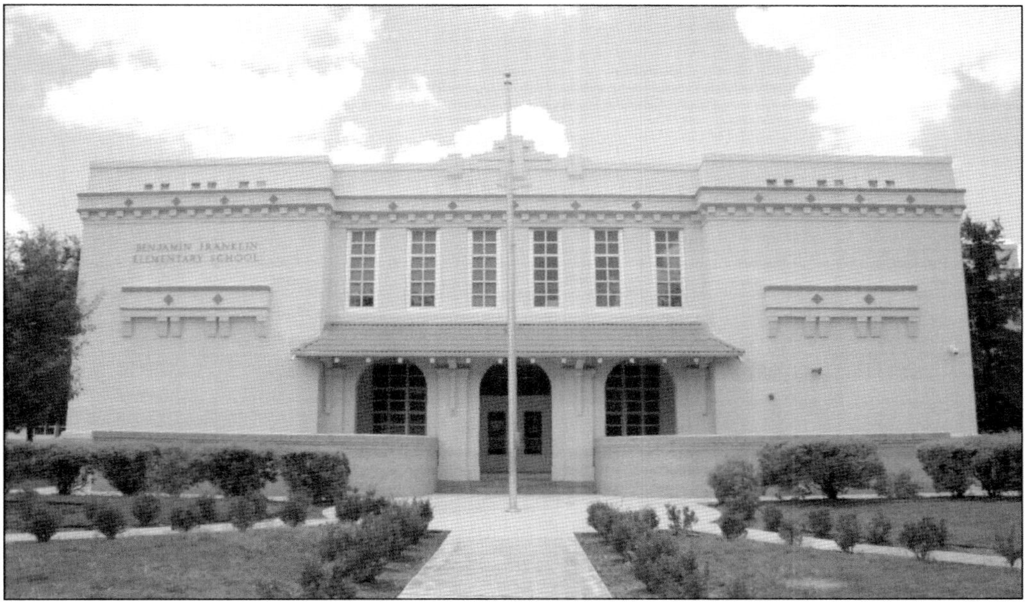

Los Angeles Heights School. Built in 1915, the original brick eight-room school features a recessed arched portico dressed with a red barrel-tile roof. Students voted unanimously to change the name to Benjamin Franklin Elementary School sometime after a new high school was built in 1929 on nearby Edison Drive. The Los Angeles Heights neighborhood is located directly east of the Monticello Park Historic District. (SAPA.)

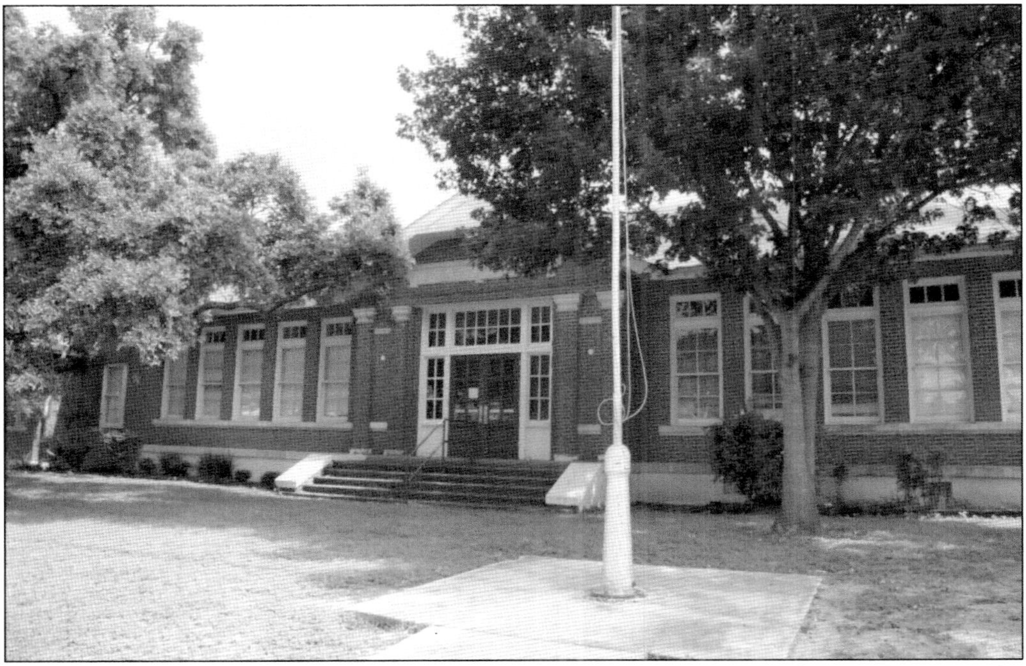

Robert B. Green School. The single-story schoolhouse was constructed around 1910 in the Huntstock Addition neighborhood and is named for Sen. Robert Green. The school has had two other additions resembling the original that date to the early 20th century. (SAPA.)

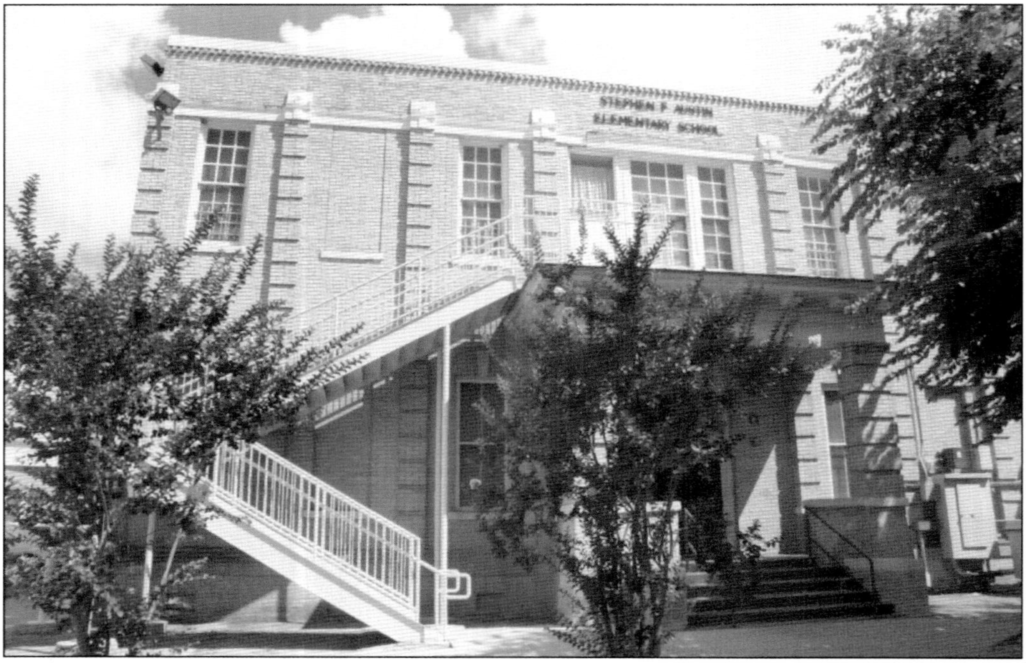

STEPHEN F. AUSTIN SCHOOL. Educating students for well over 100 years, Stephen F. Austin School has been a fixture of the Five Points area since 1878. With its history of providing special education needs since 1915, it was the first school of its kind in the state of Texas. This early 20th-century addition is just one of several buildings that has been in continuous operation since its inception. (SAPA.)

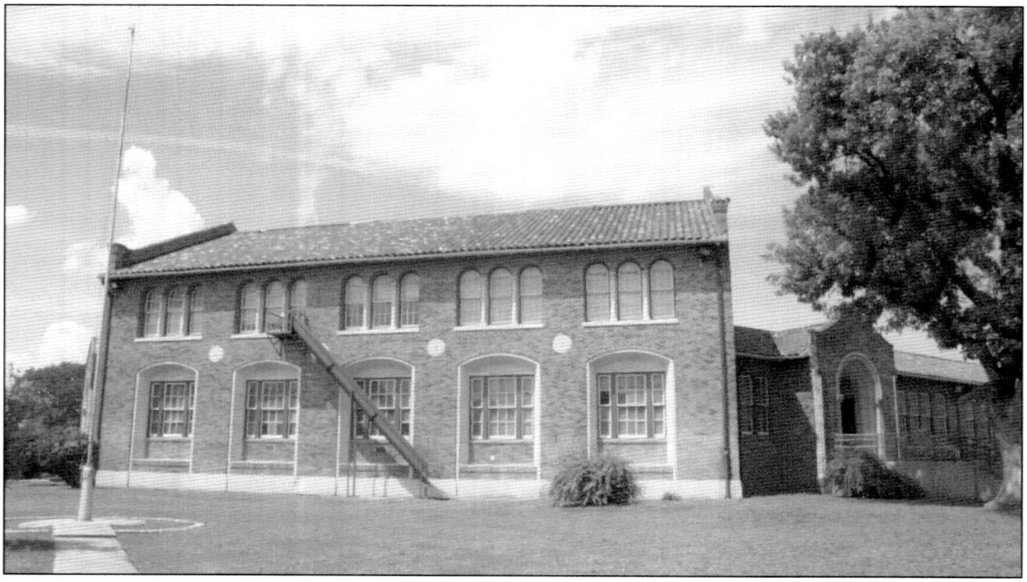

THOMAS NELSON PAGE SCHOOL. Named for American writer and US ambassador to Italy during World War I, Thomas Nelson Page School was constructed in 1925 in the Highland Park neighborhood. Engaged spiral arches occur at the entryways, and the spiral detail repeats between the tripartite, upper-story windows. (SAPA.)

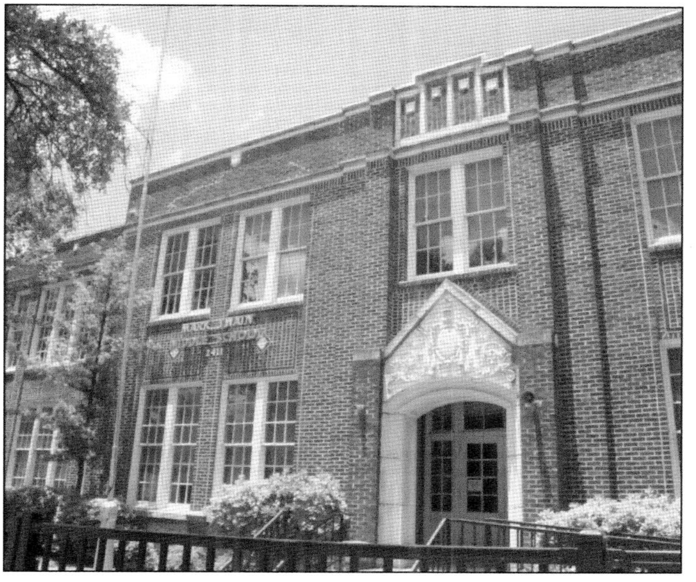

Mark Twain School. Situated on the western edge of the Monte Vista Historic District, Mark Twain School was constructed in 1923. Utilizing brown brick, decorative detailing surrounds cast stone tiles between windows, and the entrance employs a cast stone door surround, pediment with floral motifs, and a medallion displaying the school's name. Also built in 1923, Ben Milam School no longer operates as classrooms but retains a similar, yet less decorative, name medallion. (SAPA.)

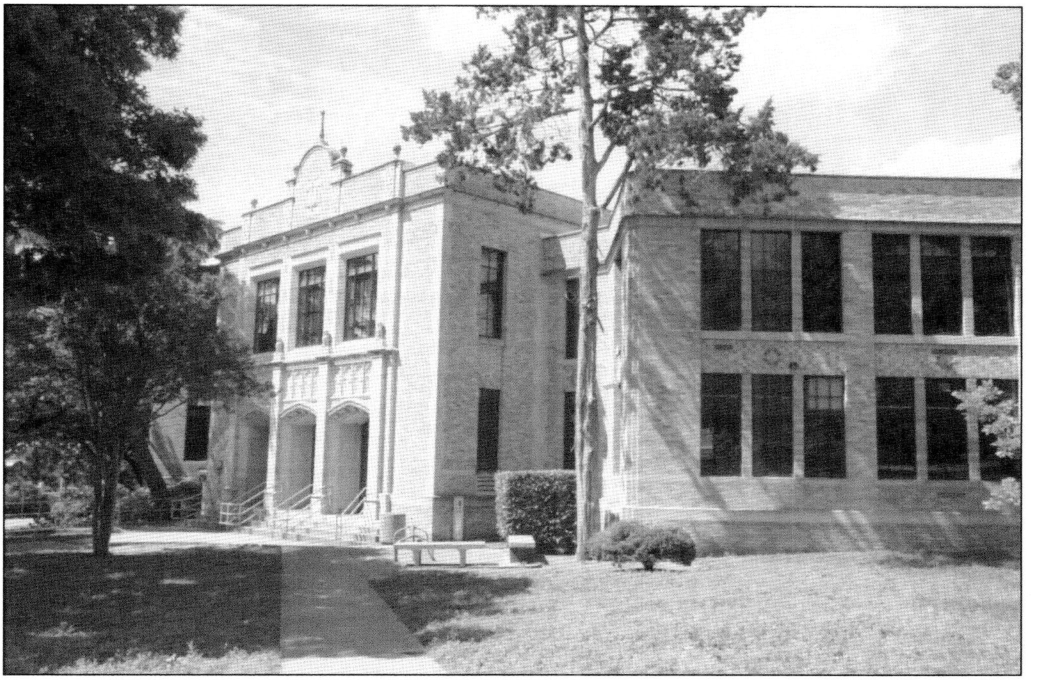

Alamo Heights School. Cambridge Oval in Alamo Heights has been the location of this area's school since 1909. The original high school was constructed in 1922 and has castellated embellishments above the entry. The existing entrance, west of the high school building, faces Townsend Avenue as seen here. The result of a later addition, the entrance features three cast stone vestibules adorned with owl statuaries and other cast stone ornamentation. (SAPA.)

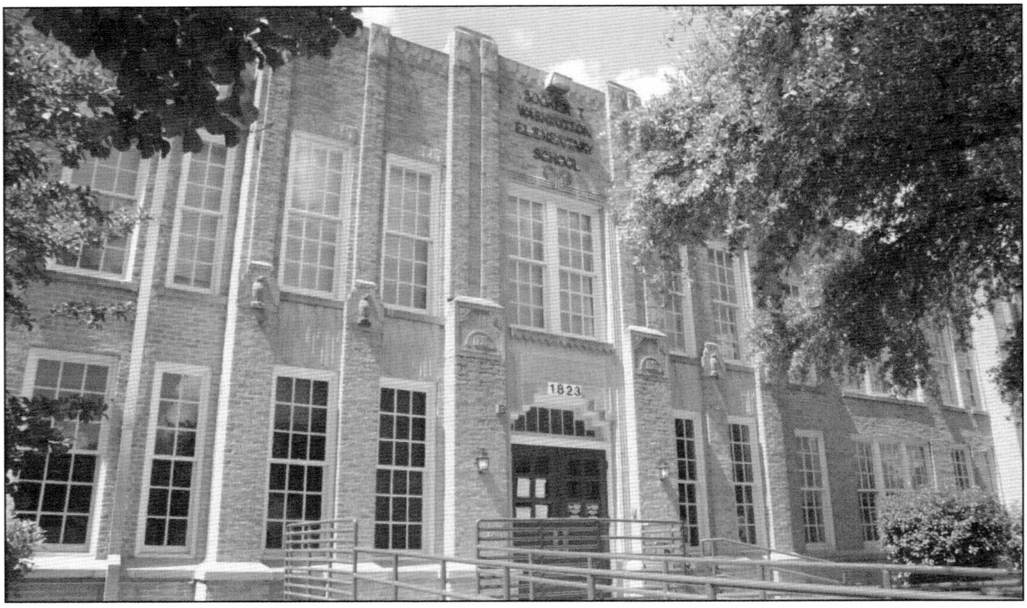

Booker T. Washington School. Named for the influential American educator and author, the east side school opened its doors in the Jefferson Heights neighborhood in 1930. The school's facade is punctuated by Art Deco details and cast stone owls. An open book sits before the sunrise on each side of the main entry. (SAPA.)

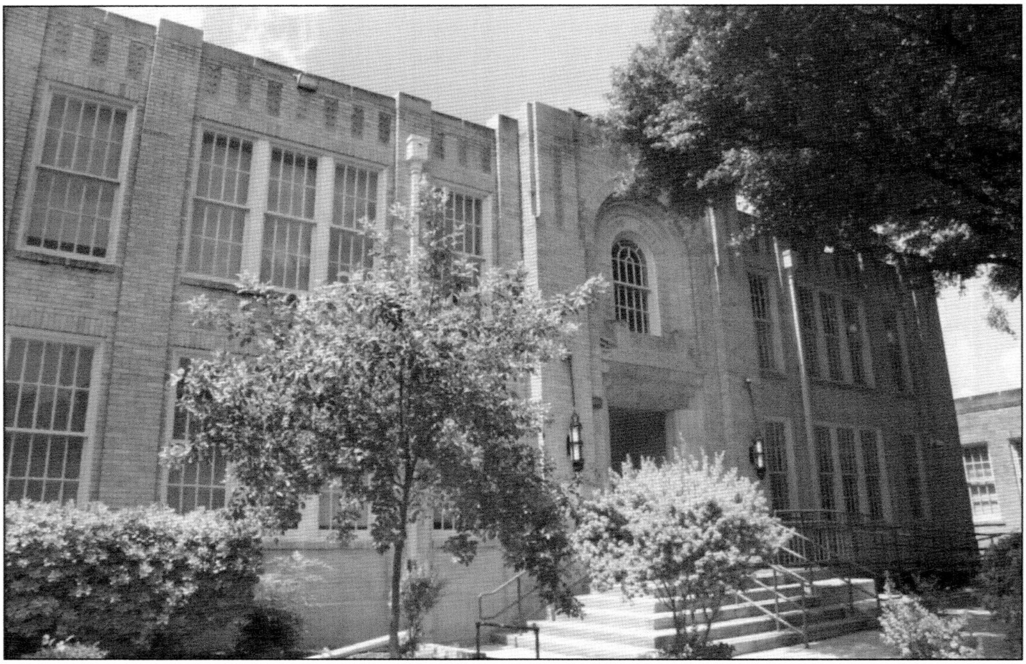

Charles Graebner School. Prominent businessman and school advocate Charles Graebner donated land to the San Antonio Independent School District, and his namesake school was opened in 1932. Also known as School No. 37, the two-story buff brick building has a decorative arched doorway and upper-story window surrounded by laurel leaf motifs. (SAPA.)

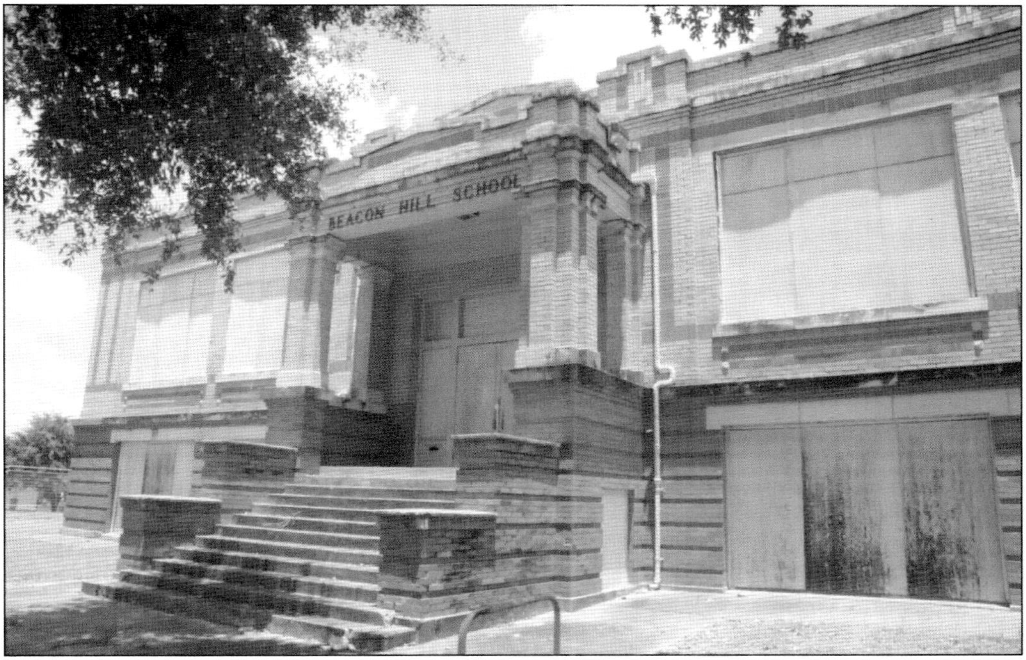

Roberts Beacon Hill School. Elevated on a base of banded brick, the school built in 1915 employs multiple colors to express ornamentation. No longer in service, the building has survived despite growth and expansion of Beacon Hill School at the same location. (SAPA.)

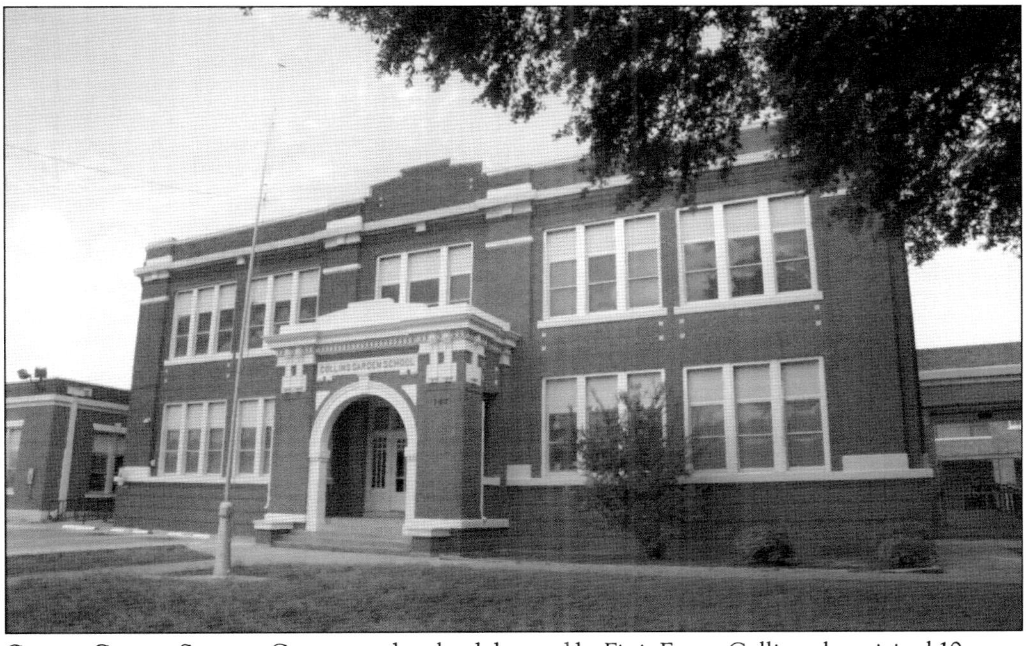

Collins Garden School. Constructed on land donated by Finis Foster Collins, the original 10-room schoolhouse at 167 Harriman Place within the Collins Garden neighborhood was completed in 1915. Several additions were completed in 1930, designated by a plaque that specifies it as School No. 27. The decorative entry features an arched doorway with a recessed foyer. (SAPA.)

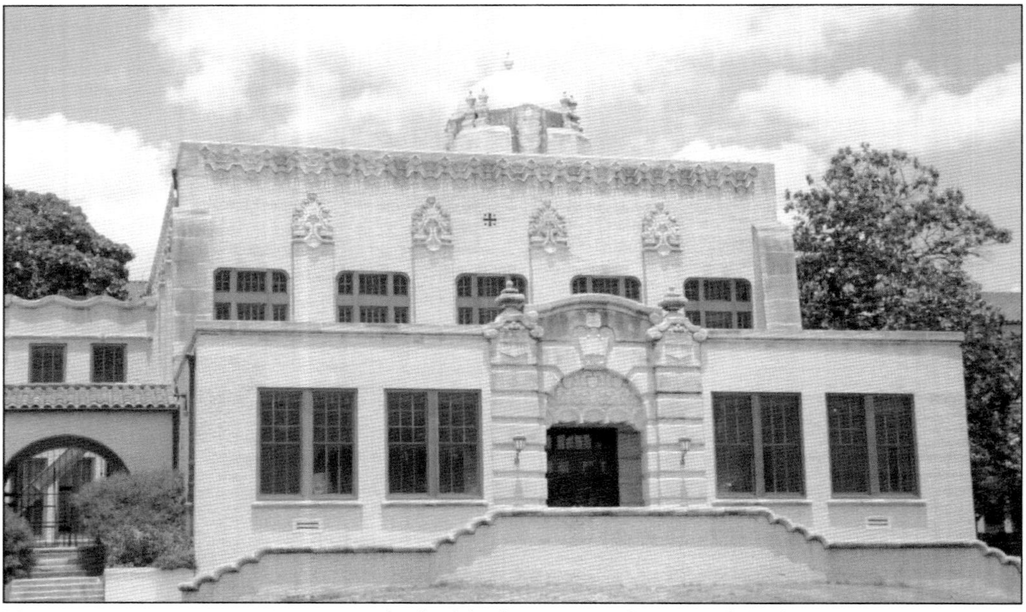

THOMAS JEFFERSON HIGH SCHOOL. The highly decorative educational facility was constructed in 1932 for the city's northwest side near Woodlawn Lake. Situated in the Monticello Park Historic District, the structure displays a combination of Art Deco and Spanish Colonial Revival architecture, resulting in a stylistically unique civic structure that embodies unique craftsmanship and artistic skill. (SAPA.)

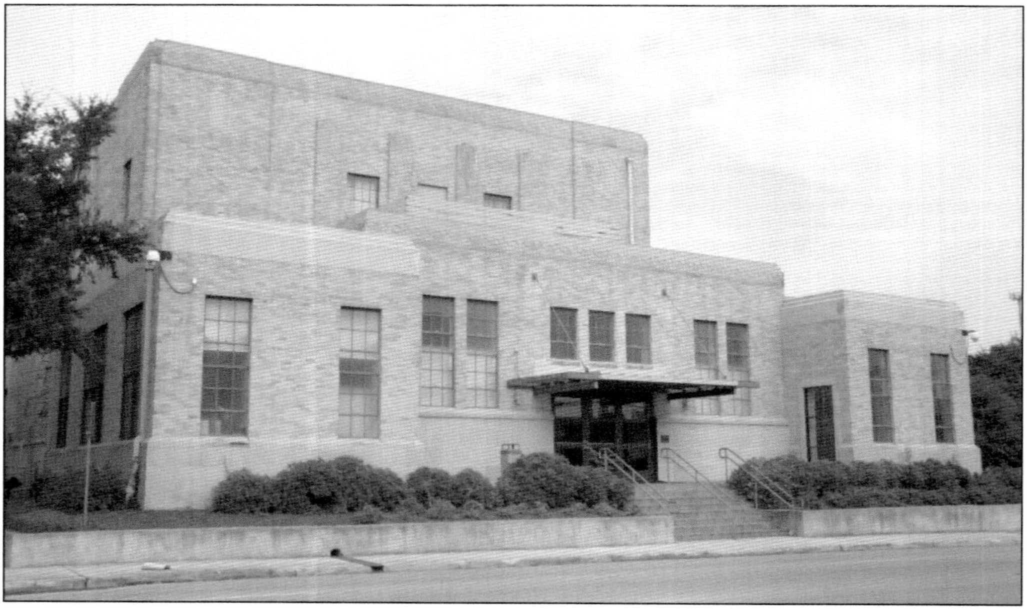

NORTH HACKBERRY STREET SCHOOL. Less elaborate than other Art Deco buildings of the period, the school expresses what few decorative details it has in cast stone. The building's base is executed in cut stone blocks, which visually anchor the basic rectilinear forms. The structure was assimilated in 2001 by the private educational foundation known as Carver Academy, which was founded by David Robinson, formerly of the San Antonio Spurs. (SAPA.)

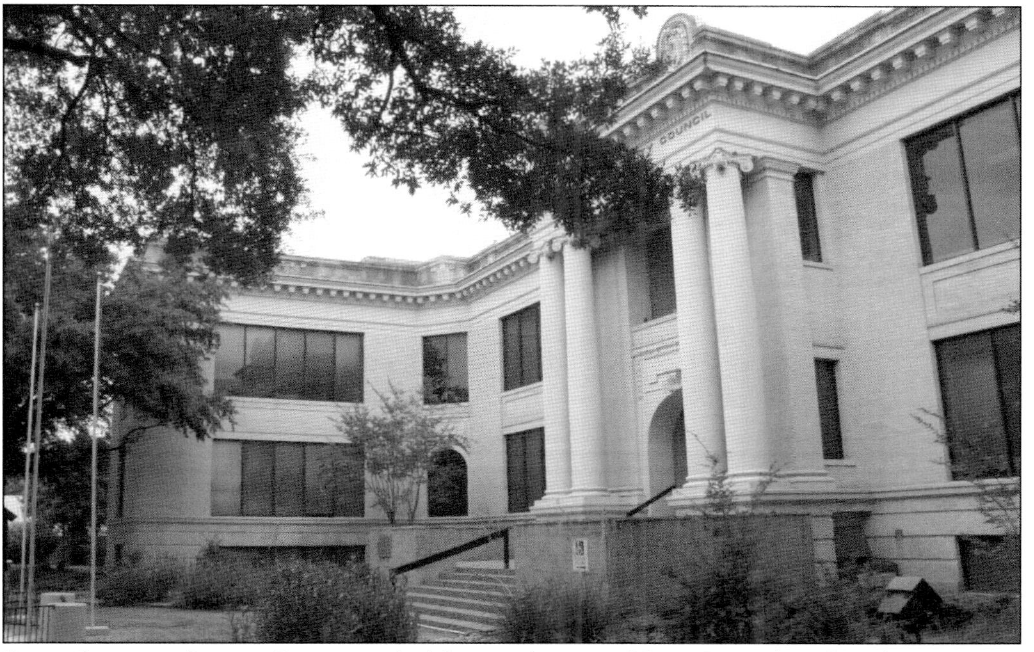

DAVID CROCKETT SCHOOL. Becoming the Mexican American Unity Council in 1977, the impressive structure served as a school on the city's west side until 1967. Most-known for his church designs, San Antonio native Leo M. J. Dielmann conceived the structure in 1911. It remains one of San Antonio's most monumental educational facilities for a city public school designed in the early 20th century. (SAPA.)

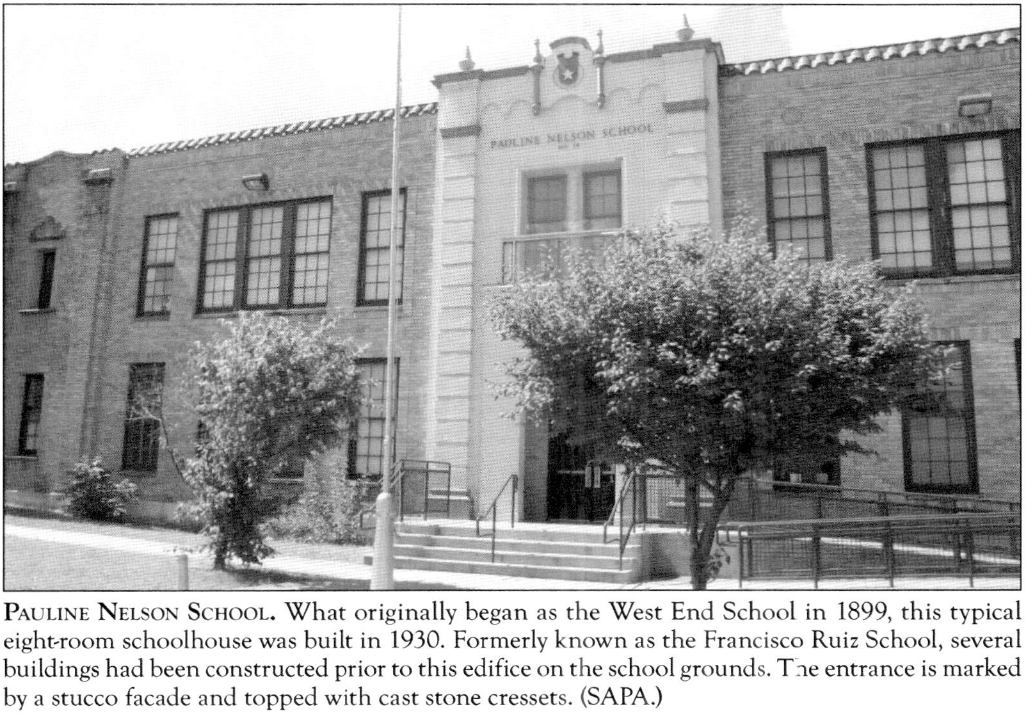

PAULINE NELSON SCHOOL. What originally began as the West End School in 1899, this typical eight-room schoolhouse was built in 1930. Formerly known as the Francisco Ruiz School, several buildings had been constructed prior to this edifice on the school grounds. The entrance is marked by a stucco facade and topped with cast stone cressets. (SAPA.)

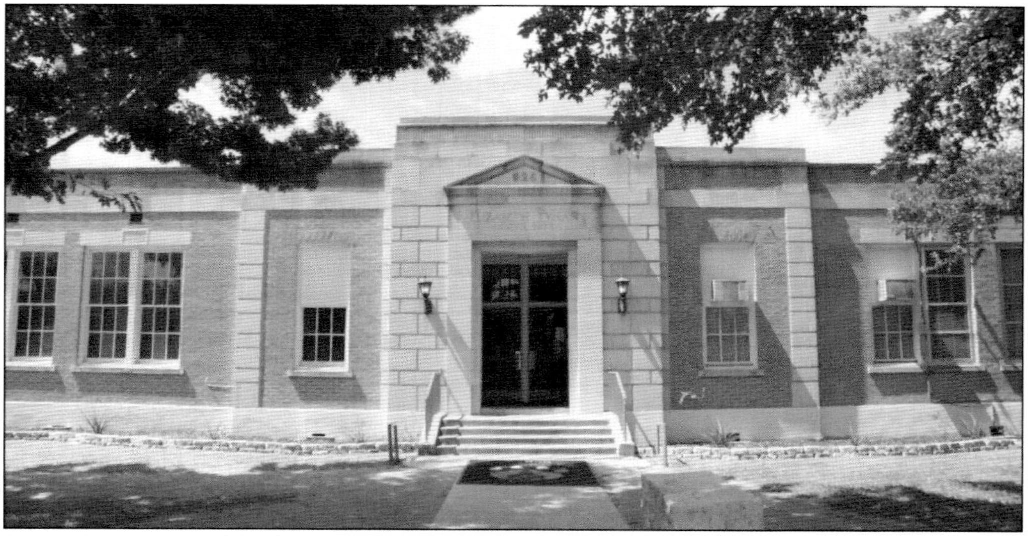

Tynan School. Neighborhood residents petitioned the district for a new school to serve Houston Heights on the city's east side. The original four-classroom school opened in 1932 and is named for Elizabeth Tynan, a local teacher and principal who served 23 years in the San Antonio Independent School District. The entrance to the single-story structure exhibits a cut stone facade flanking the basic doorway, which is topped with a modest pediment. (SAPA.)

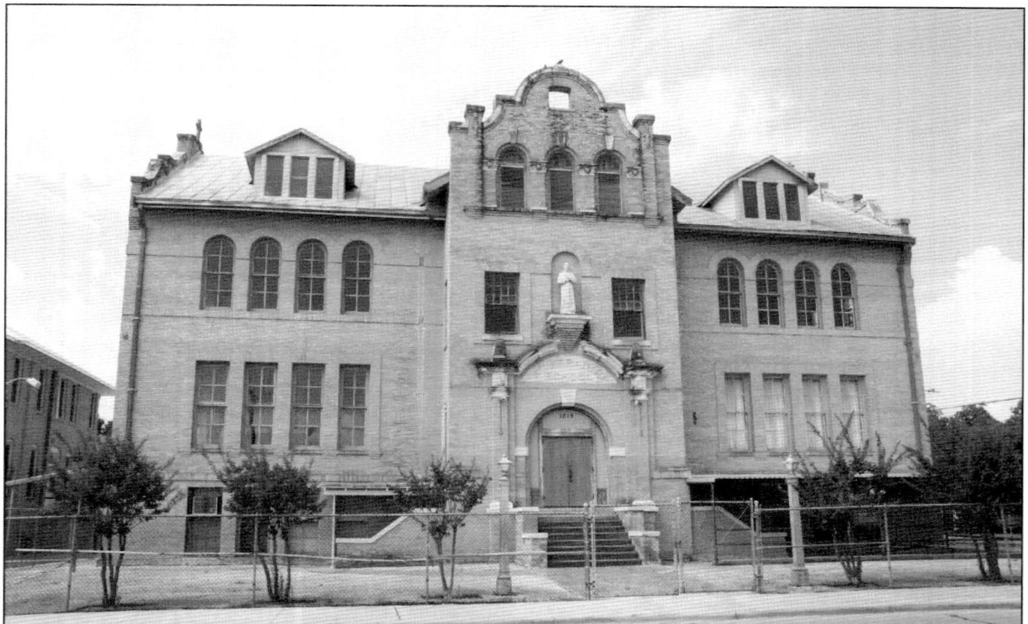

St. Gerard School. Although the Catholic high school was not founded until 1927, this school building was constructed 15 years earlier. In what was then called South Heights, two buildings date to this era, marked on the school building's entry keystone as 1912. The adjacent rectory is constructed of the same brick as the school, with a less prominent parapet, but has undergone significant alterations. St. Gerard School is located just one block north of the Knob Hill Historic District, near the Denver Heights neighborhood. (SAPA.)

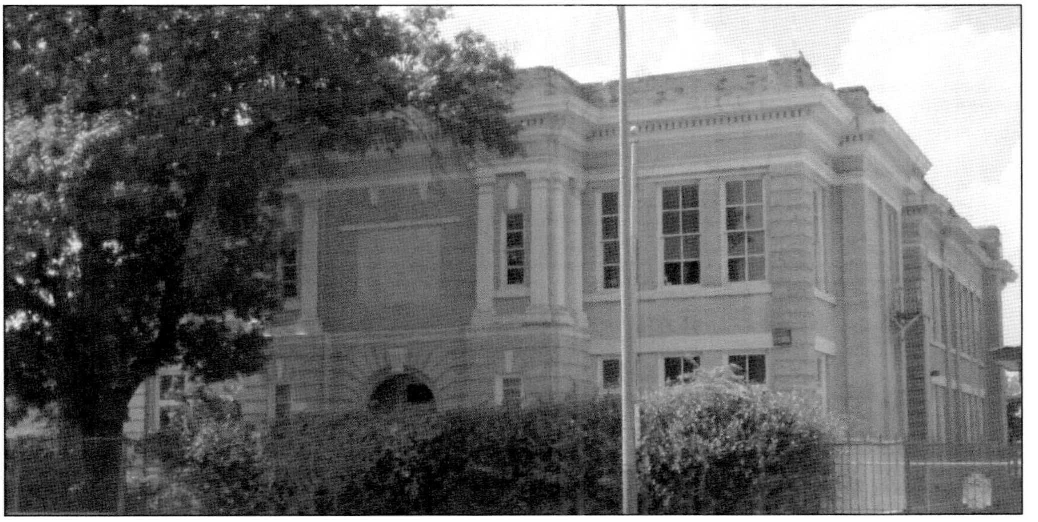

SAM HOUSTON SCHOOL. Constructed in 1907, the main entry facing Travis Street features highly decorative banding, utilizing buff-colored brick and upper-story pilasters, while the corners are embellished with quoins. Although executed entirely in brick, the detailing imitates Beaux-Arts styling. (SAPA.)

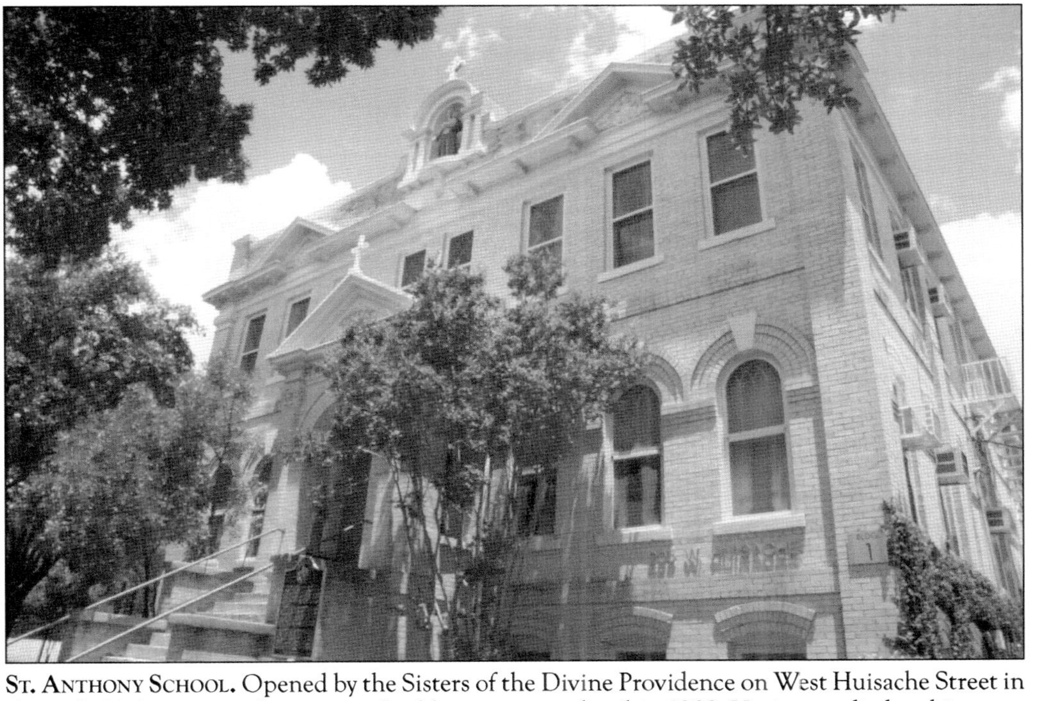

ST. ANTHONY SCHOOL. Opened by the Sisters of the Divine Providence on West Huisache Street in the early 20th century, this campus building was completed in 1909. Having studied architecture at the Massachusetts Institute of Technology, local architect Fred B. Gaenslen designed the eight-classroom building. A statue of St. Anthony resides in the parapet niche directly above the entry. (SAPA.)

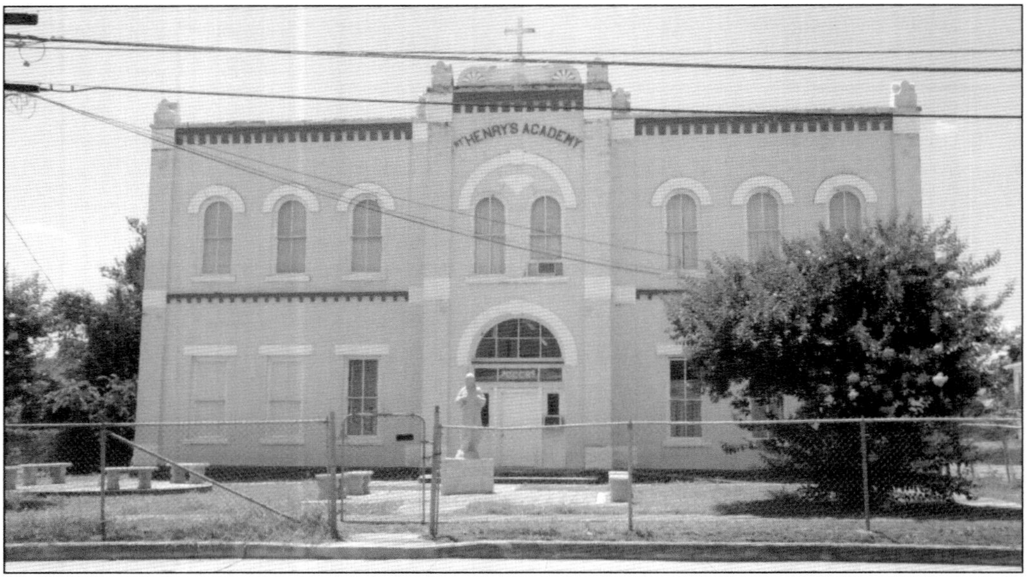

St. Henry's Academy. Resulting from a need to expand into the German-speaking Catholic neighborhood on South Flores Street, the St. Henry's Academy was founded in 1893. An offshoot from the St. Joseph Catholic Church downtown, the school was founded under the guidance of Rev. Henry Pefferkorn. Continuing expansion of St. Joseph led to the establishment of St. Henry Catholic Church in 1904. (SAPA.)

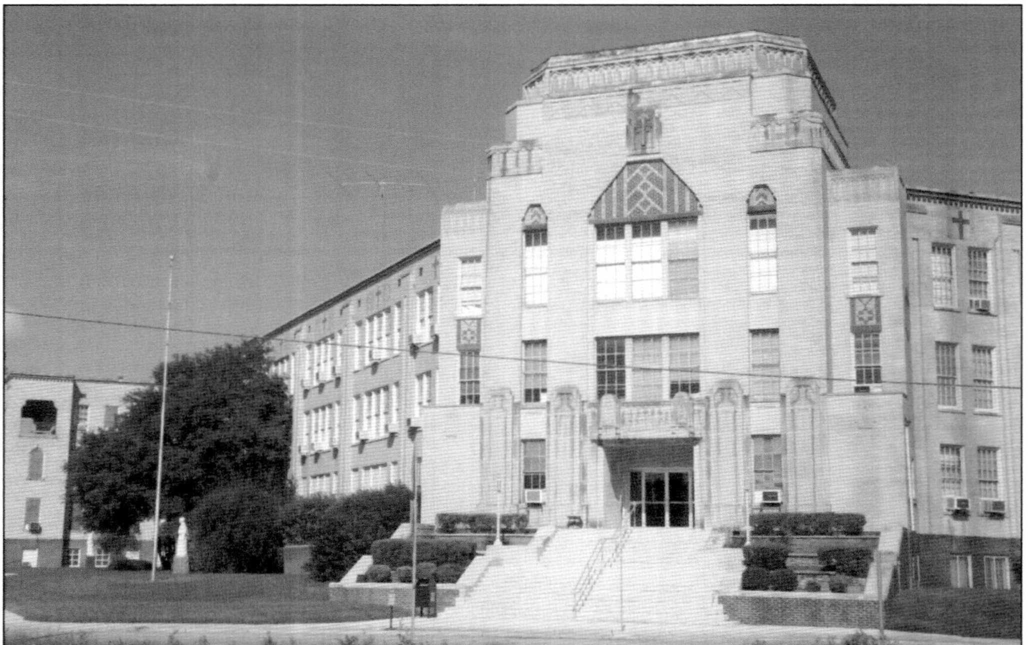

Central Catholic High School. The school's origin dates to 1853, when French educators from the Society of Mary were prompted by Bishop Jean-Marie Odin to open a school for boys, which later evolved into St. Mary's Institute. Built in 1932, Central Catholic High School features Art Deco styling in combination with ecclesiastical ornamentation executed in contrasting brick. (SAPA.)

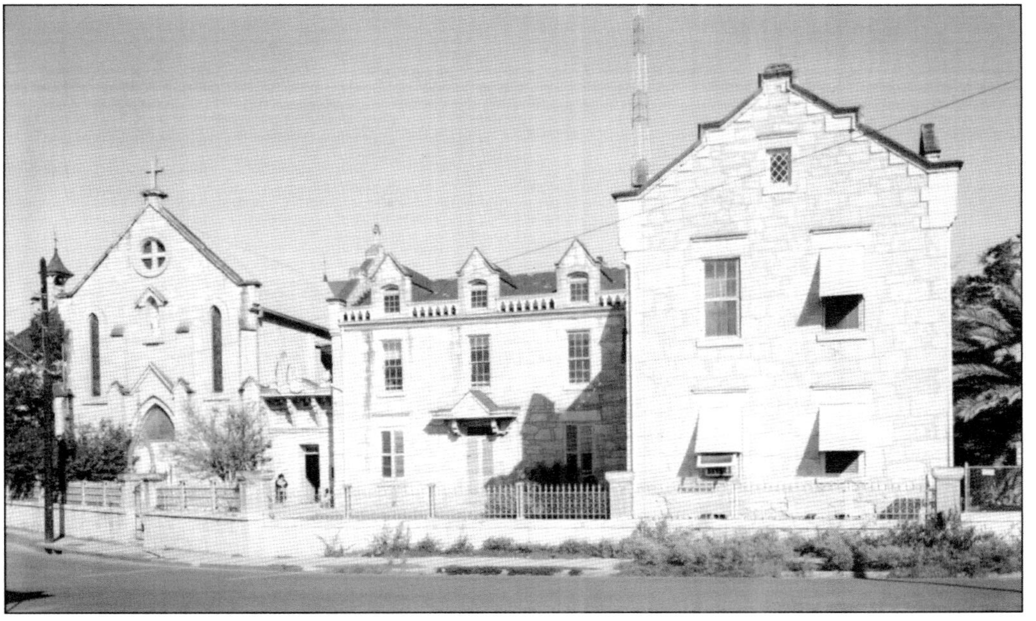

Ursuline Academy. Originally a Catholic school for girls, the Ursuline Academy was founded in 1851 by Bishop Jean-Marie Odin, Fr. Claude Dubuis, and the Sisters of the Ursuline Order of New Orleans. This photograph, taken in 1961, captures the west facade of an addition to the campus from the late 19th century. French architect Francis P. Giraud is credited with the design for several of the campus buildings, including some structures that date from 1851 through 1910. The Ursuline Academy is now home to the Southwest School of Art. (HABS.)

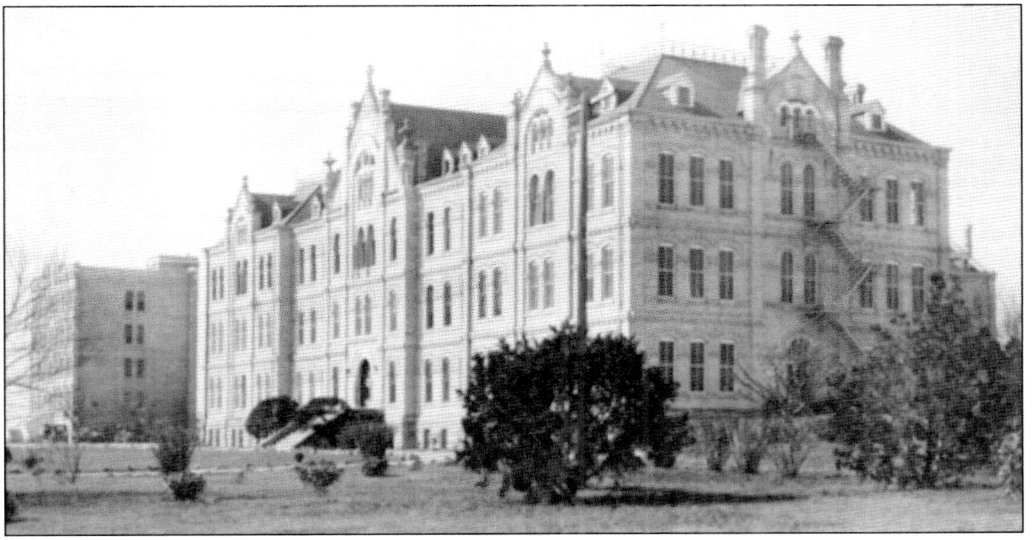

St. Mary's University. The origins of the university date to 1852, when the Brothers of the Society of Mary opened St. Mary's Institute in downtown San Antonio. In 1894, the Marianist educators constructed what was then St. Louis College near Woodlawn Lake to deal with exponential growth. By 1927, a total of three structures had been completed on campus, and the school was renamed St. Mary's University. This photograph from the late 1920s depicts St. Louis Hall and the 1908 Reinbolt Hall to the left. (UTSA.)

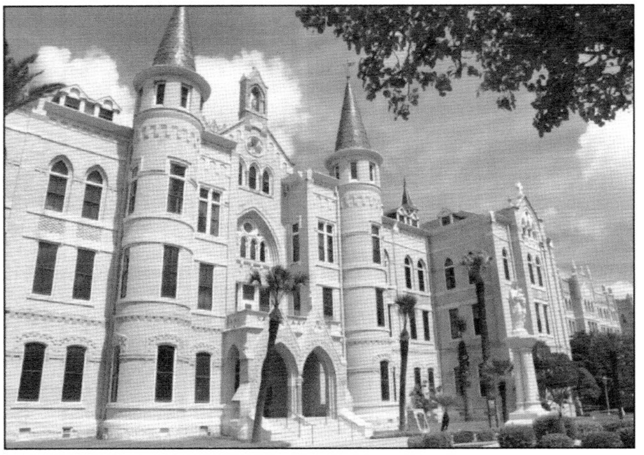

Our Lady of the Lake University. Founded by the Sisters of the Congregation of the Divine Providence at the edge of Lake Elmendorf in the former West End development, the main building originally opened as a school for girls in 1896. The Châteauesque structure exhibits exceptional brick detailing as well as a double-entry vestibule with clover motifs. The central parapet also features a cast stone clover window centerpiece. (SAPA.)

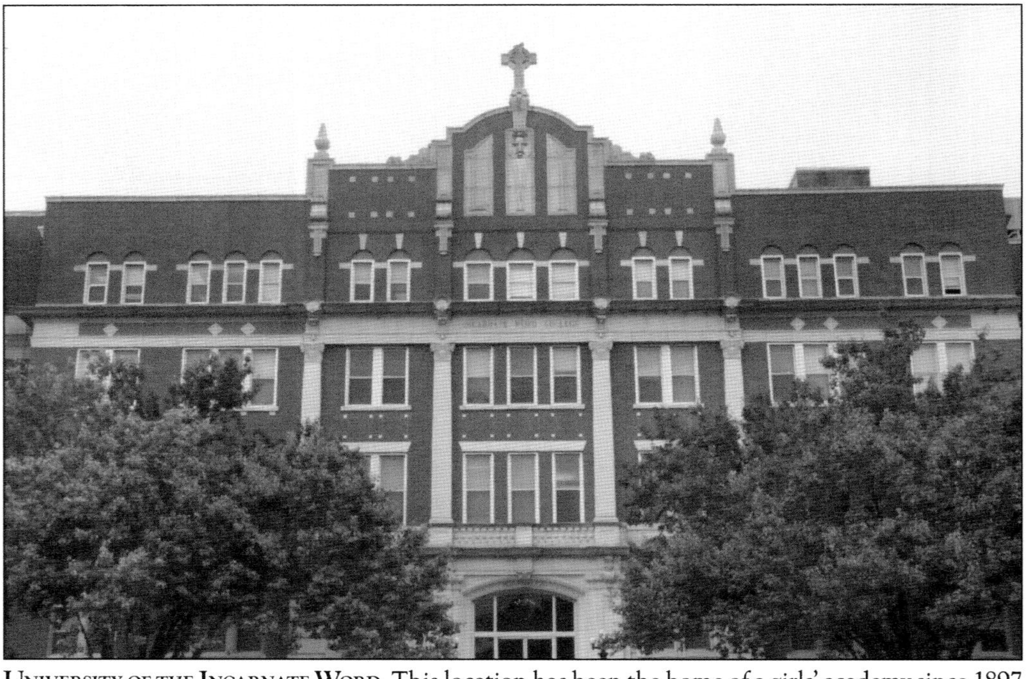

University of the Incarnate Word. This location has been the home of a girls' academy since 1897 and was founded by the Sisters of Charity of the Incarnate Word. Constructed on land formerly owned by local philanthropist George W. Brackenridge, the redbrick administration building was constructed in 1921, just one year before the surrounding neighborhood incorporated as Alamo Heights. (SAPA.)

Six

Religious Structures

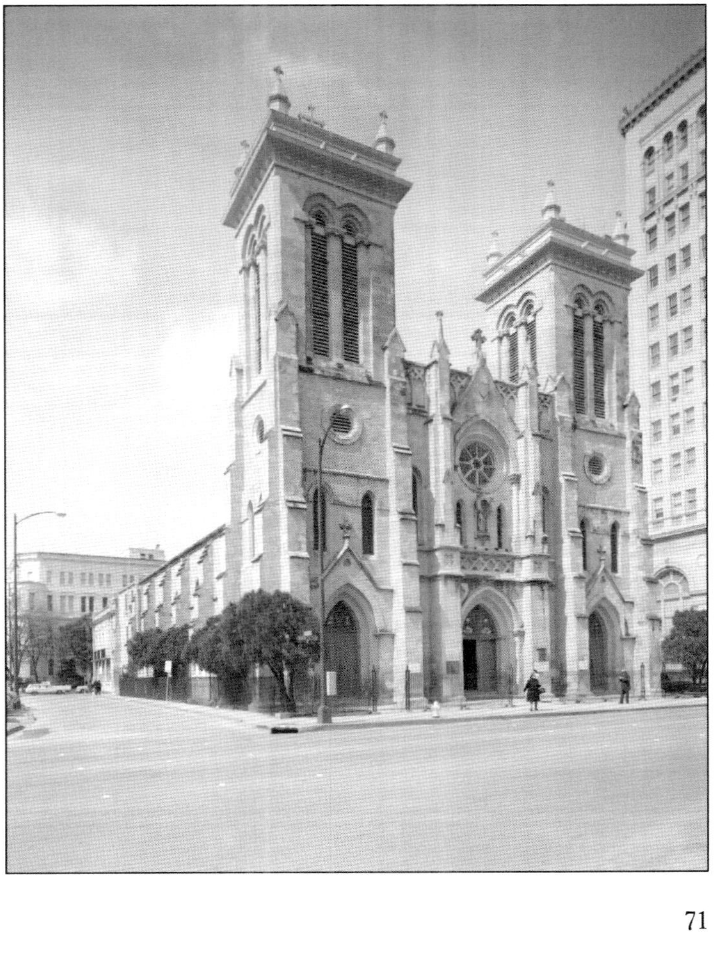

San Fernando Cathedral. Also known as the Church of the Nuestra Señora de la Candelaria y Guadalupe, the building traces its roots to the 1730s, when Canary Islanders settled the city. The original church walls were constructed between 1738 and 1750 and can be seen when looking at the rear of the cathedral. Many alterations have drastically changed its appearance, most affected by the designs of architect and politician Francis P. Giraud in 1868. To the right, the Frost Bank Building was constructed in 1922. (HABS.)

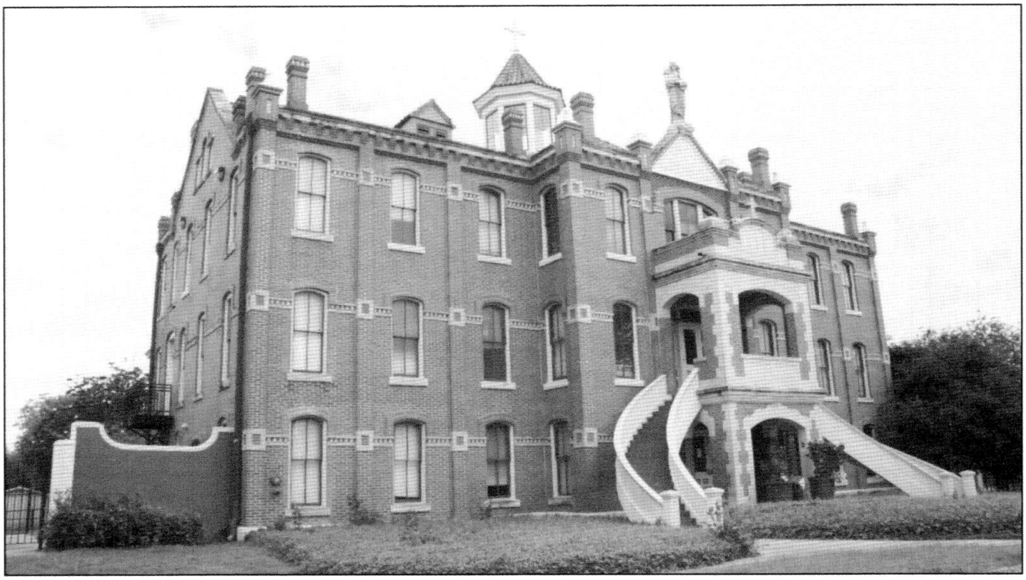

Monastery of Our Lady of Charity. Located on the east side of San Antonio, the redbrick monastery was constructed on Montana Street in 1899. Notable for the dual-entry staircase leading to the second level, the three-story building utilizes cast stone and contrasting brick to delineate horizontal details. The structure was designed by San Antonio architect Leo M. J. Dielmann and features a glass cupola on the roof. (SAPA.)

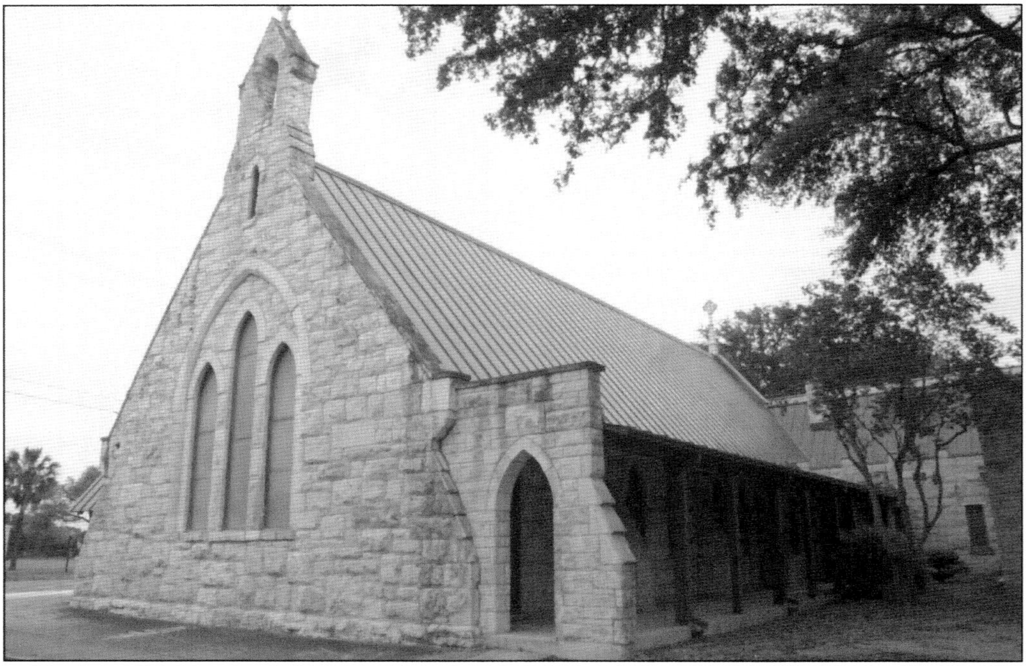

St. Paul's Episcopal Church. Constructed in 1885 of local limestone, the neo-Gothic church served the nearby community of Fort Sam Houston. Located in what is now the Government Hill Historic District, the church is a basic rectilinear plan with stone buttressing. The roofline terminates on each side, with a Celtic cross and bell tower at the western edge. (SAPA.)

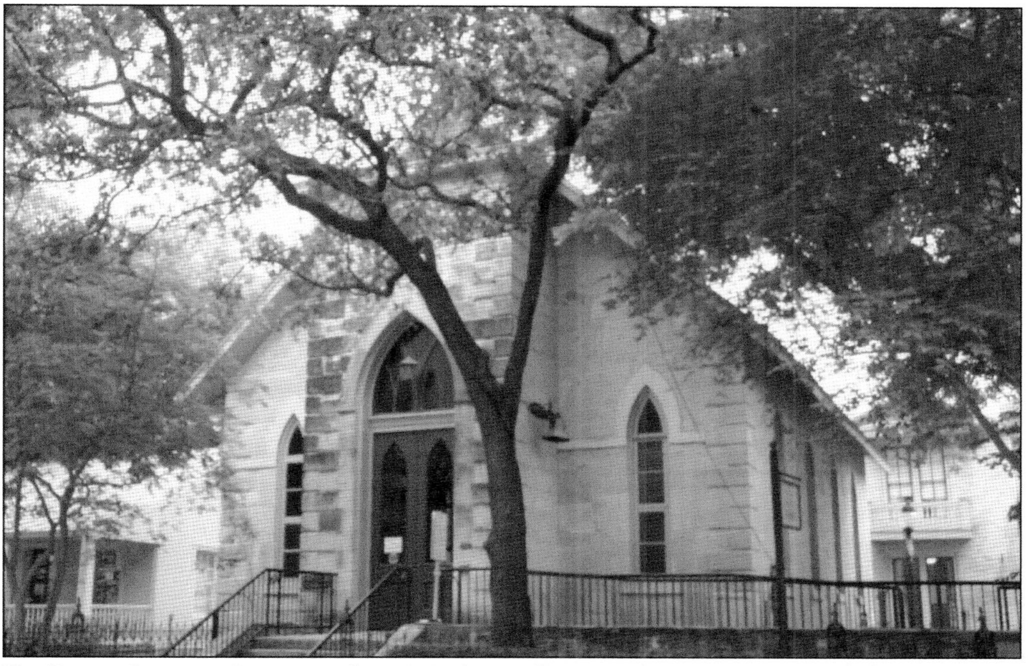

The Little Church. Constructed in 1879, the small neo-Gothic structure struggled to maintain a permanent worshipping community and was vacant during the early 1920s. As part of the La Villita Historic Arts Village, the church now conducts nondenominational services and is an event venue. The stone building features an alternating quoining technique only on the front facade. (SAPA.)

St. Paul Methodist Episcopal Church. Named for this church that was constructed during the 1870s, the neo-Gothic church employs local limestone and features buttressing on its northern facade. A replacement structure for the previous wood-frame building, this stone building was erected in 1884 in what is now known as the St. Paul Square Historic District. (SAPA.)

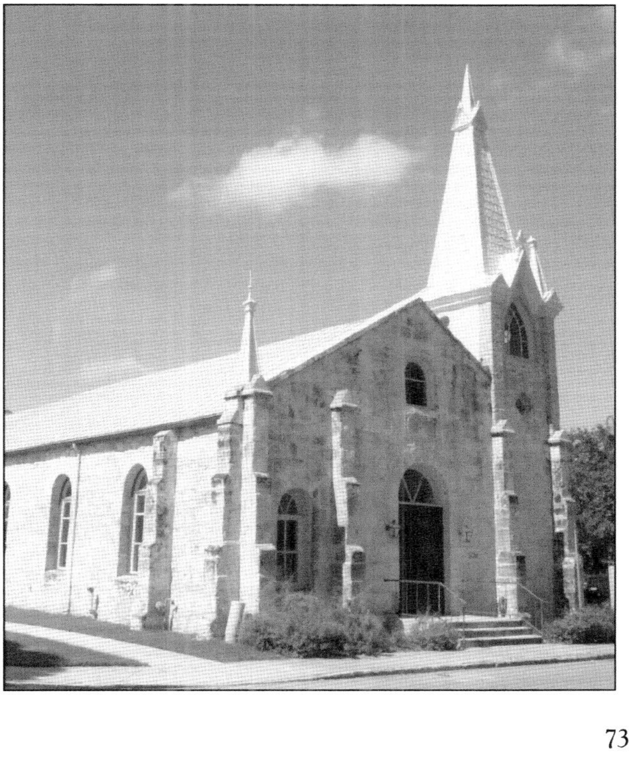

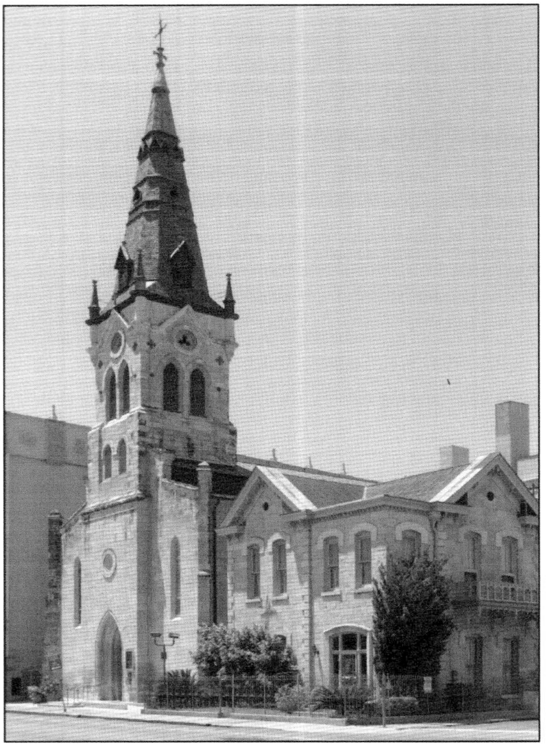

St. Joseph Catholic Church. The cornerstone of St. Joseph's, nestled in the heart of downtown, was laid in 1868. Founded by Catholic immigrants from Germany, the neo-Gothic church has art glass, fabricated in 1902 by German immigrant Emil Frei. Despite being threatened by encroaching commercial developments, the church remains intact. (Carol M. Highsmith and HABS.)

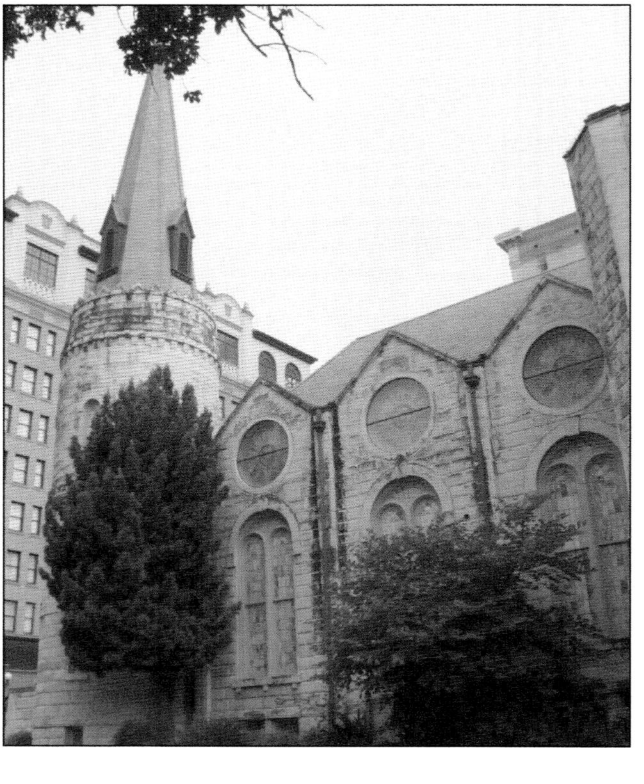

Travis Park Methodist Church. Founded in 1846 by Rev. John Wesley DeVilbiss, the church was not completed at this location until 1886. Rapid congregation growth required an expansion in the early 1900s, and the church is now capable of seating 480 patrons. The circular tower was topped with a low turret during this period but was later replaced with a taller one that remains today. The St. Anthony Hotel is visible just beyond the church's spire. (SAPA.)

MADISON SQUARE PRESBYTERIAN CHURCH. Rev. William Howell Buchanan purchased several lots adjacent to Madison Square Park in downtown and established this church in the 1880s. The sanctuary was expanded and a new steeple was added after a storm damaged the building in 1886, just four years after its completion. (SAPA.)

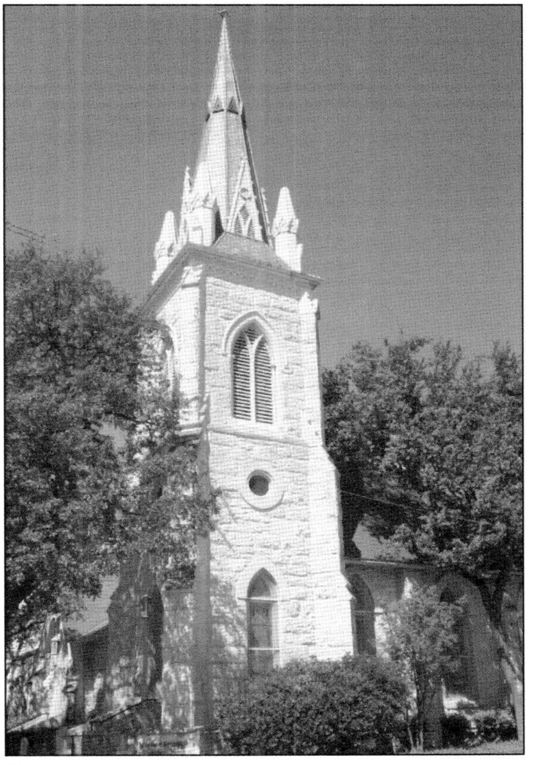

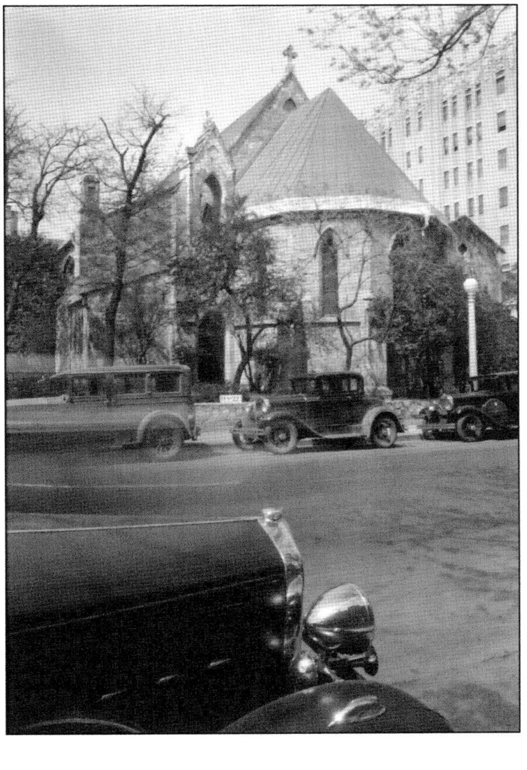

ST. MARK'S EPISCOPAL CHURCH. Designed by British architect Richard Upjohn, St. Mark's church is an excellent example of Upjohn's well-known Gothic Revival style. Work began on the church before the onset of the Civil War, but the limestone building was not completed until 1875. An expansion occurred during the prosperous 1920s, and by 1950, the church underwent a major interior renovation and also added the carillon and Gothic-style tower. This view of the apse was taken in 1936 by Arthur W. Stewart. (HABS.)

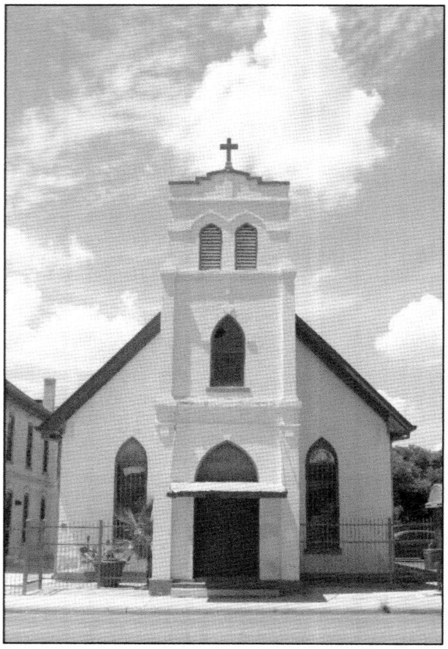

St. Peter Claver Church. Founded in 1888 by Irish immigrant Margaret Mary Healy-Murphy as the first institution in Texas built for African American Catholics, the modest church structure and school buildings were assembled at the corner of Live Oak and Nolan Streets. Community disapproval made staffing and fundraising efforts difficult. To remedy this, Healy-Murphy established the Sisters of the Holy Ghost. Still in operation as the Healy-Murphy Center under the guidance of the State of Texas at its original location, the school serves students at risk regardless of ethnicity and is designated locally as the Healy-Murphy Historic District. (SAPA.)

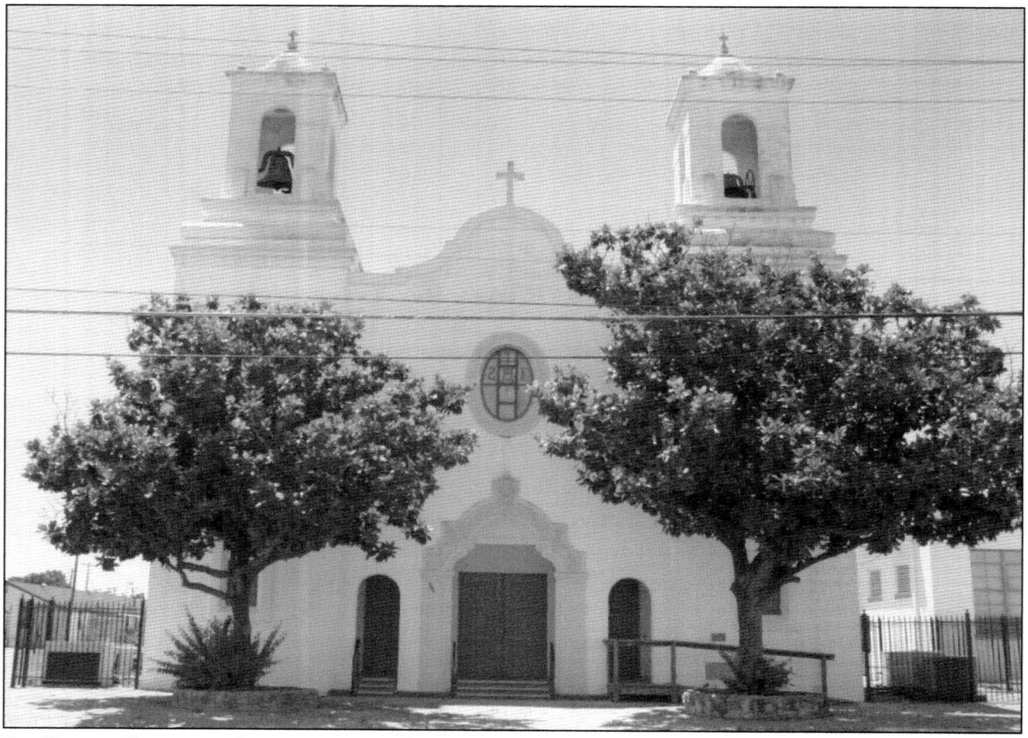

St. Henry Catholic Church. Named for its first pastor, Rev. Henry M. Wirtz, the church was established from a need to expand St. Joseph Catholic Church downtown. St. Henry's Academy was previously established in the 1890s, adjacent to the church structure. Constructed in 1929, the modest Spanish Colonial Revival facade is evidence of the influential Mission architecture so favored during this era. (SAPA.)

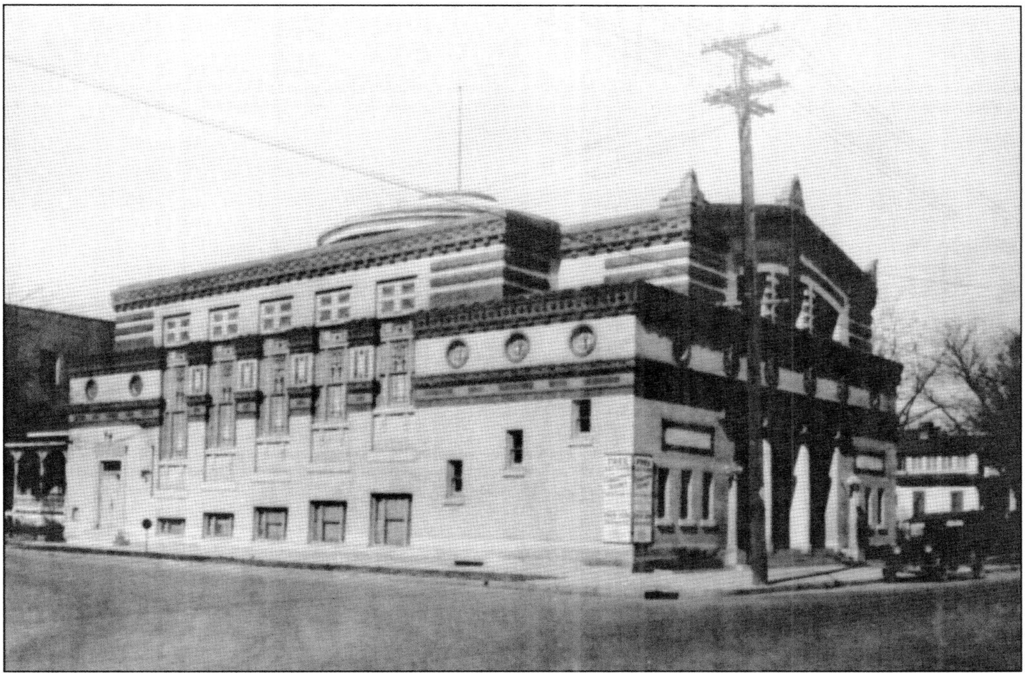

CHRIST, SCIENTIST. These photographs taken in 1927 show an advertisement near each building's entrance offering free lectures on Christian Science. Completed in 1916 at the intersection of North Alamo Street and McCullough Avenue, the highly decorative facade of the First Church of Christ, Scientist (above) features brick construction with a contrasting ornamental cornice, corner banding, and a central dome. The Second Church of Christ, Scientist (below) is located at 230 West Magnolia Avenue in what is now known as the Monte Vista Historic District. This photograph depicts the monumental, north-facing entrance. (Both, Ann Russell and UTSA.)

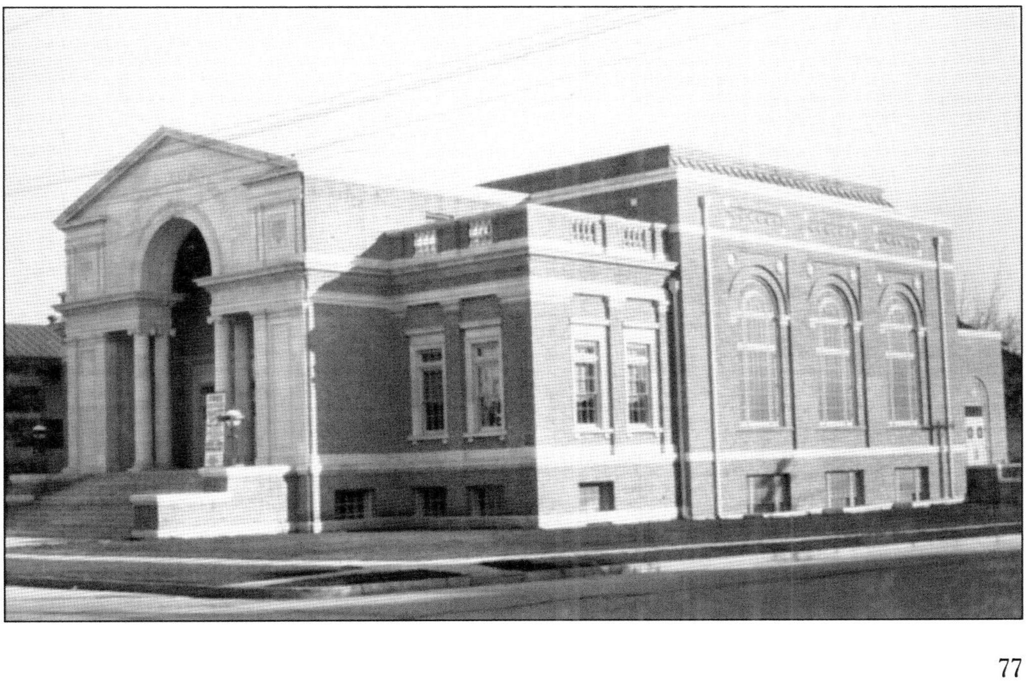

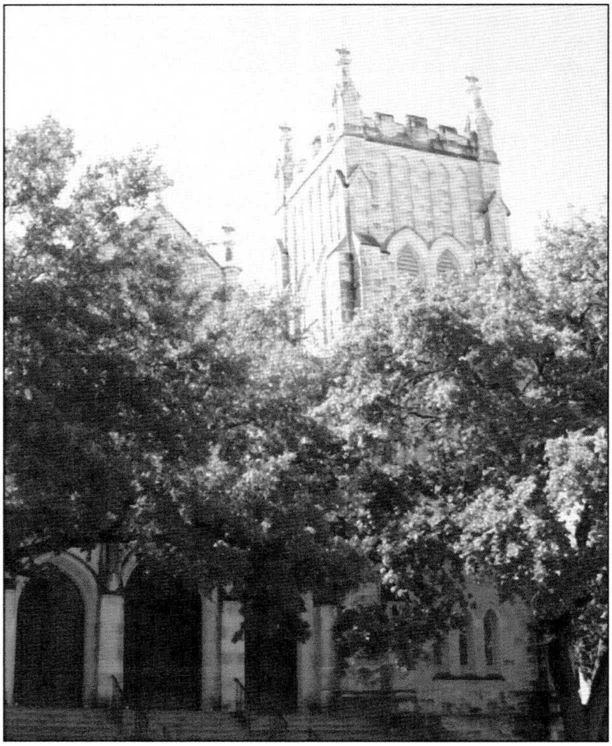

First Presbyterian Church. Founded by pastor John McCullough in 1846, First Presbyterian was the first Protestant congregation organized in San Antonio. This neo-Gothic structure, designed by Atlee B. Ayers, was completed at the corner of North Alamo and Fourth Streets. The prominent tower at the southwest corner has the 1909 cornerstone at its base. (SAPA.)

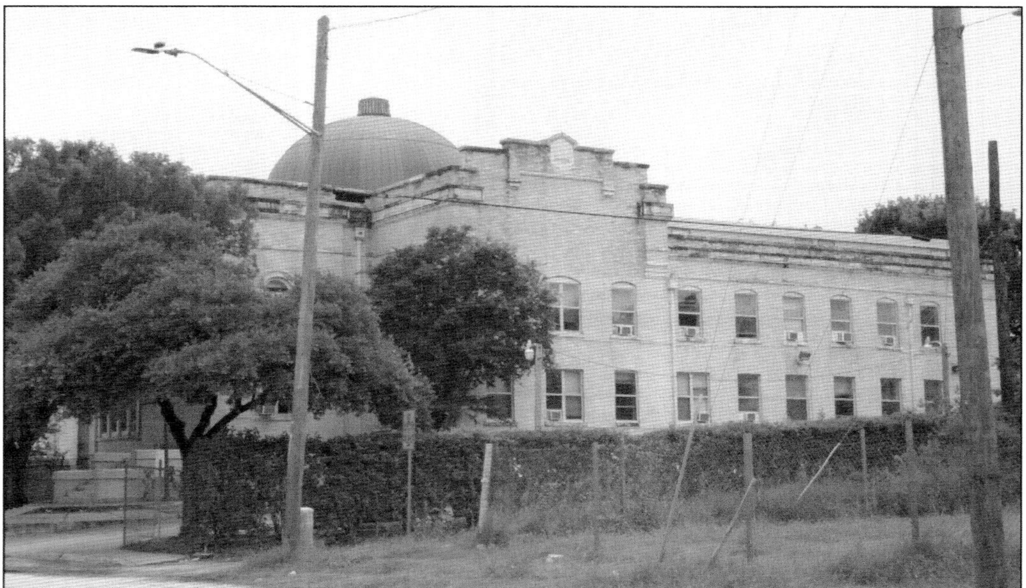

Prospect Hill Missionary Baptist Church. Designed by architect Henry J. Harker of Arkansas, the 1911 church building utilizes a central rotunda or worship space, surrounded by classrooms on multiple levels. This floor plan was popularized by architect Jacob Snyder. Restoration efforts in the 1980s restored the original exterior massing of the dome that was destroyed by fire, and the building has since been utilized as apartments. (SAPA.)

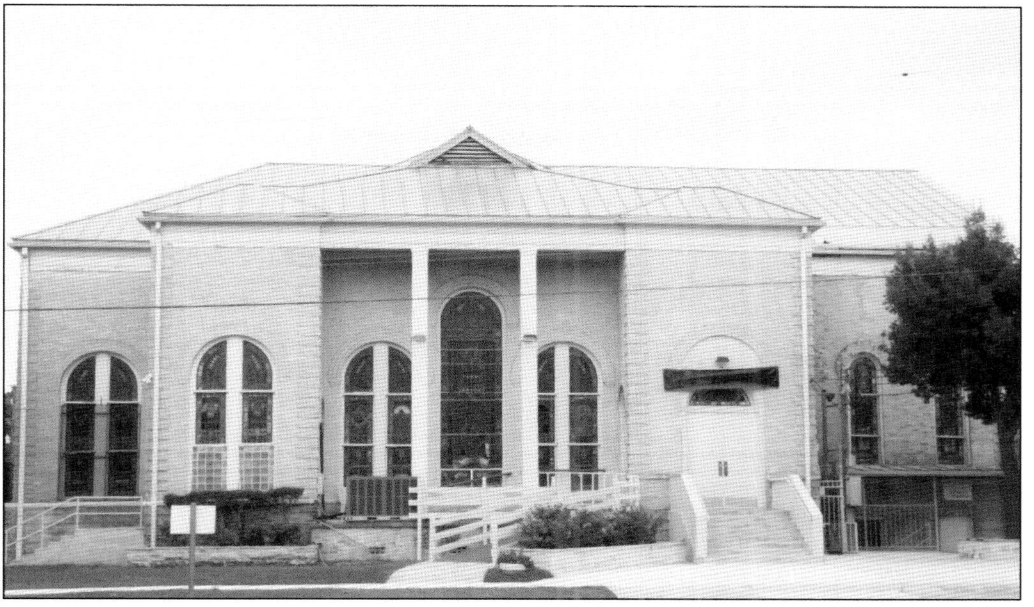

GERMAN METHODIST EPISCOPAL CHURCH. Designed by local architect W.N. Hagy in 1911, this structure, originally founded in 1889, was a rebuild for the church community. Extensive art glass is featured within the semicircular arched windows and doorways. (SAPA.)

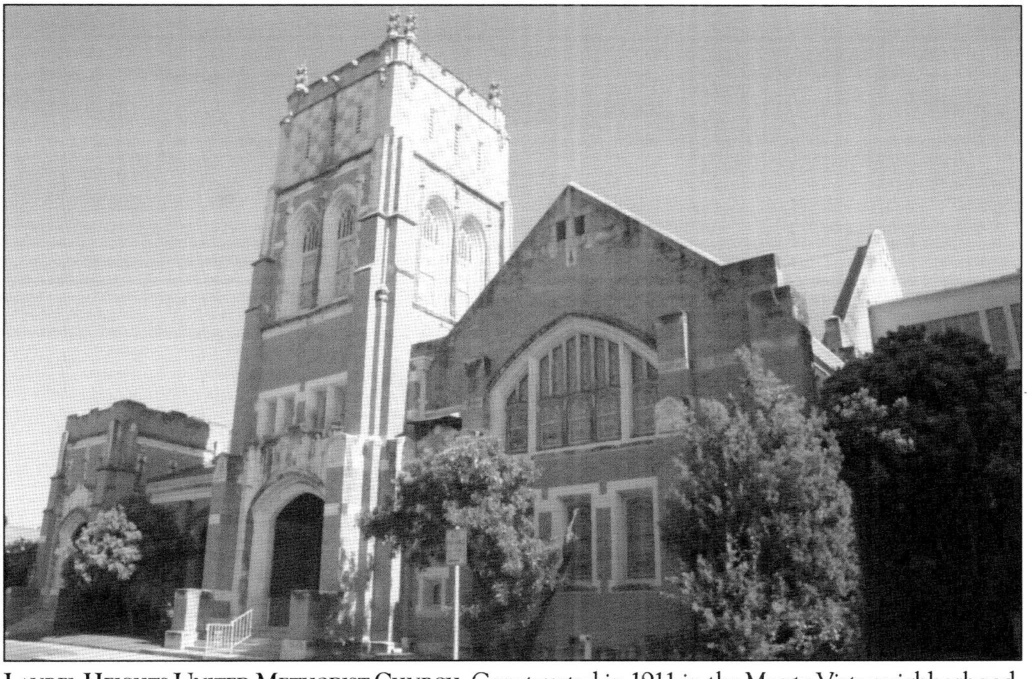

LAUREL HEIGHTS UNITED METHODIST CHURCH. Constructed in 1911 in the Monte Vista neighborhood, the church was designed by prominent local architect Atlee B. Ayers. Neo-Gothic in style, the main tower is now patterned with decorative cast stone elements but originally boasted a steeple. Due to problems with deterioration, an expansion in the late 1920s removed the steeple and heightened the tower. (SAPA.)

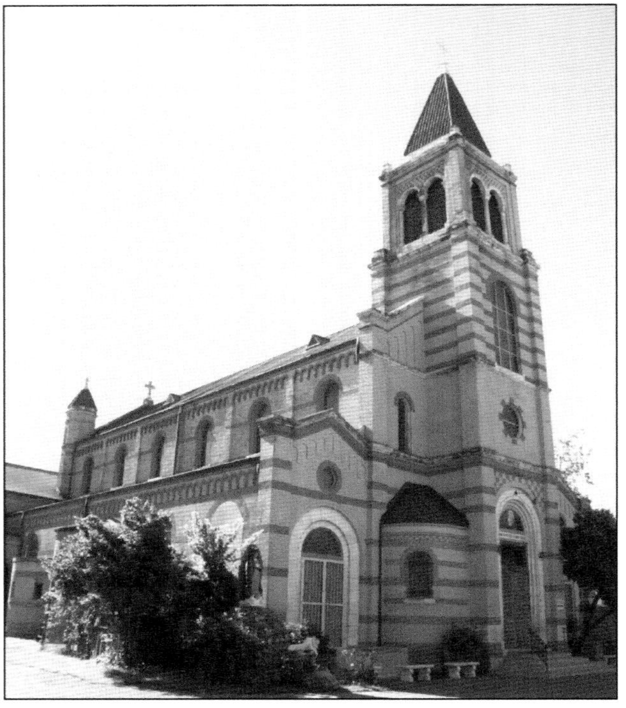

Immaculate Heart of Mary Catholic Church. Distinctly decorated with elaborate stenciling and artwork throughout the interior, the decor is heavily inspired by Byzantine influences. Constructed in 1912, the contrasting brick banding de-emphasizes the building's verticality on the entrance and tower. (SAPA.)

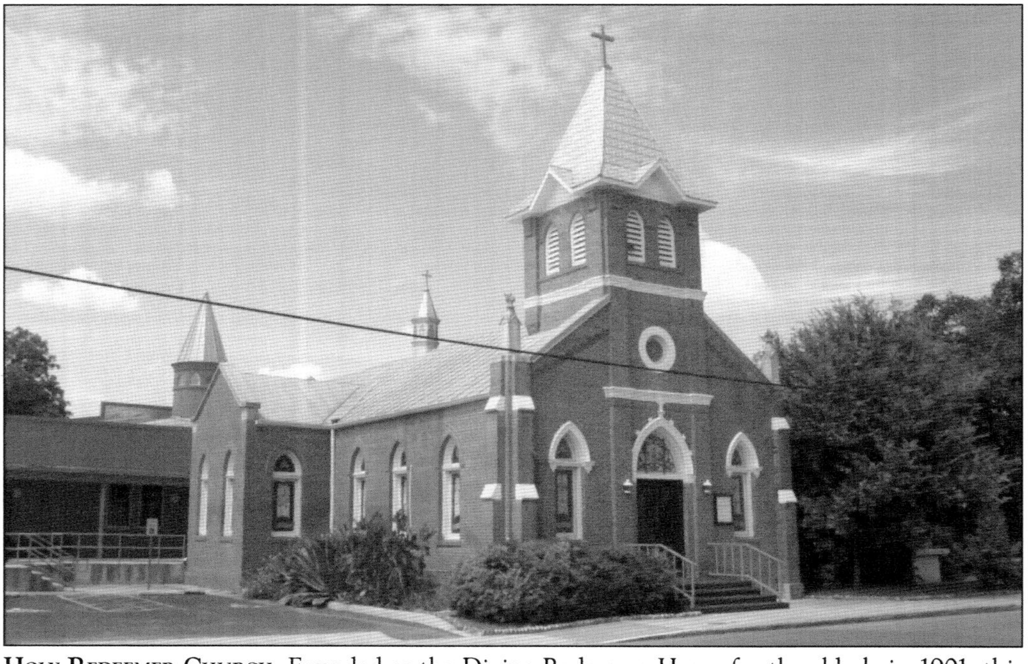

Holy Redeemer Church. Founded as the Divine Redeemer Home for the elderly in 1901, this structure later underwent a name change, and an education center was built. Coordinated efforts with the Sisters of the Holy Ghost assisted in teaching in 1913—the same year the church's plaque indicates completion. The simple redbrick structure is cruciform in plan and features a solitary oculus between the single-arched entry and belfry. (SAPA.)

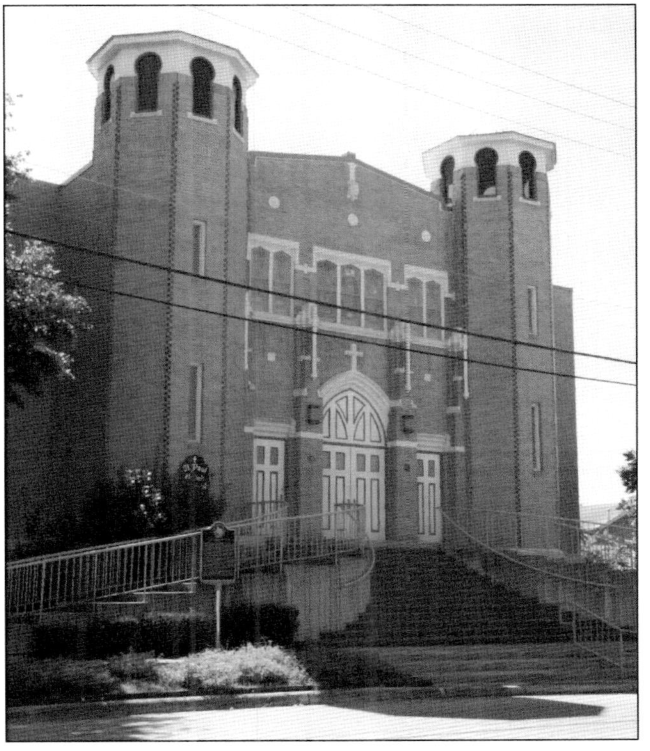

St. Paul United Methodist Church. Originally known as the Colored Methodist Church, the St. Paul congregation was founded by Rev. A. Larkin Carper in 1864. Moving the congregation from St. Paul Square to the corner of Mesquite and Center Streets occurred in 1922, when this brick sanctuary was built. The octagon bell towers vertically emphasize the elevated front facade. (SAPA.)

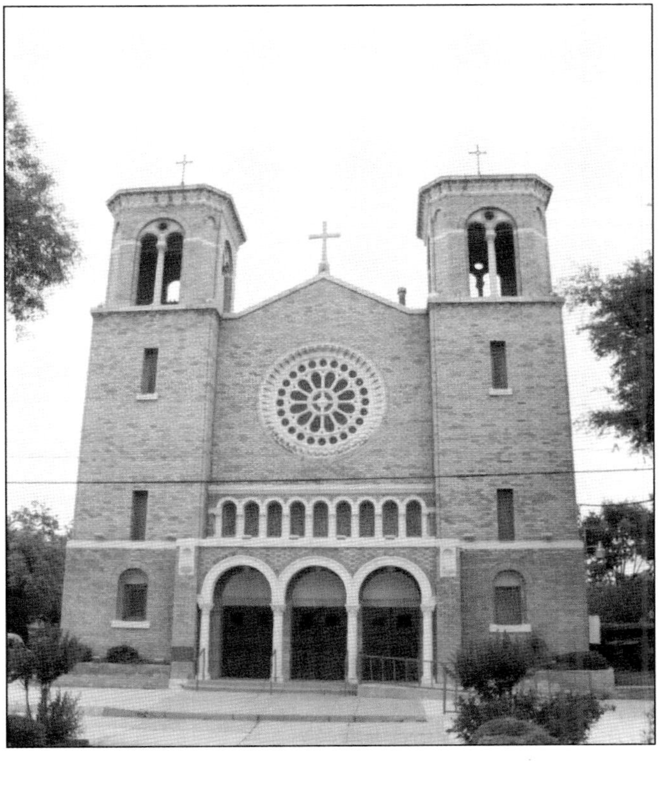

St. Patrick Roman Catholic Church. Constructed in 1895, the original building was destroyed by fire in 1922. In service to the Fort Sam Houston area in historic Government Hill, this church building was completed by 1923. The brick structure features a large rose window and a tripartite entry with circular arches. (SAPA.)

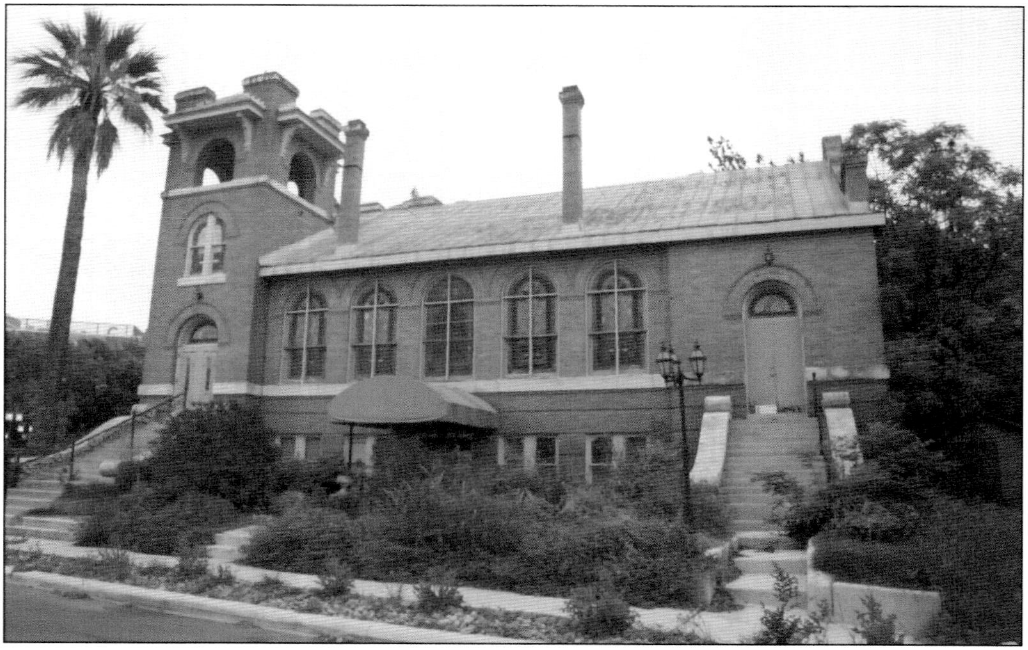

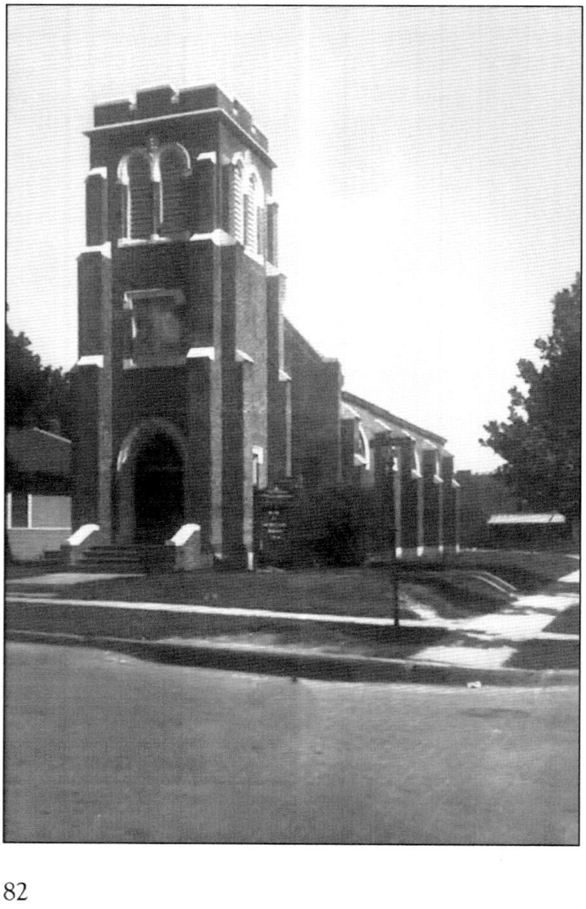

Alamo Methodist Church. Completed in 1912 on South Alamo Street in the King William Historic District, the Mission Revival church was designed by Texas-born architect B.W. Spillman. Disbanded in the 1960s for declining membership, the church was sold and later became a restaurant and live entertainment venue. The building retains much of its original art glass. Although not visible in this perspective, the parapet stylistically imitates the silhouette of the Alamo. (SAPA.)

St. Paul's Evangelical Lutheran Church. Captured by photographer Albert Schaal in 1929, the modest neo-Gothic church on South Presa Street is constructed of red brick. The massive single bell tower dominates the facade at the main entrance. The church was founded in 1913, but this structure was not completed until 1925. (Linda Mercer and UTSA.)

St. Mary's Catholic Church. The original downtown Gothic-style structure built in 1857 was badly damaged by major flooding in 1921. Deciding to replace the church, a new structure was designed by architect Fred. B. Gaenslen and completed in 1924. With a total seating capacity of over 1,200 people, the interior was finished by the Greiwe Decorative Company of Cincinnati in the mid-1950s. (SAPA.)

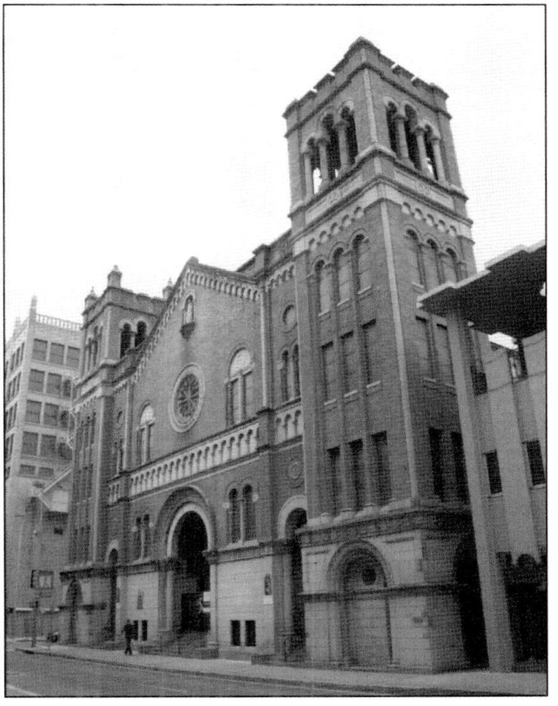

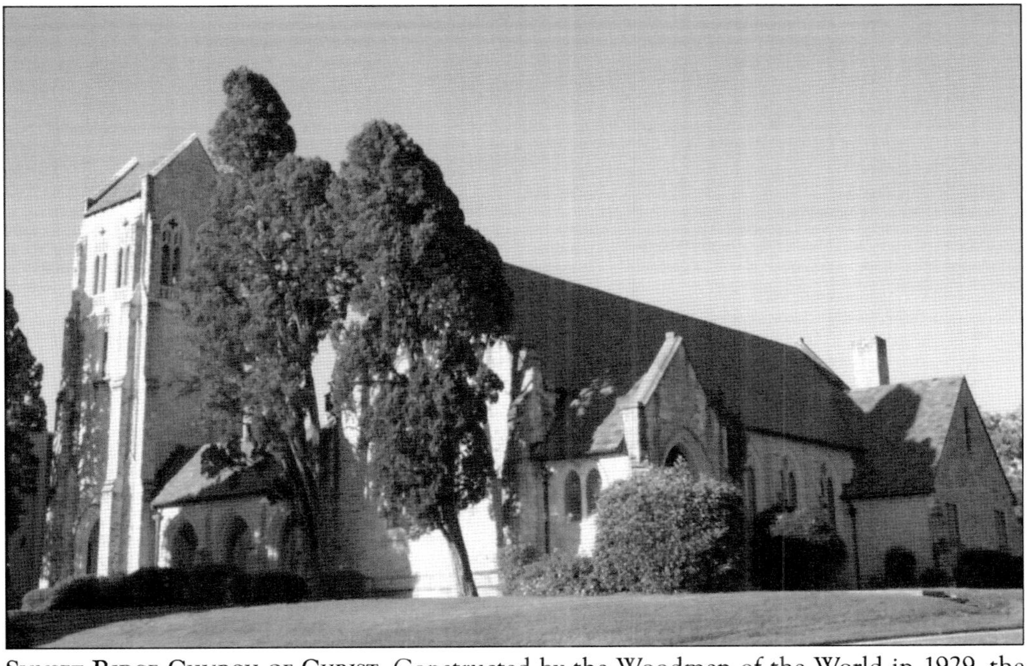

Sunset Ridge Church of Christ. Constructed by the Woodmen of the World in 1929, the limestone chapel was part of a hospital complex that no longer stands. Dedication plaques to the fallen Woodmen of World War I adorn the entryway. Purchased by the Sunset Ridge Church of Christ, the main church building was constructed in 1965, mirroring the neo-Gothic architectural details of the original chapel. (SAPA.)

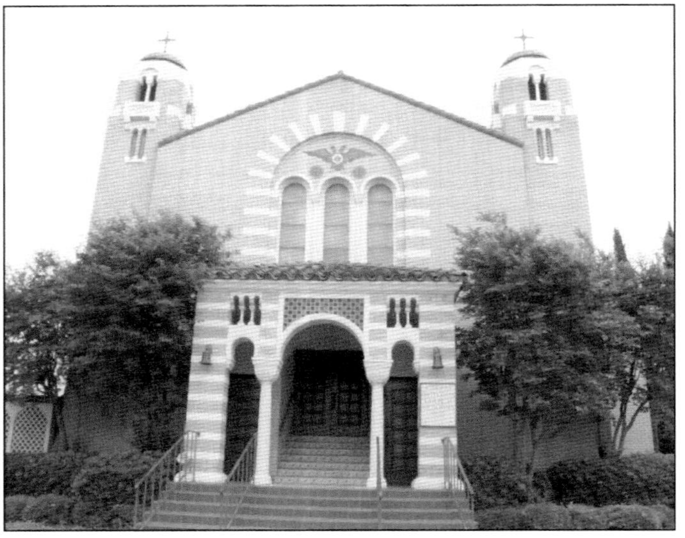

St. Sophia Greek Orthodox Church. Constructed in 1926, the decorative exterior of St. Sophia alternates the use of stone and brick surrounding the main entryway, while uniquely patterned columns and tile work complete the decorative finish. The building was designed by local architect Emmett Jackson, and the iconography and furnishings were received from Mount Athos, a monastic establishment and spiritual center in Greece established in 1054. (SAPA.)

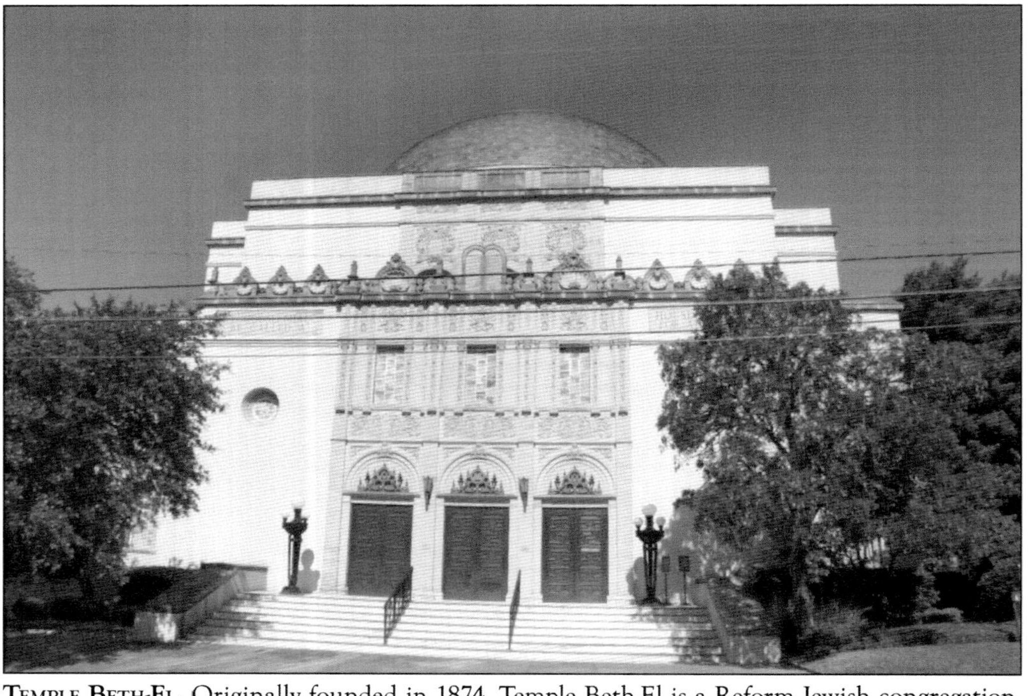

Temple Beth-El. Originally founded in 1874, Temple Beth-El is a Reform Jewish congregation. Located in historic Monte Vista, the structure's tile dome is supported by large, austere vaults designed by American architect Harvey Lindsley Page. The entry on Belknap Street is marked with scalloped ornament and floral motifs. Existing as the oldest synagogue in South Texas, this temple was completed in 1927. (SAPA.)

Church of San Francesco Di Paola. Listed as a Texas Historic Landmark, the small Catholic church was founded by Italian Immigrants in 1927 on land donated by the Christopher Columbus Italian Society. Neighboring the church is the society's meeting hall, which opened in 1928 on Columbus Square. Constructed of red brick, the contrasting entry arch contains decorative bas-relief detailing. (SAPA.)

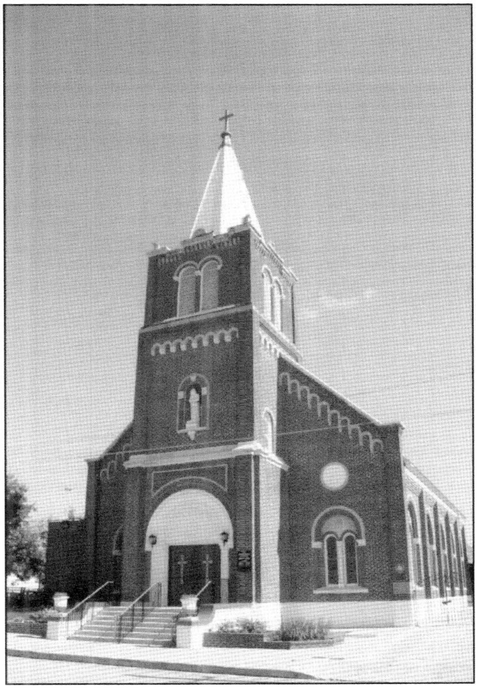

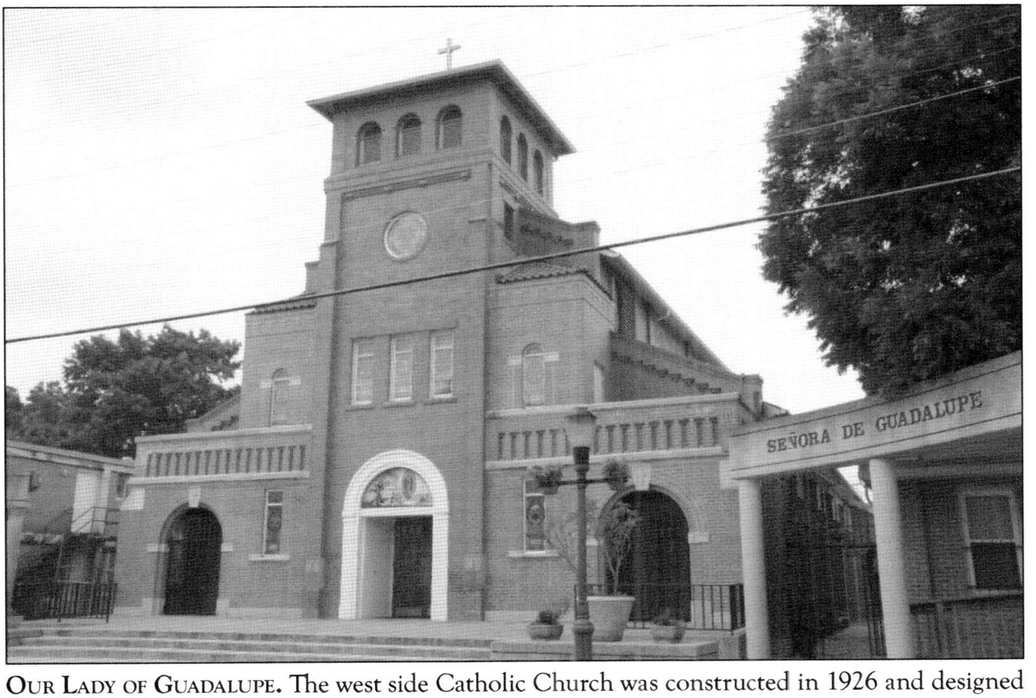

Our Lady of Guadalupe. The west side Catholic Church was constructed in 1926 and designed by local architect Leo M.J. Dielmann. A Texas native and prolific church designer in south Texas, Dielmann was a graduate of St. Mary's College and the son of a stonemason. The four-story tower balances the front facade's broad base, and the interior displays highly decorative vaults and clerestory windows. (SAPA.)

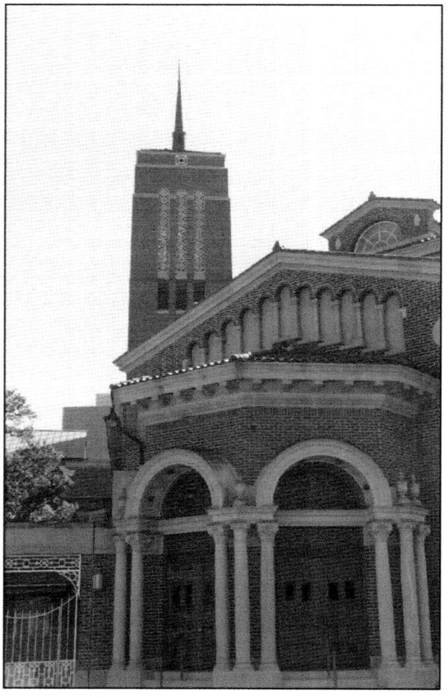

First Baptist Church. One block southeast of the San Antonio River on McCullough Avenue in downtown, First Baptist Church was designed by architect Will N. Noonan and was completed in 1925. The octagonal auditorium was built collaboratively with W.E. Simpson Company and L.T. Wright, who were engineers and general contractors. (SAPA.)

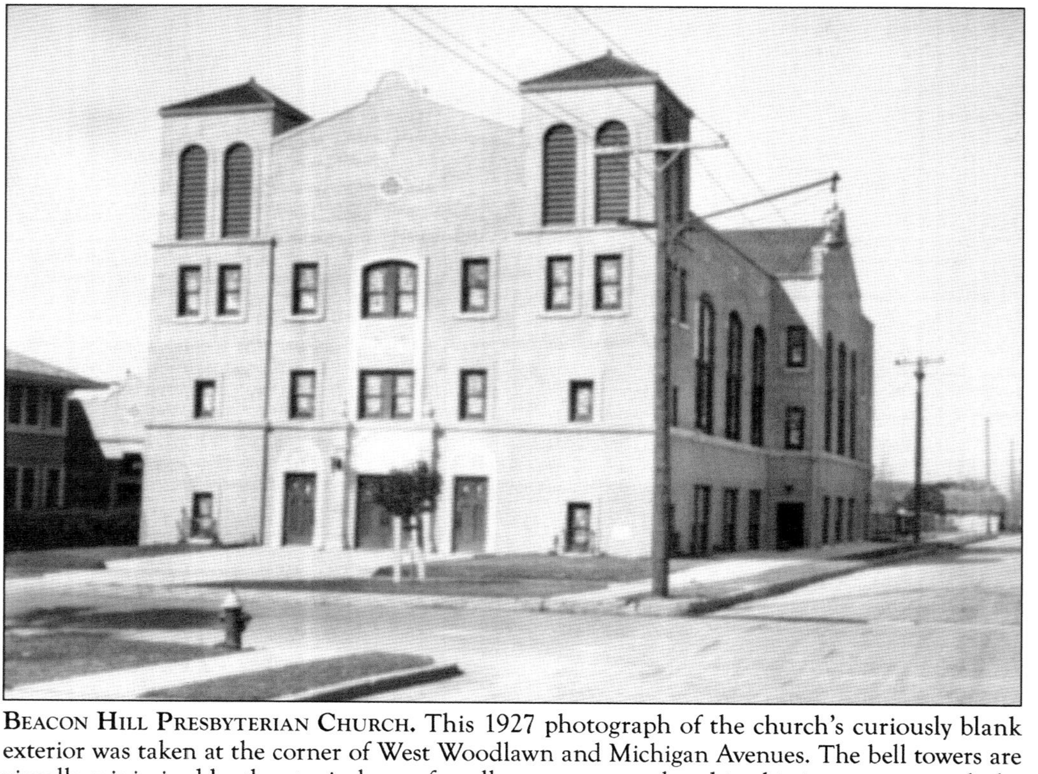

Beacon Hill Presbyterian Church. This 1927 photograph of the church's curiously blank exterior was taken at the corner of West Woodlawn and Michigan Avenues. The bell towers are visually minimized by the atypical use of a taller parapet, employed in this instance to mask the roof structure beyond. (Ann Russell and UTSA.)

St. John's Evangelical Lutheran Church. Sitting directly south of the La Villita Historic Arts Village on Nueva Street, this structure was completed in 1932 and was called the "Lutheran Cathedral of the West," known for its grandeur and craftsmanship. It was founded in the mid-19th century by pastor Phillip Zizelmann for the German immigrant community, and the original church cornerstone dates to 1860. (SAPA.)

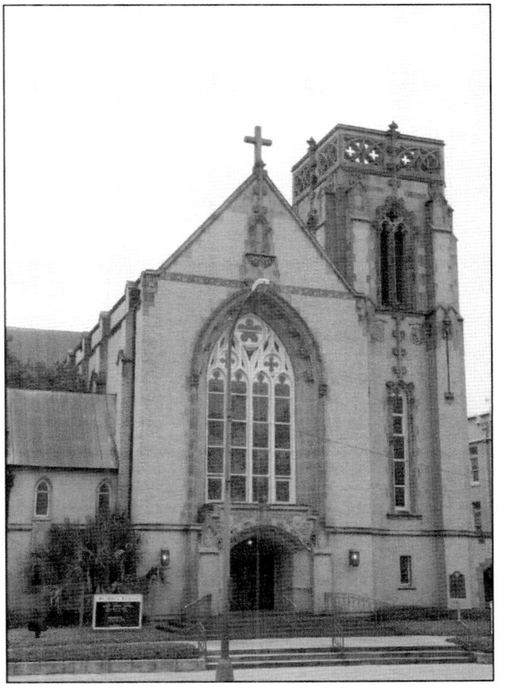

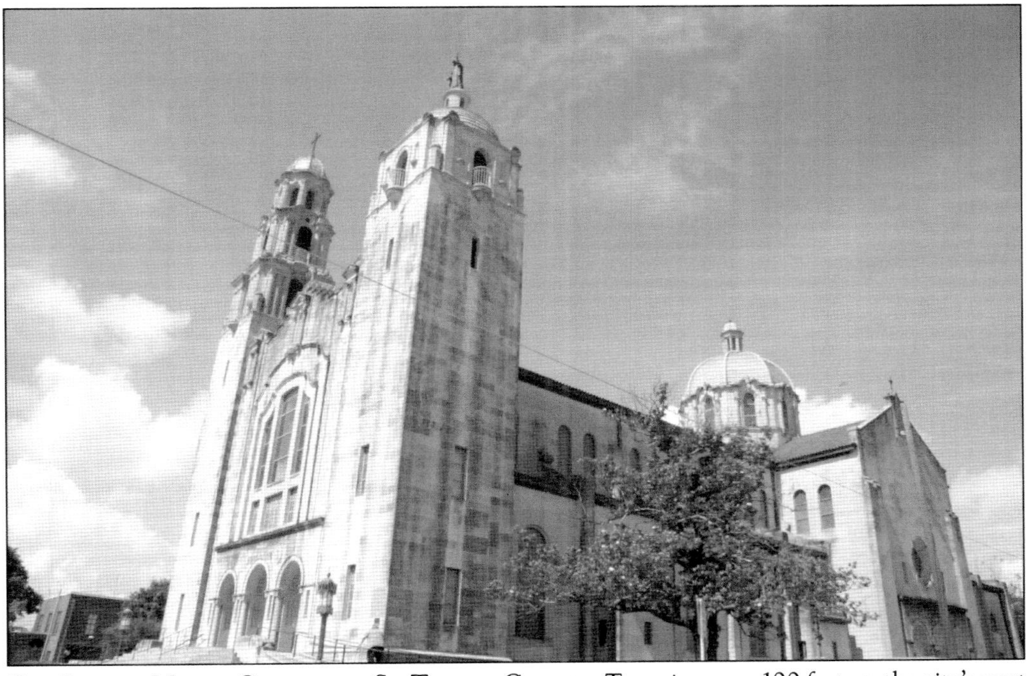

Our Lady of Mount Carmel and St. Therese Church. Towering over 100 feet on the city's west side, the Spanish Colonial Revival church was constructed in 1931. Cruciform in plan and capped with a dome at the transept, the limestone structure is also known as the Basilica of the National Shrine of the Little Flower. It was designed by architect Charles Lester Monnot of Oklahoma City. (SAPA.)

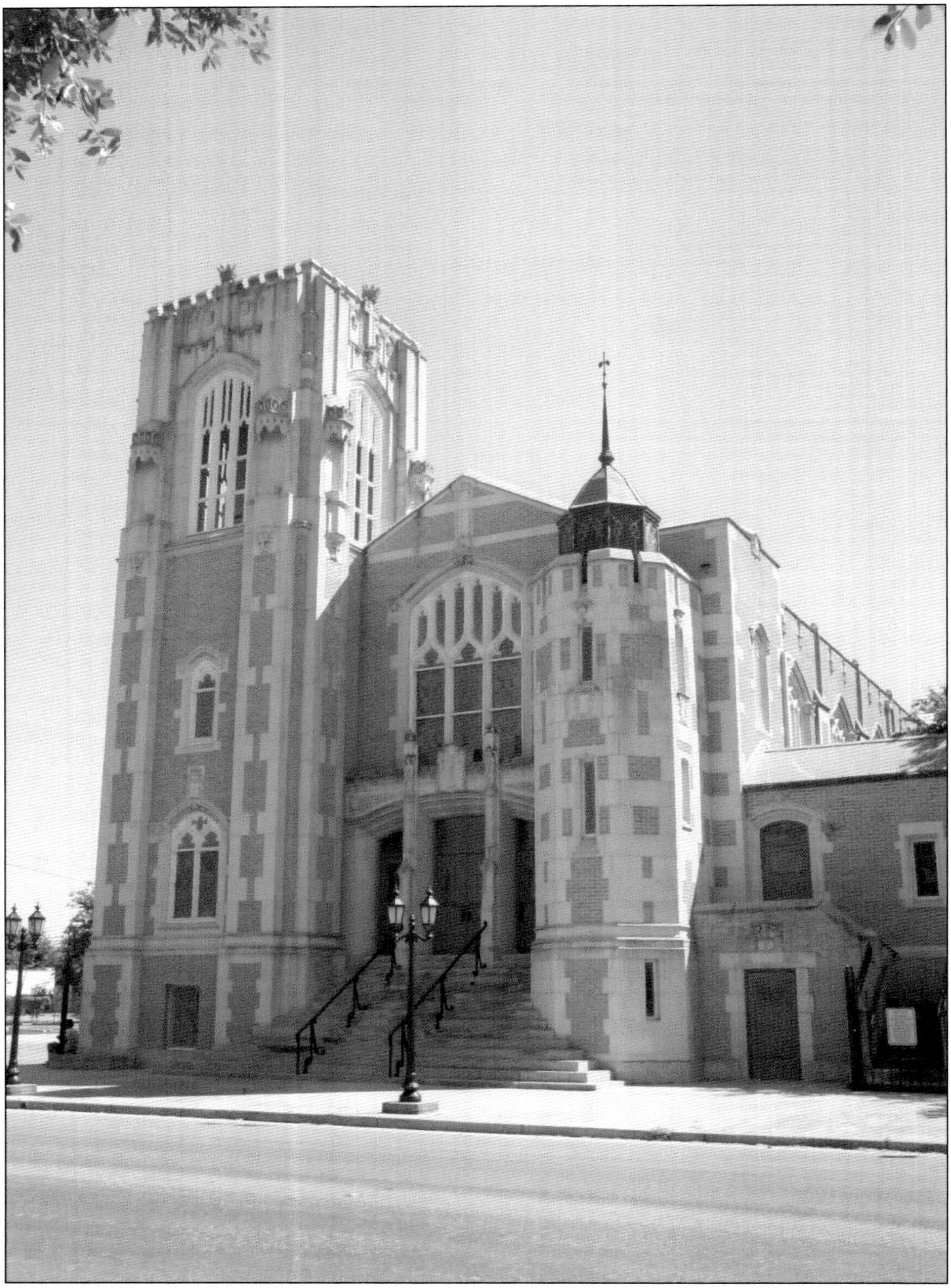

GRACE LUTHERAN CHURCH. Located at the corner of Avenue E and McCullough Avenue downtown, the brick structure utilizes cast stone detailing on both towers and prominent window tracery. The facade's asymmetry is anchored at the western corner by a neo-Gothic belfry and balanced by the smaller, more decorative turret to the right of the main doorway. (SAPA.)

Seven

Commercial and Industrial Architecture

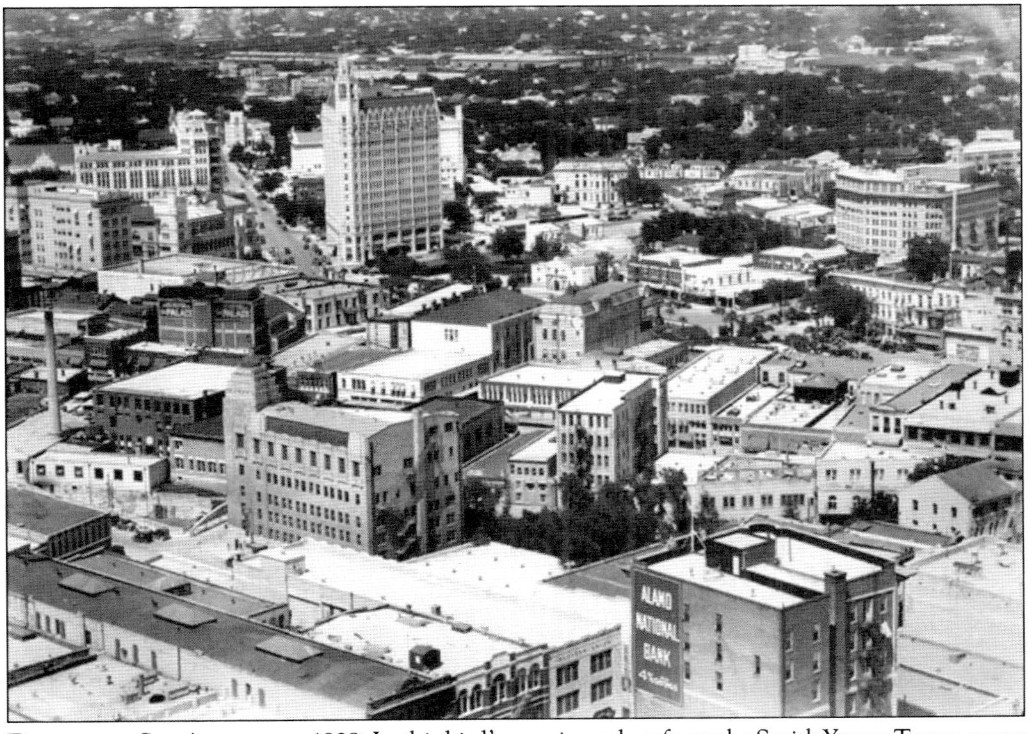

DOWNTOWN SAN ANTONIO IN **1929.** In this bird's-eye view taken from the Smith-Young Tower, many notable structures are visible. The San Antonio Express-News and the Medical Arts Buildings are just to the left of the Alamo (center). The Casino Building is to the lower left of center; in the foreground, the back of the Alamo National Bank is identified by a painted advertisement. (Ann Russell and UTSA.)

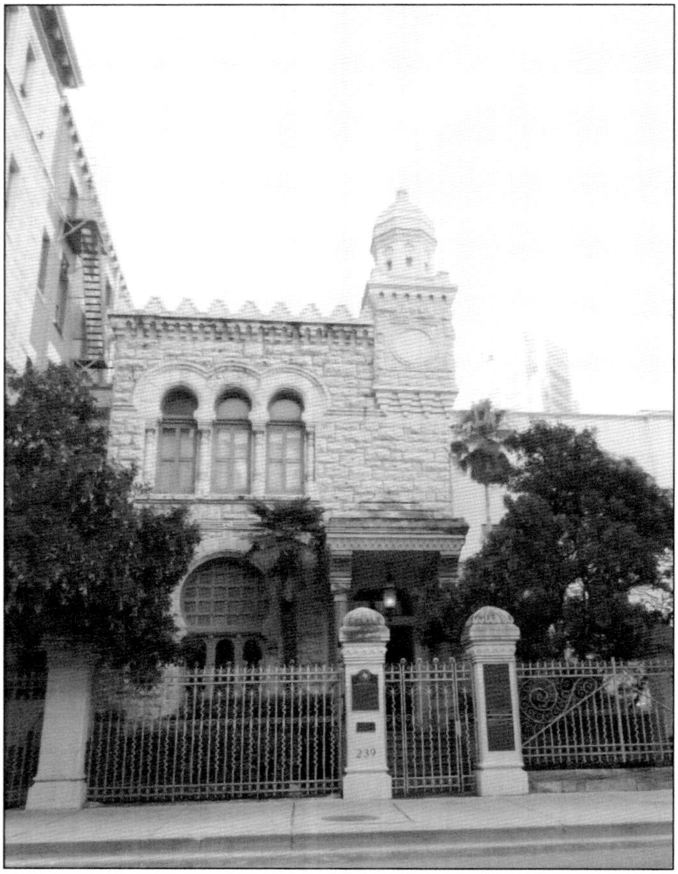

First National Bank. Designed by New York architect Cyrus Lazelle Warner Eidlitz in 1886 for banker George W. Brackenridge, the two-story Exotic Revival–style bank features horseshoe arches, rusticated stone, and an offset Moorish tower at the eastern corner. The adjacent San Antonio Loan and Trust Company Building, constructed in 1903 and reaching to a height of six stories with a width of only 25 feet, was also the property of Brackenridge. (SAPA.)

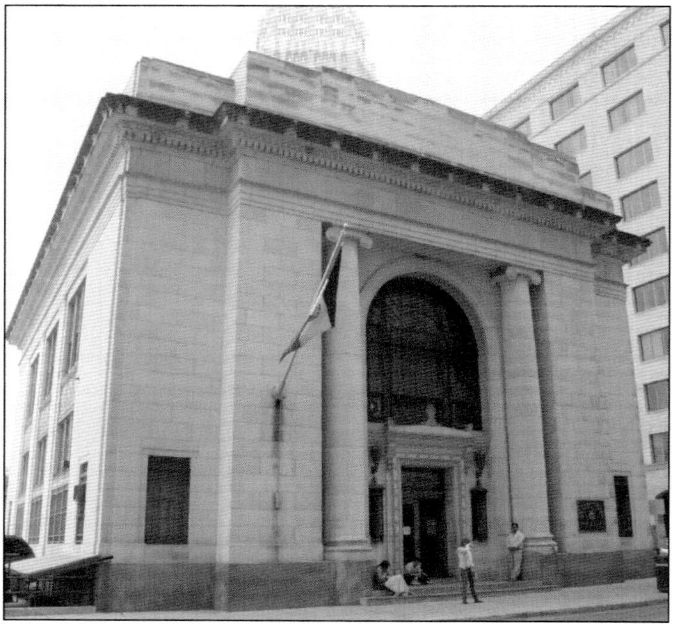

Federal Reserve Bank. Designed by local architects Altee B. Ayers and Robert Ayres and located on Navarro Street near the Smith-Young Tower, the branch bank location of the Dallas Federal Reserve was constructed in 1928. Columns of the Ionic order flank the recessed doorway within the monumental entrance. With the growing economy in South Texas, the need for a larger branch building was required, and the bank relocated to another facility in 1956. (SAPA.)

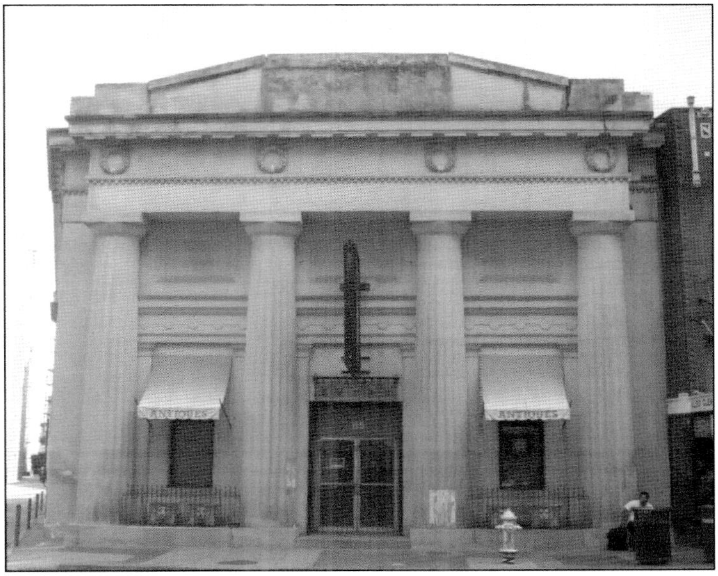

Lockwood Bank. The severe facade of this bank, which was built in 1918 on Broadway Street, features stout Doric columns with vertical fluting. Four cast stone wreaths mark the top of each column within the frieze. Later known as the Commonwealth Bank and Trust Company during the 1920s, the structure sits next to the Paris Hatters (right), which is San Antonio's oldest surviving downtown retail business. (SAPA.)

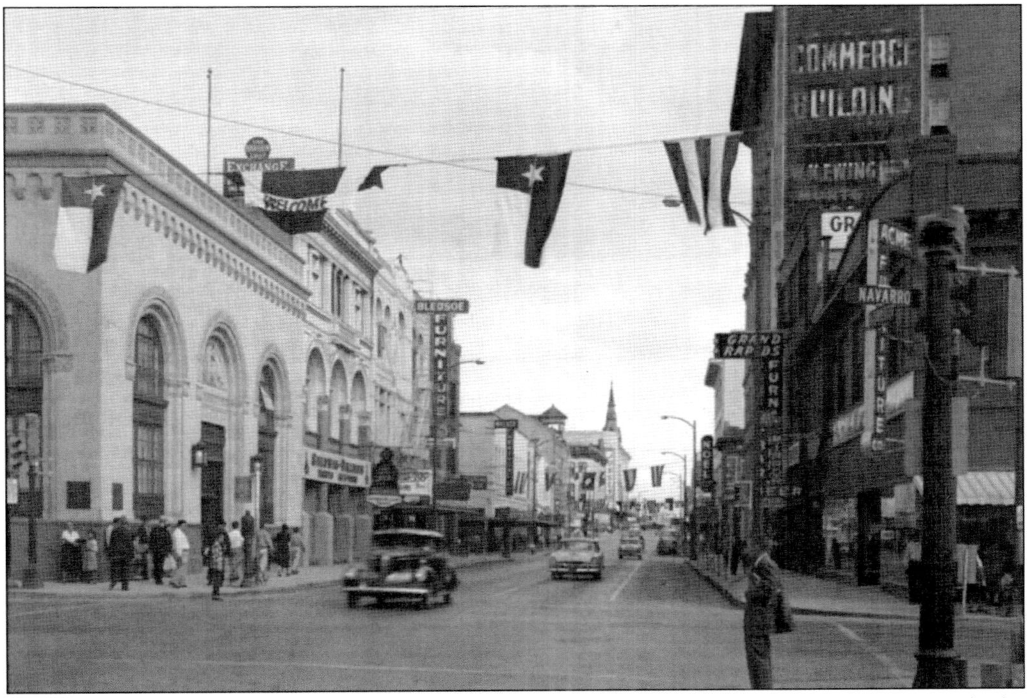

Stevens-Staacke Retail Block. This view looking east on Commerce Street in 1956 reveals the Groos Bank in the foreground at left. Directly behind the bank, the Staacke Brothers Building served as the storefront to a carriage manufacturing business, which here has a sign for Sherwin-Williams paints. Designed by James Riely Gordon in 1884, the building is notable for its use of red sandstone. Also designed by Gordon, along with D.E. Laub in 1891, the adjacent Stevens Building is missing many of its decorative details. Both buildings were saved from demolition in the 1980s with the intervention of the San Antonio Conservation Society, but the Groos Bank is no longer standing. (UTSA, Zintgraff Studio Collection.)

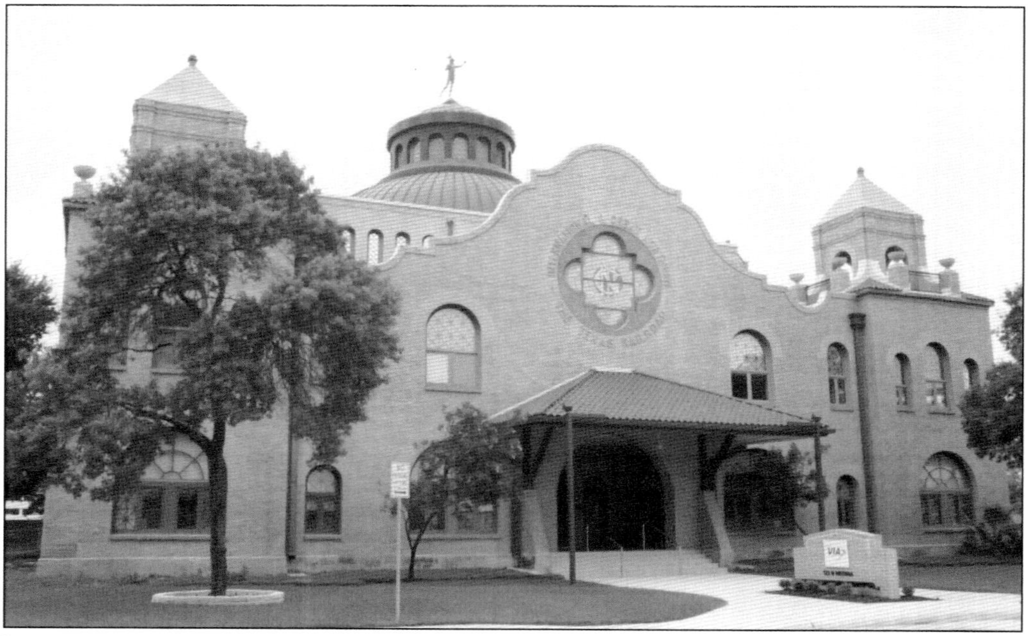

INTERNATIONAL AND GREAT NORTHERN PASSENGER STATION. The Mission-style railroad station was constructed in 1908 by contractor James Stewart and Company. Designed by American architect Harvey Lindsley Page, the station, located on Medina Street directly west of downtown, now resides in the Cattleman Square Historic District. In an area known for prosperity during the early 20th century, this passenger station is one of only two rail stations remaining in San Antonio and retains the original art-glass windows. (SAPA.)

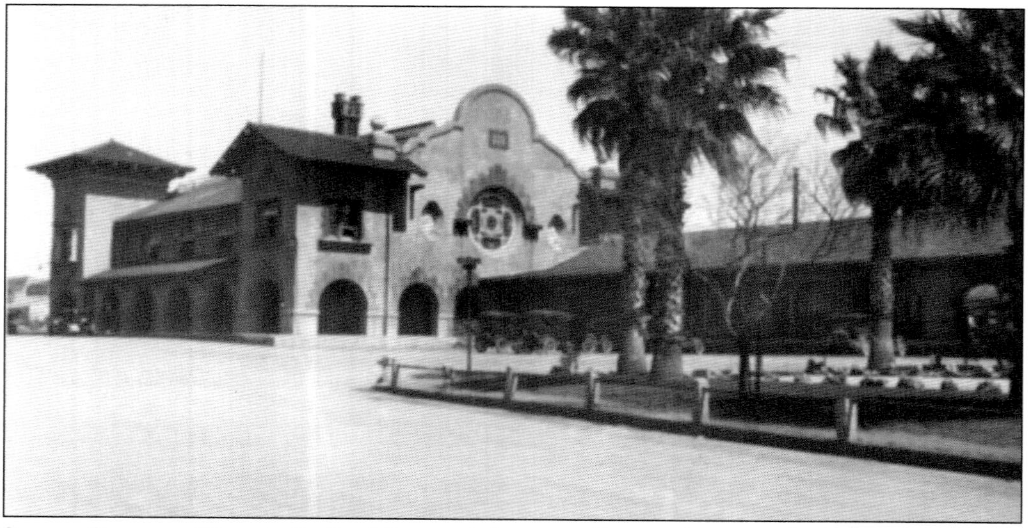

SUNSET STATION. Historic St. Paul Square is home to Sunset Station, which was constructed around 1902 by the Southern Pacific Railroad. Devastated by fire a few years later, the building was restored in 1907. The original design was created by Daniel J. Patterson, an American architect most distinguished for his railroad station designs throughout the western United States. The final design was a collaborative effort with civil engineer John D. Isaacs and architect W.E. Milwain. (Linda Mercer and UTSA.)

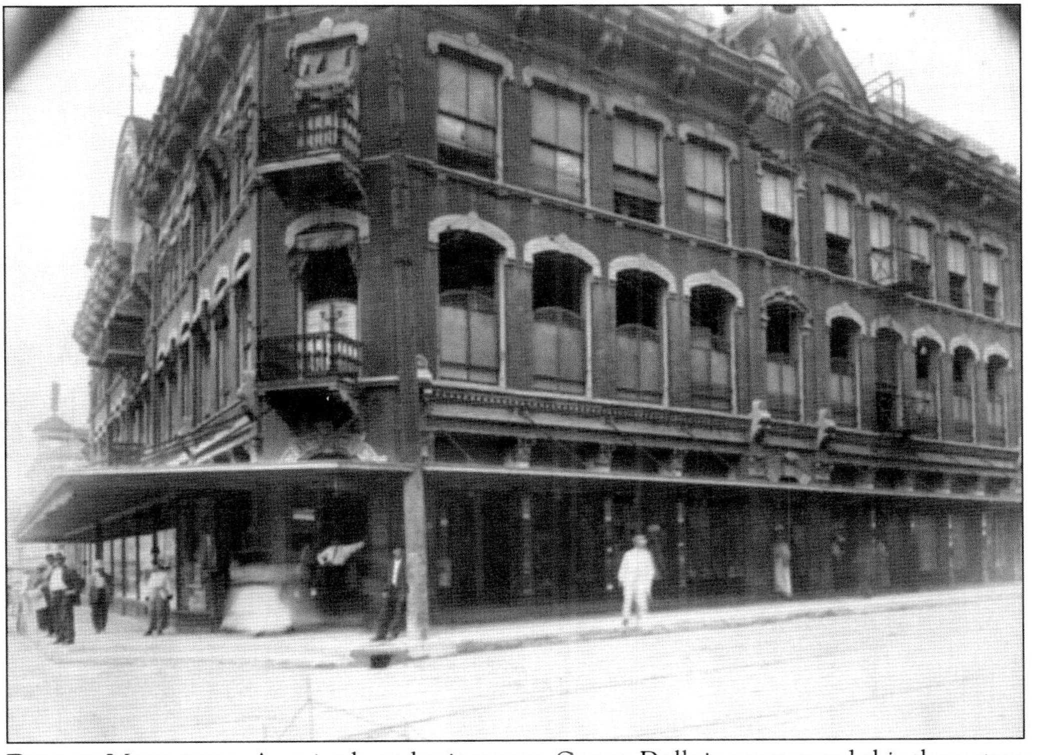

DULLNIG MERCANTILE. Austrian-born businessman George Dullnig constructed this three-story emporium at the corner of Alamo Plaza in 1883. This photograph from the turn of the century shows its large sidewalk canopy and intact roof cresting. The original design featured a two-story, rooftop cupola at the southeast corner. Neither the cupola nor the roof details presently remain. (UTSA.)

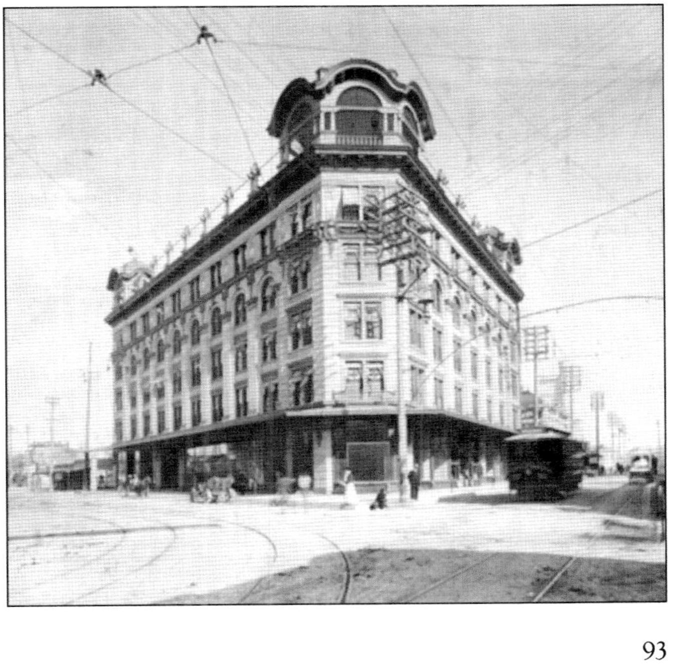

MOORE BUILDING. Successful lumber businessman and banker G. Bedell Moore relocated to Texas from Pennsylvania in the late 1800s. By 1904, Moore constructed this commercial building, which was designed by local architectural partners Charles Coughlin and Atlee B. Ayers. This view from Avenue C, later renamed Broadway Street, shows a streetcar traveling east on Houston Street. A rooftop addition displaced the corner cupolas a few years later, completing a sixth level. (Ann Russell and UTSA.)

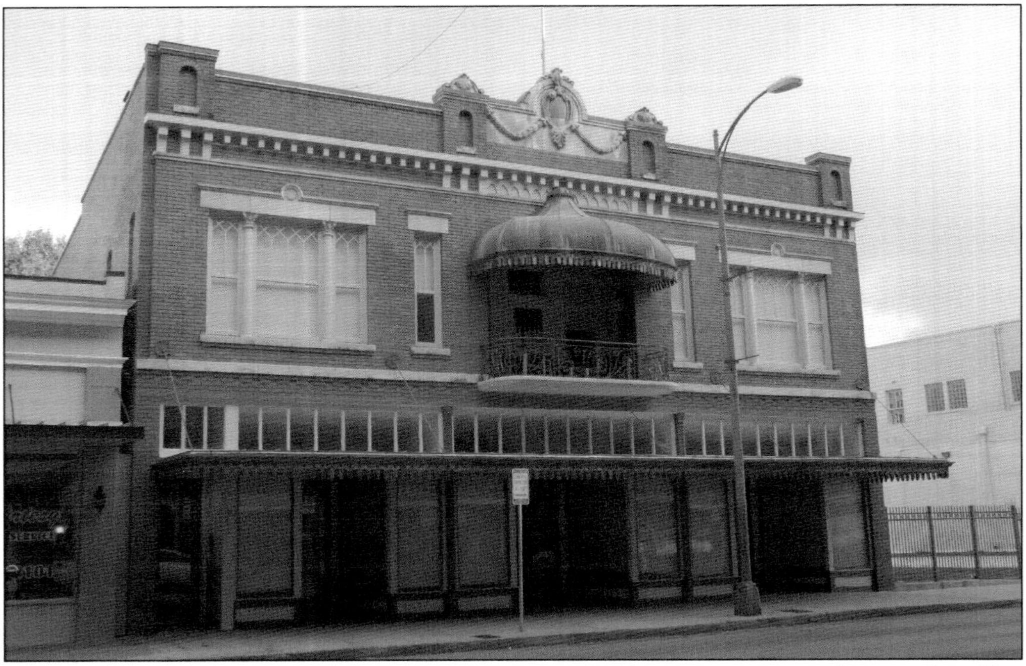

BARR BUILDING. Designed by prominent San Antonio architect Leo M.J. Dielmann, the office and retail building was commissioned for local photographer David Perry Barr around 1908. The symmetrical facade is punctuated by a balcony and capped with a distinctive metal awning. Decorative metal banderoles line the sidewalk canopy along the front of the building. (SAPA.)

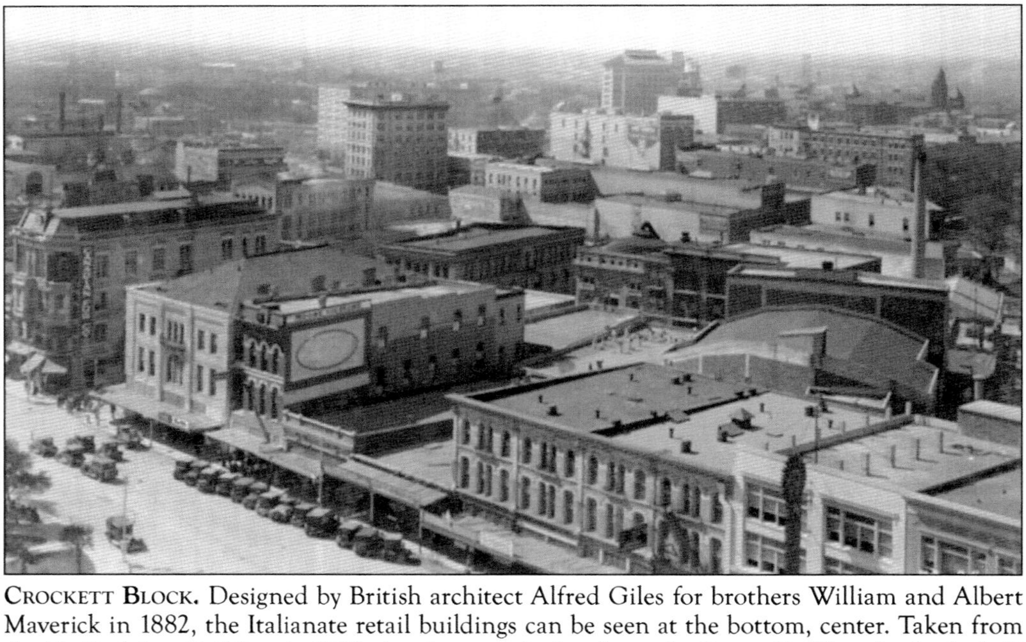

CROCKETT BLOCK. Designed by British architect Alfred Giles for brothers William and Albert Maverick in 1882, the Italianate retail buildings can be seen at the bottom, center. Taken from the Medical Arts Building in 1927, the photograph also shows the Reuter Building (at the far left) designed by local architects James Wahrenberger and Albert Beckmann, seen here as the Canadian Fur Co. (Ann Russell and UTSA.)

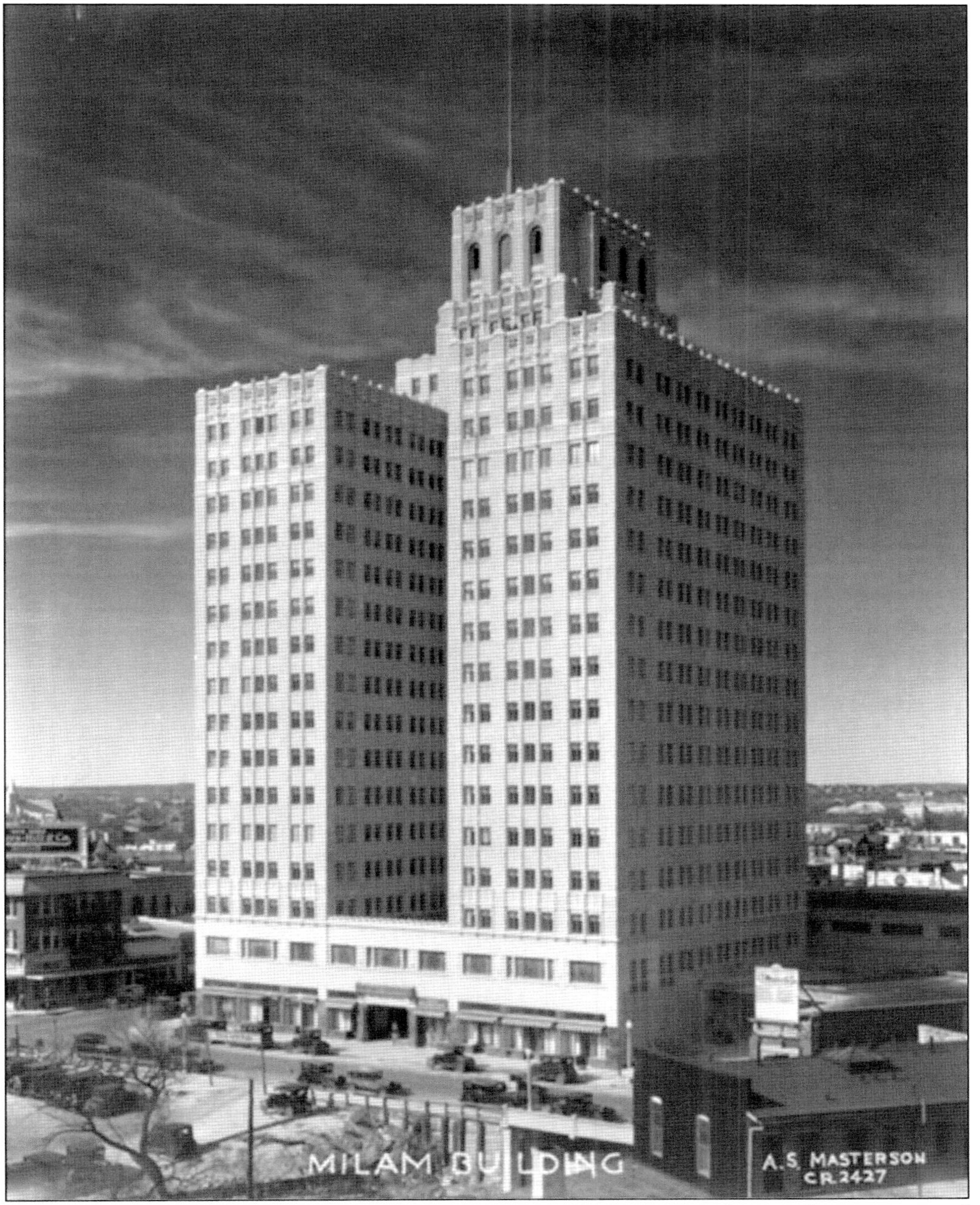

MILAM BUILDING. Named for Col. Benjamin Milam of the Texas Revolution, the concrete and steel-frame building was the first fully air-conditioned high-rise in the United States. Seen newly completed in this 1928 photograph, the building was designed by Chicago-born architect George Rodney Willis. The neo-Gothic skyscraper has a distinctive U-shaped floor plan and is also a National Mechanical Engineering Heritage Site. (Martha N. Bradley and UTSA.)

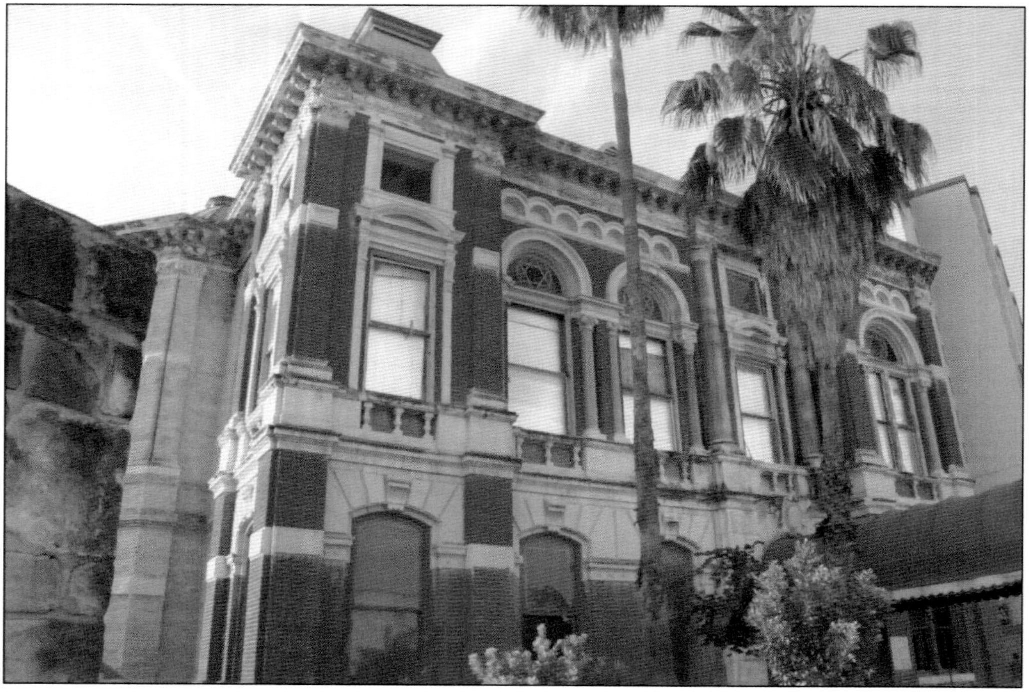

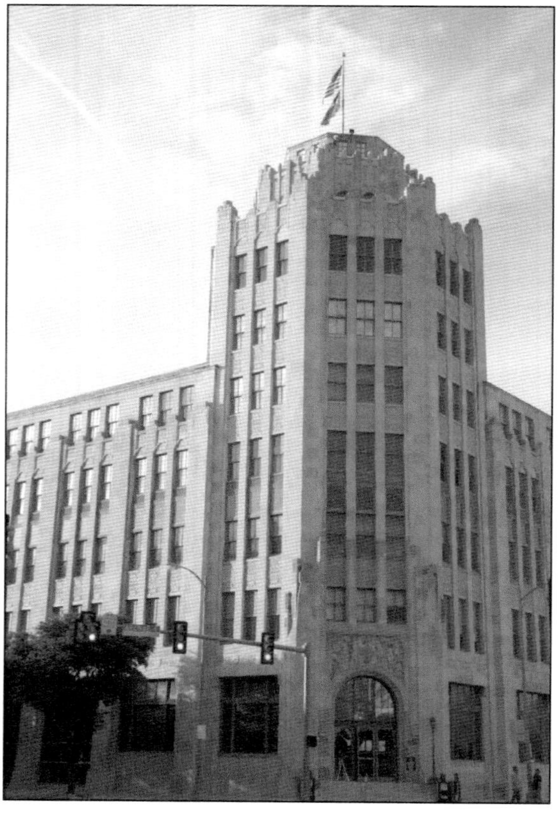

SAN ANTONIO TURN VEREIN. Established in Germany in 1811 by Friedrich Ludwig Jahn, this gymnastics club was brought to the United States by German immigrants during the 19th century. Also known as a social and philanthropic organization, San Antonio's Turn Verein was founded around 1860. Texas architects James Wahrenberger and Albert Beckmann, who designed the unique building in 1891, utilized contrasting brick detailing and a variety of materials to create the excessively decorative Italianate structure. (SAPA.)

SAN ANTONIO EXPRESS-NEWS BUILDING. Designed by local architect Herbert S. Greene in 1929 for local publisher and philanthropist Frank Granger Huntress, the dominant corner tower is 12 stories tall. Just above the south-facing main entry at the intersection of Third Street and Avenue E are bas-reliefs executed by Italian artist Pompeo Coppini. (SAPA.)

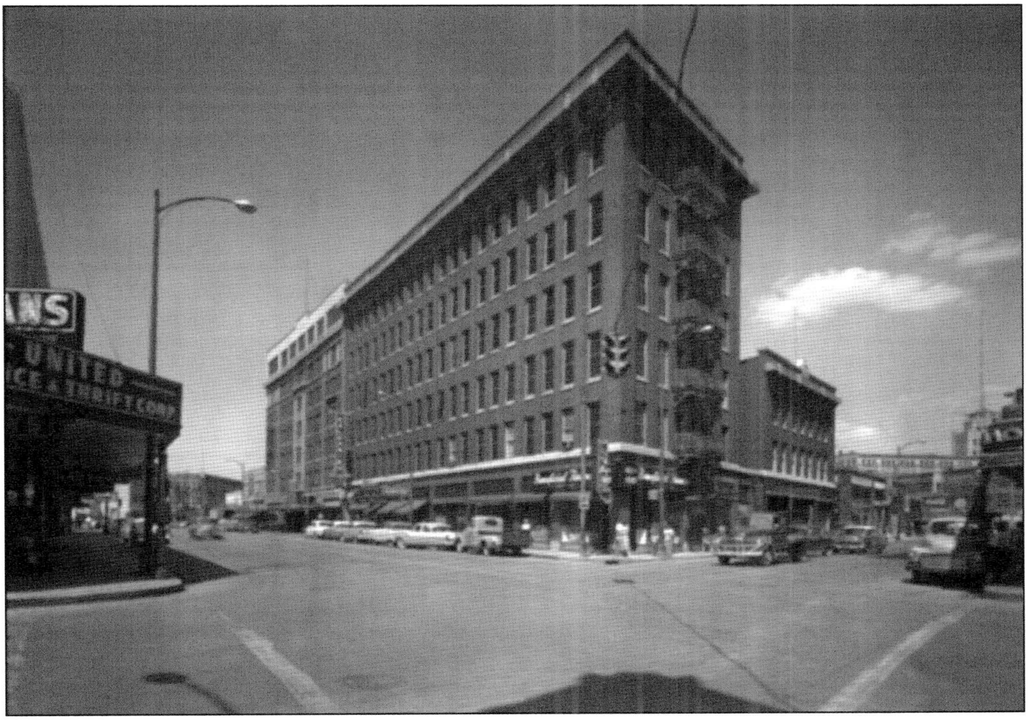

Calcasieu Building. Constructed in 1914, this commercial design by local architect Atlee B. Ayers housed offices and retail. The building was later converted to efficiency apartments, as seen here in 1956, and the ground floor retains its retail space. Directly behind the Calcasieu Building, to the right, is the former 1920s San Antonio Light Building, which faces Travis Street. Further up Broadway Street, to the building's left, is the Travelers Hotel built in 1910. (UTSA.)

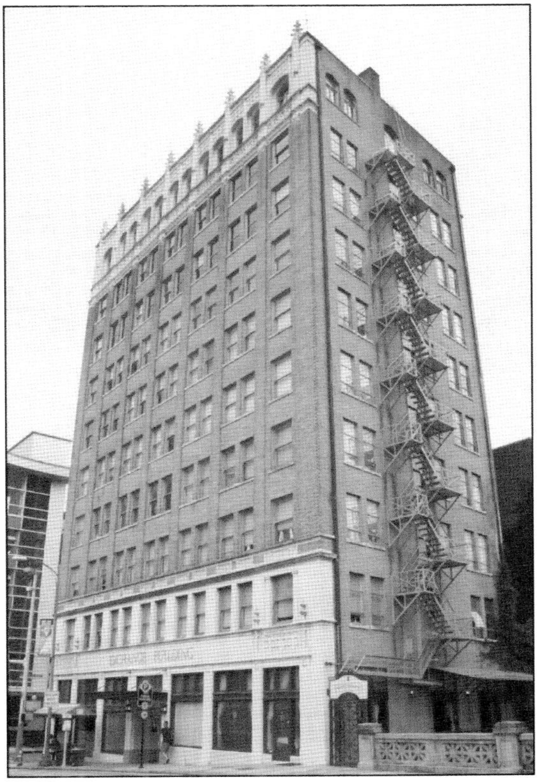

San Antonio Exchange Building. Designed by architects George Rodney Willis and Emmitt Jackson to serve as the local Builder's Exchange headquarters in 1925, the high-rise served the collaborative group at this location until 1950. Having studied architecture in Chicago, Willis was influenced by skyscraper master Louis Sullivan, as evident in the tripartite delineation of the facade. (SAPA.)

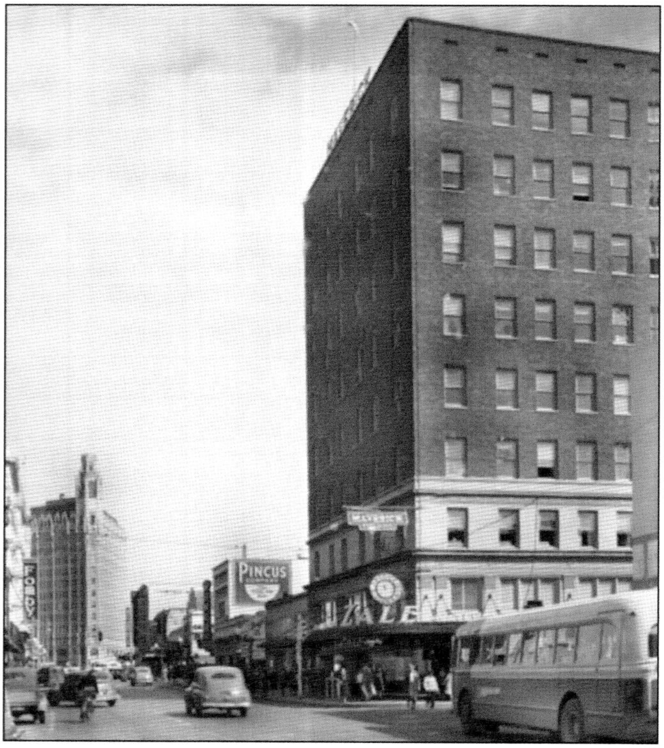

Maverick Building. Constructed during a high-rise boom, the new structure replaced the old Maverick Hotel, which was originally constructed on this site during the mid-19th century. The 1922 structure is notable for its simplicity. Design credit goes to the local firm of L. Harrington Company, Architects. (UTSA, Zintgraff Studio Collection.)

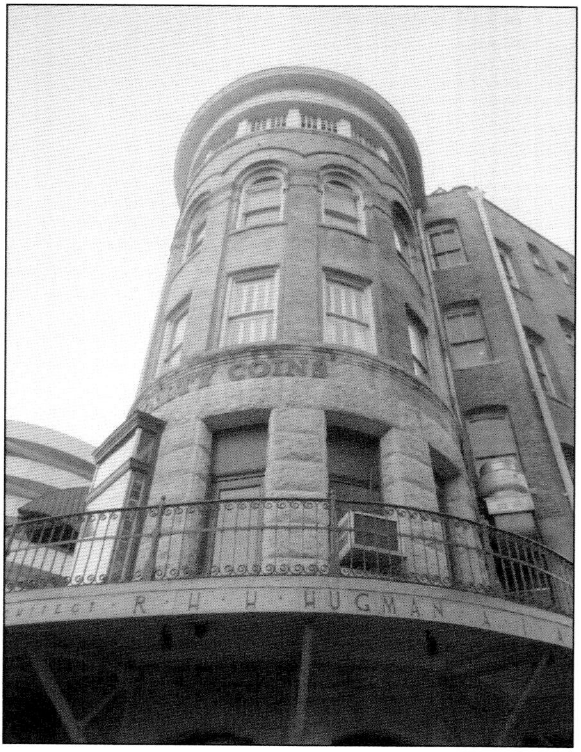

Clifford Building. Erected for local attorney Charles Clifford in 1893, the building was also later used as an office by San Antonio architect Robert Harvey Harold Hugman. Recognized as the creator of the city's famous River Walk, Hugman completed his education at the University of Texas at Austin and the Massachusetts Institute of Technology. Designed by James Riely Gordon, the Clifford Building is situated where the River Walk meets the Commerce Street Bridge. (SAPA.)

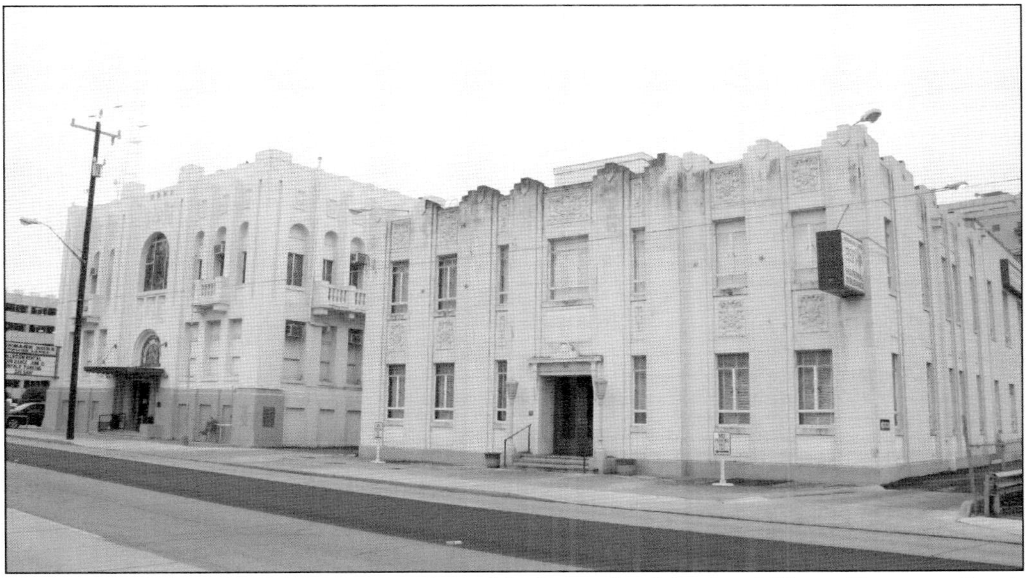

HERMANN SONS GRAND LODGE. Located two blocks south of the Smith-Young Tower on South St. Mary's Street, the Grand Lodge was designed by San Antonio architect Leo M. J. Dielmann in 1938. The Order of the Sons of Hermann was first established in New York City in the 1840s, when there was with an influx of German immigrants. By 1896, fifteen states had constructed Grand Lodges, including Harmonia Lodge No. 1 in San Antonio, first built in 1861. By 1920, the Texas Order declared itself independent of the national fraternity and was the first to combine the male and female lodges nationwide. (SAPA.)

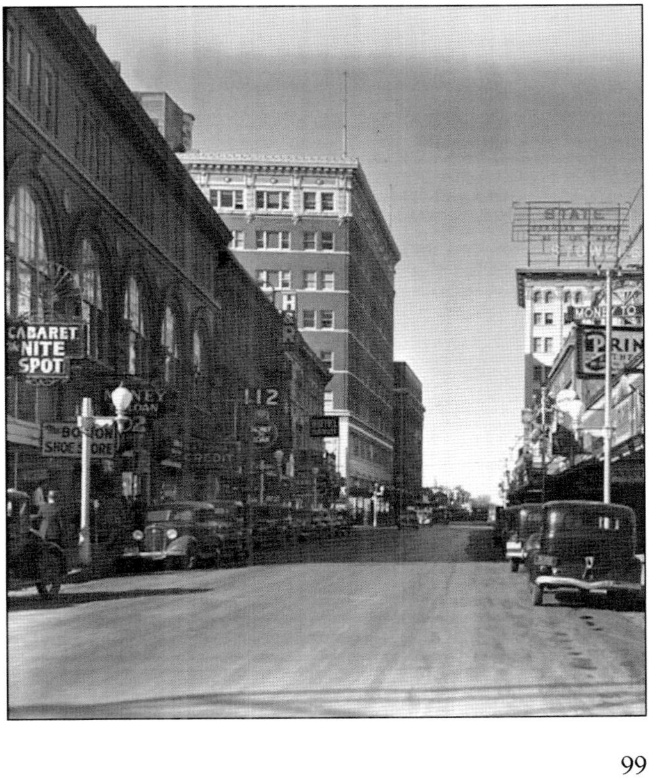

RAND BUILDING. The 1913 retail structure was home to the department store Wolff and Marx, which occupied the building until the mid-1960s. Saved from demolition by the San Antonio Conservation Society in 1981, the steel-framed high-rise was designed by Sanguinet and Staats of Fort Worth, Texas, known throughout the state for their skyscraper designs prior to the 1930s. Their design exemplifies the Chicago school of architecture. In this street scene from 1938, the Book Building featuring the Nite Spot cabaret is on the left. In the near distance, the taller Rand Building is visible in this view looking west on Houston Street. (UTSA, Zintgraff Studio Collection.)

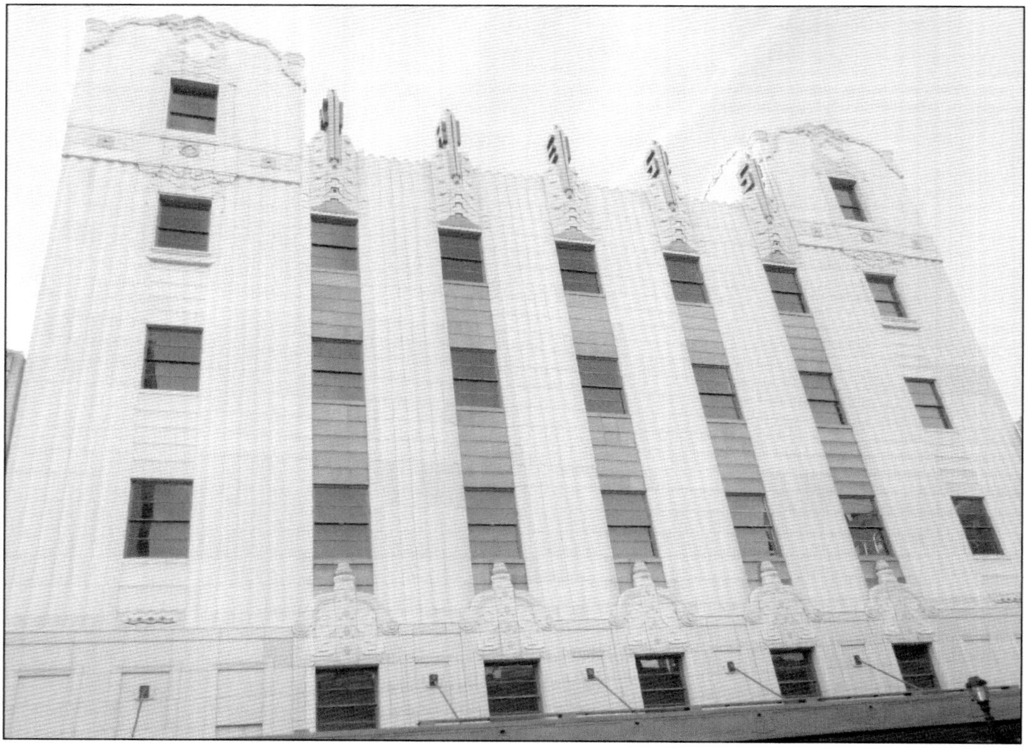

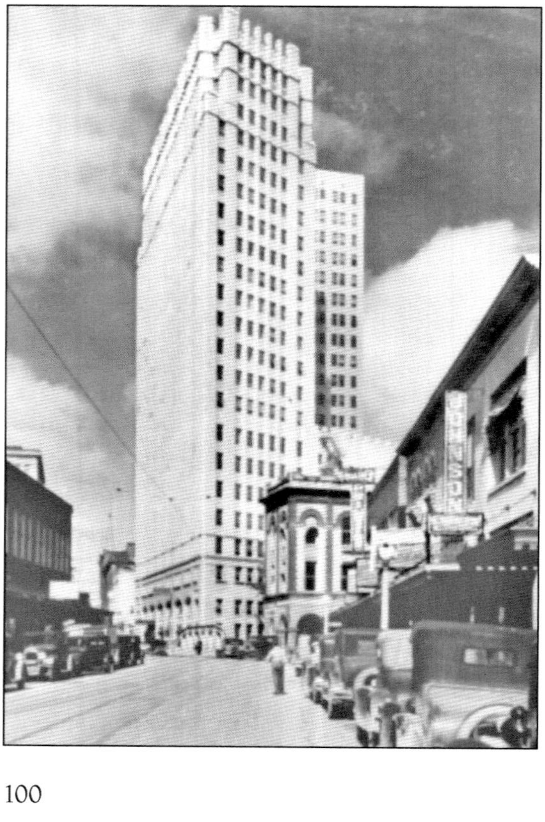

S.H. Kress & Company. Over 200 S.H. Kress & Company five-and-dime stores nationwide were known for their distinctive architectural style. Kress's new chief architect as of 1929 was Edward Sibbet from Brooklyn, New York. A graduate of the architecture program at Cornell University, he created a consistent style for the Kress franchise. Utilizing terra-cotta ornamentation and an emphasis on verticality, Sibbet is responsible for over 50 Art Deco Kress stores constructed over a period of 15 years. (SAPA.)

Nix Professional Building. The medical complex was the realization of visionary Joseph M. Nix in 1930. Containing not only a hospital, it also houses medical offices and incorporates a parking structure designed by Texas-born architect Henry Truman Phelps. This photograph from 1932 captures the 23-story hospital in a view looking north over the Navarro Street bridge. (*San Antonio Express-News* and UTSA.)

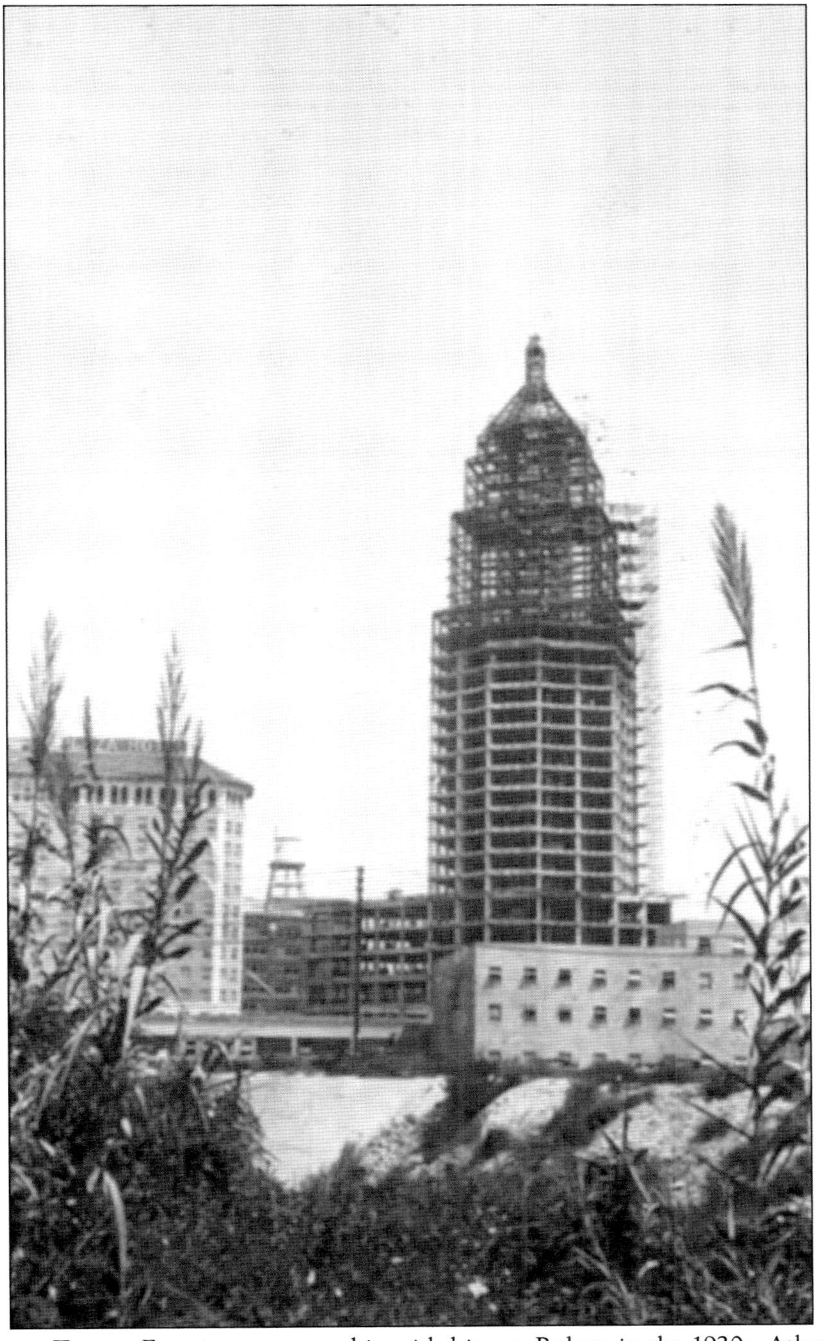

SMITH-YOUNG TOWER. Forming a partnership with his son Robert in the 1920s, Atlee B. Ayers was a native of Ohio and was educated at New York's Metropolitan School of Architecture. The father-son team designed the Smith-Young Tower in 1929. The facade of the 30-story octagonal high-rise is executed in brick and terra-cotta, conveying neo-Gothic detailing. The Plaza Hotel to the left was completed in 1927, another Ayers and Ayers design, photographed by Albert Schaal during construction. (Linda Mercer and UTSA.)

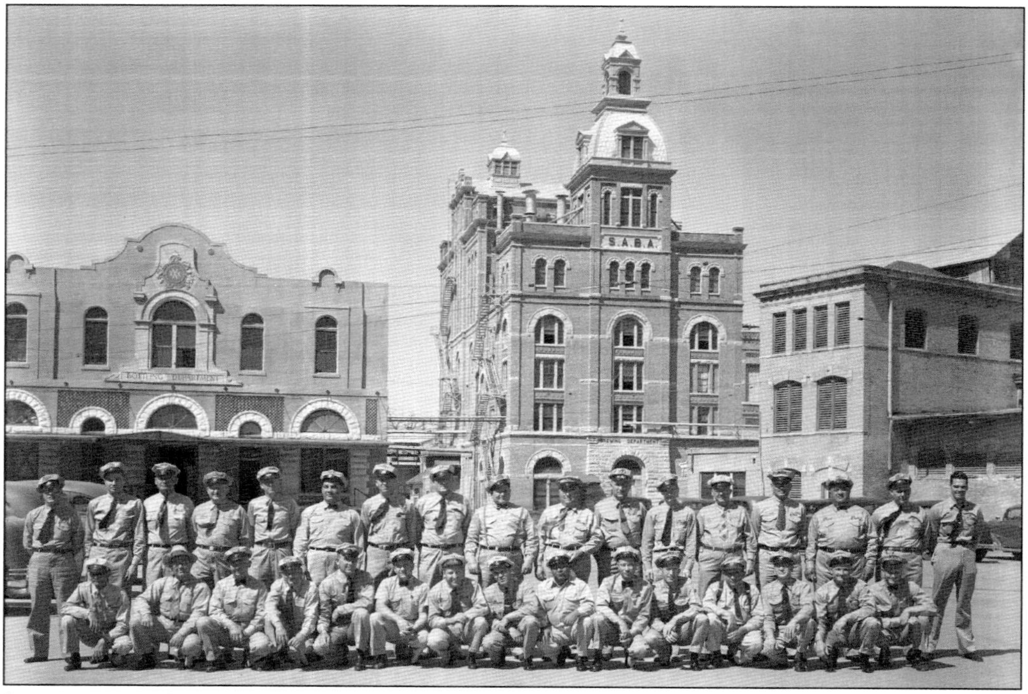

SAN ANTONIO BREWING ASSOCIATION. More commonly known as the Pearl Brewery, the 1883 structure began to produce the Pearl label in 1886. By 1916, it was the largest brewery in Texas, and the name was formally changed to the Pearl Brewing Company in the 1950s. Drivers of regional beer routes line up in front of the building in their uniforms labeled "Pearl Pride." (UTSA.)

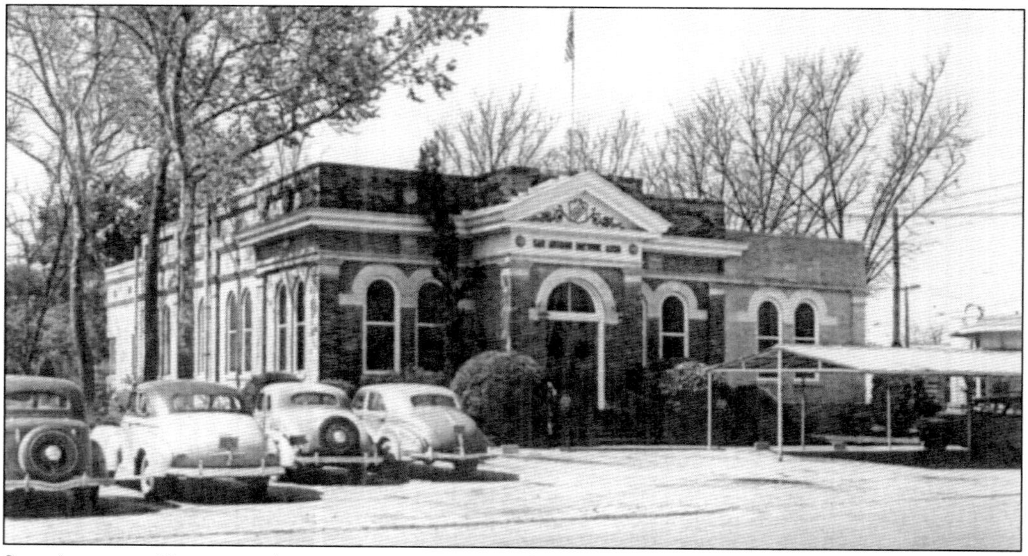

SAN ANTONIO BREWING ASSOCIATION OFFICES. The administrative offices of the brewery were constructed in 1904 as Otto Koehler expanded the company nationally. After his death a few years later, Koehler's wife, Emma, took over and fulfilled her husband's strategy to become the largest brewery in the state. Seen here around 1940, the office building has one addition that successfully mimicked the original building, but it no longer remains. (UTSA.)

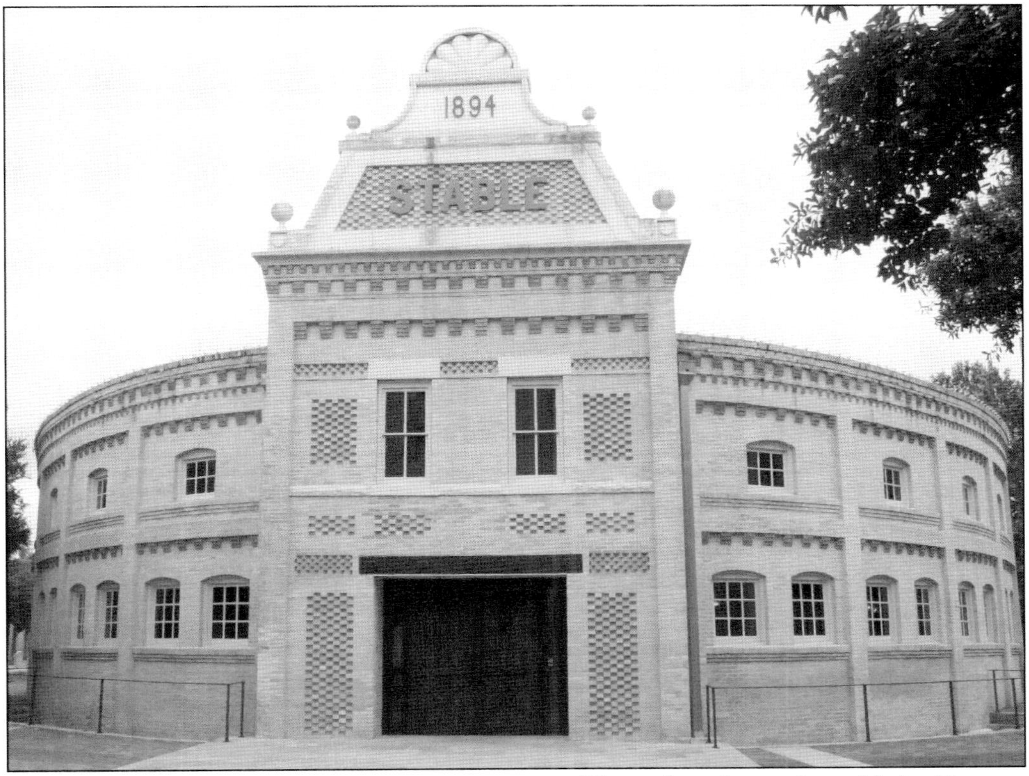

STABLE AT THE SAN ANTONIO BREWING ASSOCIATION. Elliptical in shape, the stable building on the brewery grounds exhibits well-crafted brick detailing and a tall parapet at the entrance. The large horse facility was designed by Otto Kramer, a well-known San Antonio architect in the late 19th century. The stable may have been inspired by a similar roundhouse design built in 1885 for Adolphus Busch in St. Louis. (SAPA.)

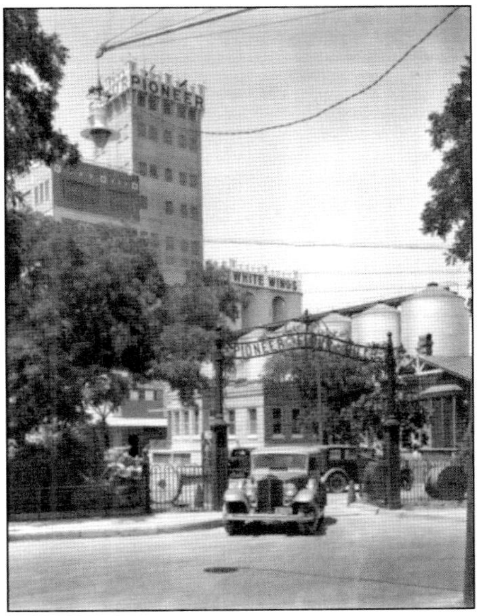

GUENTHER MILLS. German immigrant Carl Hilmar Guenther originally established his flour mill in Fredericksburg, Texas. Relocating to San Antonio due to drought, Guenther constructed his new mill along the San Antonio River in 1860. With the arrival of the railroad in the 1870s, a larger mill was constructed, and the company changed its name to C.H. Guenther and Sons in 1878. The landmark concrete grain elevator was constructed in 1922 and features the company's brand names along the castellated roof edges, as seen in this 1934 photograph by Austin Seymour Masterson. (Martha N. Bradley and UTSA.)

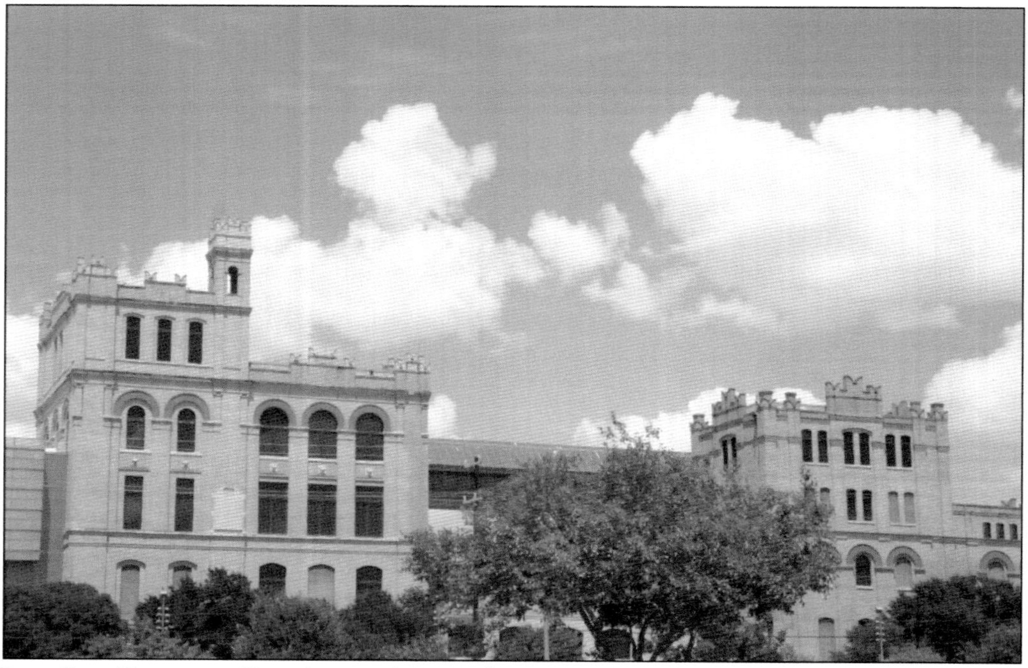

Lone Star Breweries. Texas-born architects Albert Beckmann and James Wahrenberger partnered with E. Jungenfeld and Company to create the brewing complex (above) between 1895 and 1904. Jungenfeld's design for the structure mirrors the detailing of the 1890s Anheuser-Busch structure in the historic Soulard neighborhood of St. Louis, Missouri. After Prohibition ended in 1933, Lone Star Brewing Company relocated to 600 Lone Star Boulevard, a south-town location (below) that continued under various changes of ownership through 1996. (Both, SAPA.)

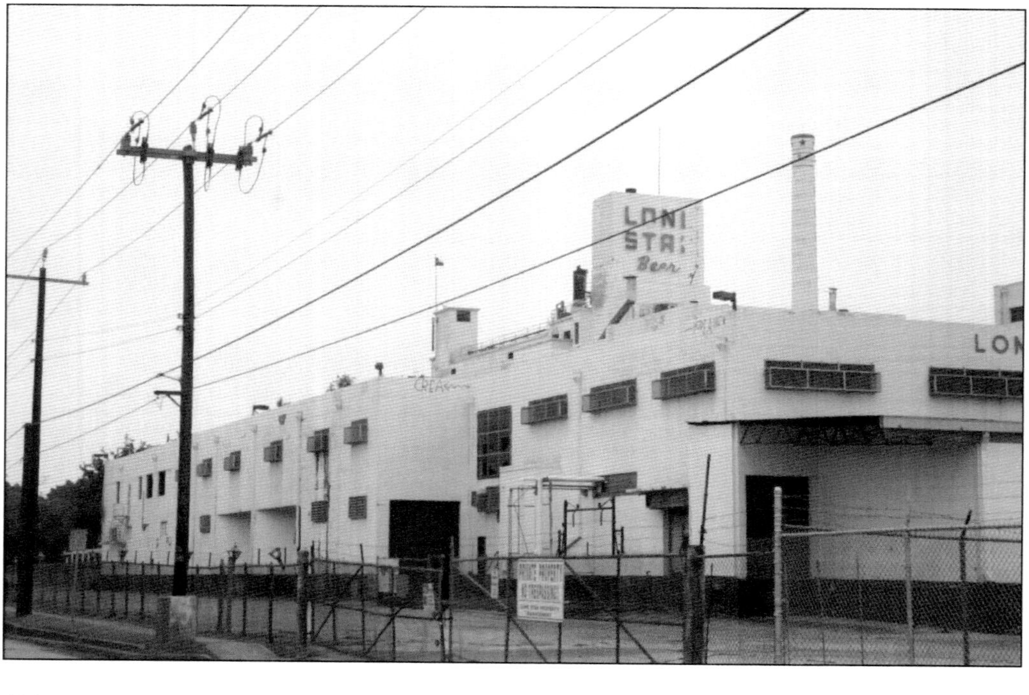

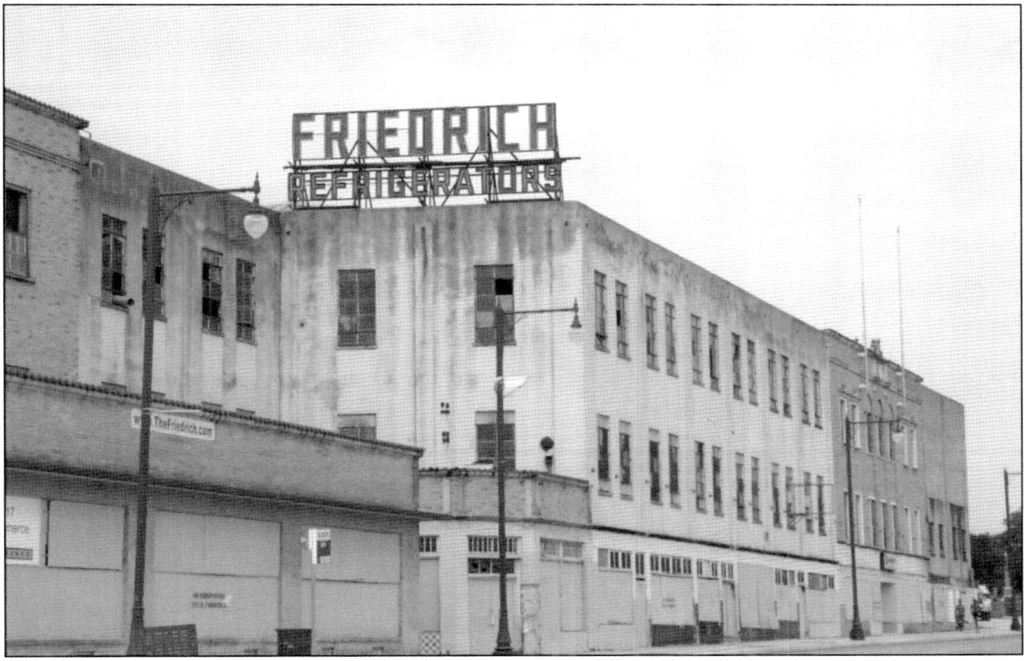

Friedrich Refrigerators. Founded by Edward Friedrich in 1883, the refrigerator company is responsible for the development of a patented commercial cooling system, refrigerated food counters, and a later expansion into single-room cooling units during the 1950s. This factory, constructed in 1923, was built on East Commerce Street to keep up with product demand. Friedrich hired architect Harvey P. Smith to design administrative offices and storefronts within the complex. Educated in Chicago, Illinois, and Paris, France, Smith moved to San Antonio in 1915 and briefly worked for local architect Atlee B. Ayers. (SAPA.)

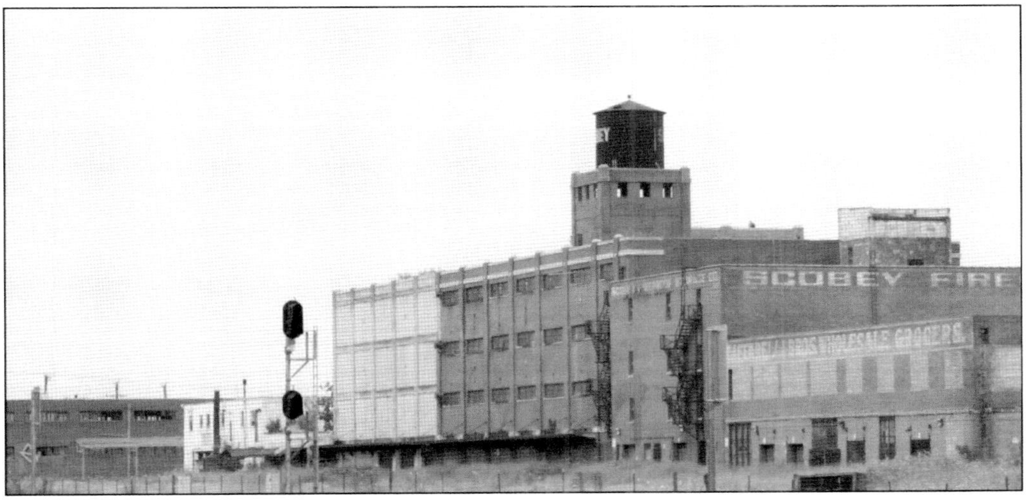

Scobey Fireproof Storage Company. The company was founded by Frank Edgar Scobey, an Ohio-born businessman who relocated to San Antonio in 1907. A personal friend of Pres. Warren G. Harding, Scobey served as director of the US Mint during Harding's administration. The west side storage facility was constructed of concrete and brick on Medina Street, just north of what is now known as Cattleman Square Historic District. (SAPA.)

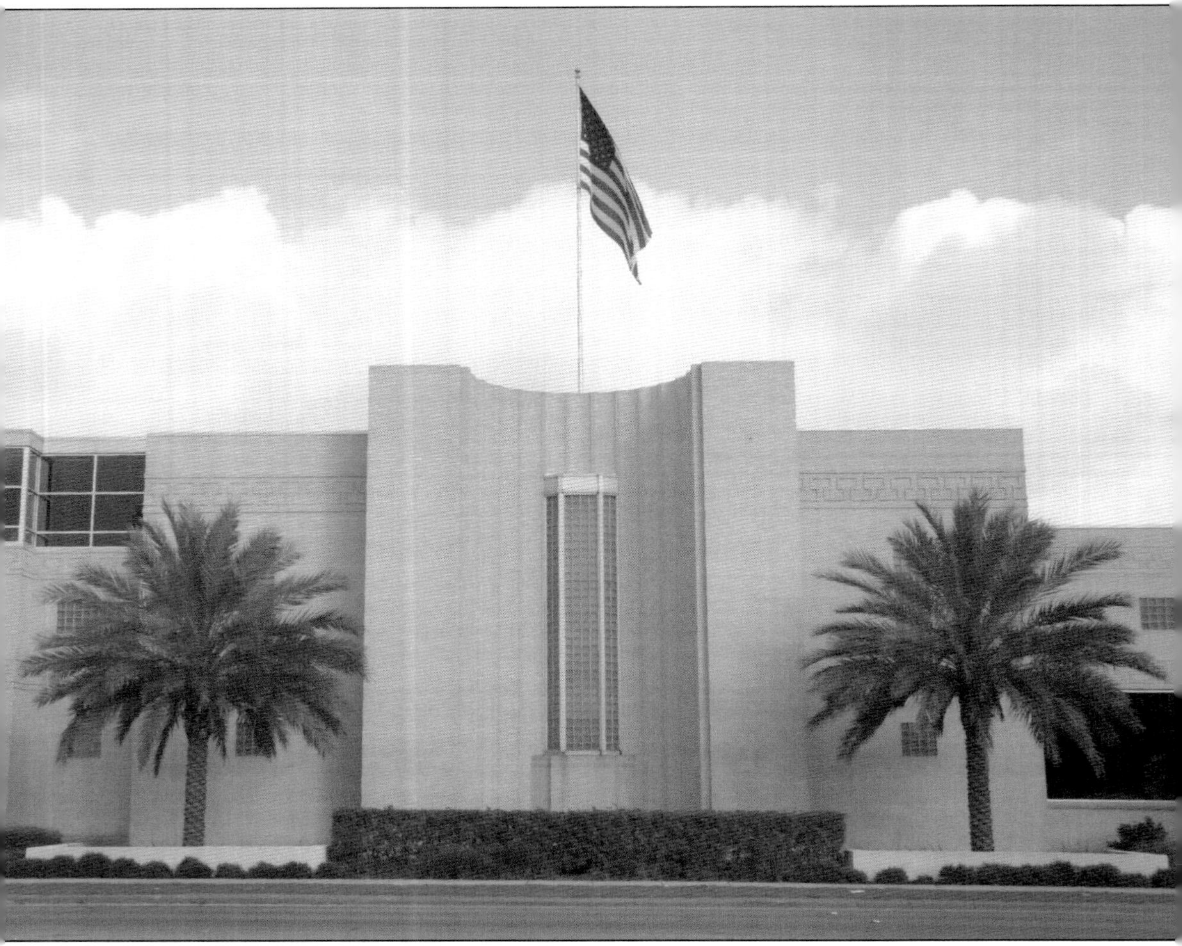

Butter Krust Bakery. Originally opening as Richter's Bakery at the corner of Laredo and Santa Rosa Streets in 1882, William and Emma Richter's successful business continued to grow, allowing them to purchase a Butter Krust Bread franchise in 1912. Constructed in 1941, this brick facility on Broadway Street was the culmination of the franchise expansion. The elongated structure features a semicircular focal point, glass block, and brick ornamentation using a variant of the Greek key pattern. (SAPA.)

Eight

MILITARY INSTALLATIONS

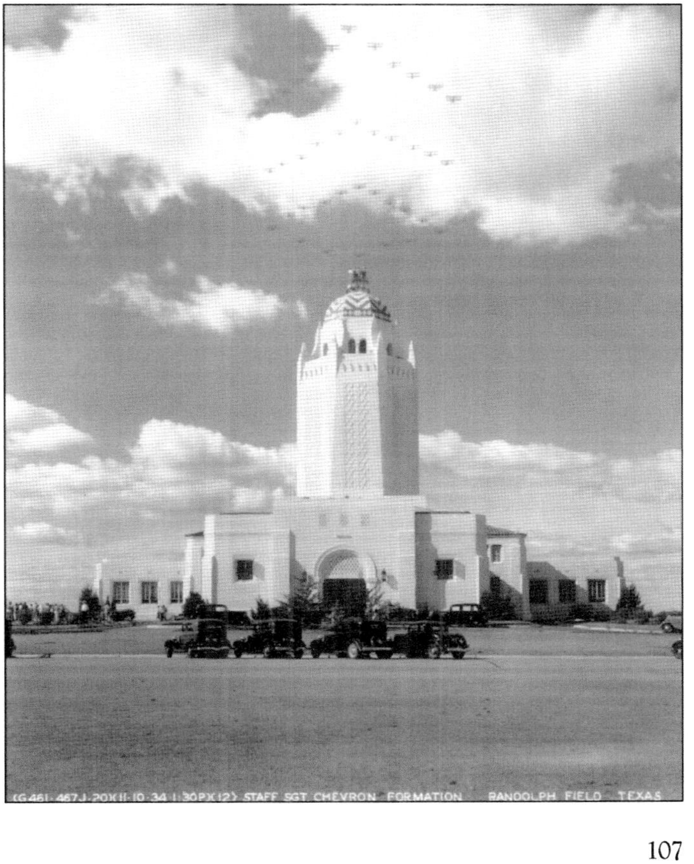

RANDOLPH ADMINISTRATION BUILDING. Formally dedicated in 1930, Randolph Field was the result of a five-year expansion of the Army Air Corps. The centerpiece to the air station is the unique administration building, designed by 1st Lt. Harold L. Clark. Prominent local architects Ayers and Ayers were consulted to create construction drawings, completing the structure in 1931. Nicknamed the "Taj Mahal," the octagonal tower actually conceals a large water storage tank. This flyby group from 1934 forms the staff sergeant chevron formation. (PTH/Tarrant.)

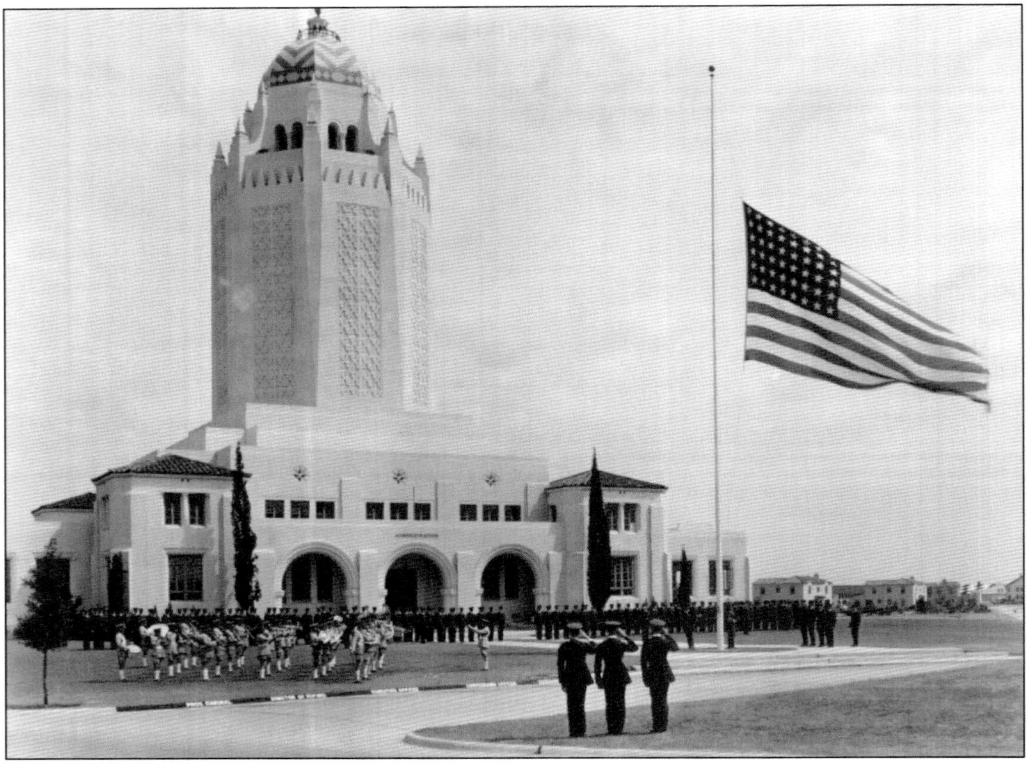

Randolph Air City. While serving as a dispatch officer at Kelly Field's motor pool, 1st Lt. Harold L. Clark began sketching his idea for the new "Air City" on the backs of dispatch sheets. Having trained as an architect prior to his military service, Clark took his drawings to Brig. Gen. Frank P. Lahm for approval. An American aviation pioneer from Ohio, Lahm granted Clark full-time status as liaison to oversee construction. Above, the Flying Cadets stand at attention while the 9th Infantry Band plays during a flag-raising ceremony. The main entrance of the small hospital, below, is marked with slender, double-spiral columns and a minimally decorated parapet. (Both, PTH/Tarrant.)

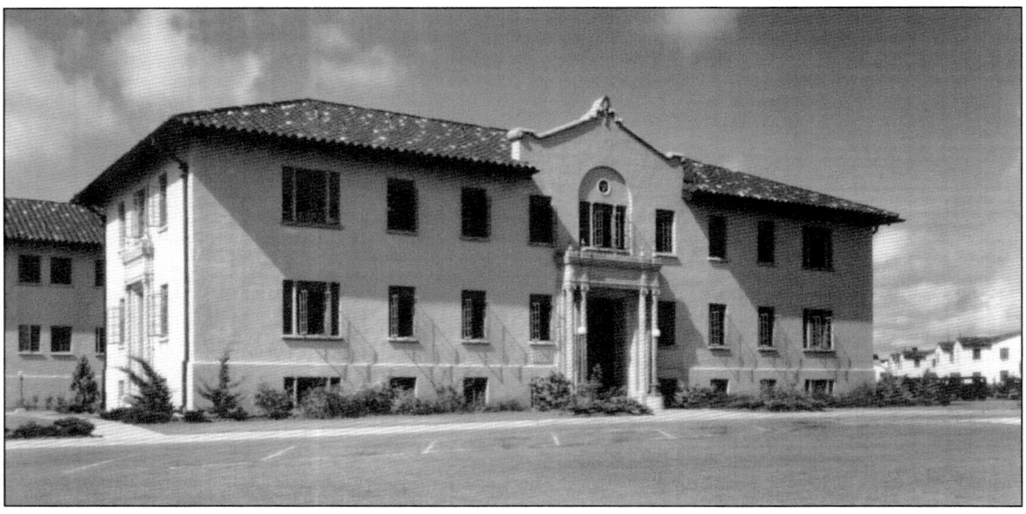

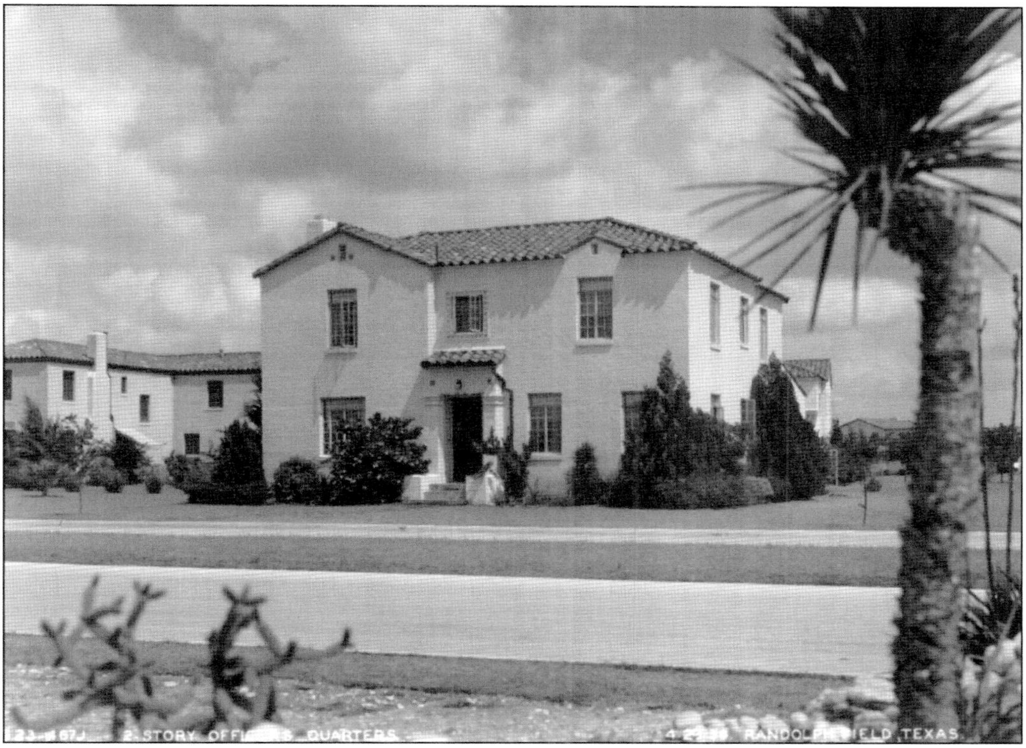

Randolph Officer's Quarters. The majority of the structures at Randolph exhibit the Spanish Colonial Revival style, an anomaly in San Antonio. Even outside government venues, the style continued in popularity throughout the city in the 1930s. This two-story residence seen here in 1936 is simple yet elegant in design. (PTH/Tarrant.)

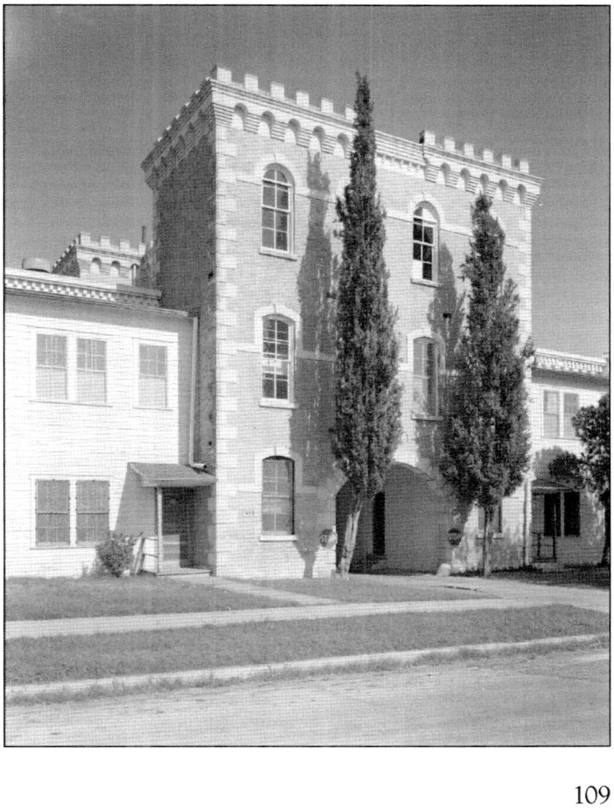

Fort Sam Houston Sally Port and Long Barracks. The three-story brick structure and long barracks were designed by engineer C.M. Ellington and local architect Alfred Giles. Typical of American frontier fort layouts, the barracks are located around a central parade ground. The sally port was originally constructed as an accommodation for band members and was completed in 1887. (HABS.)

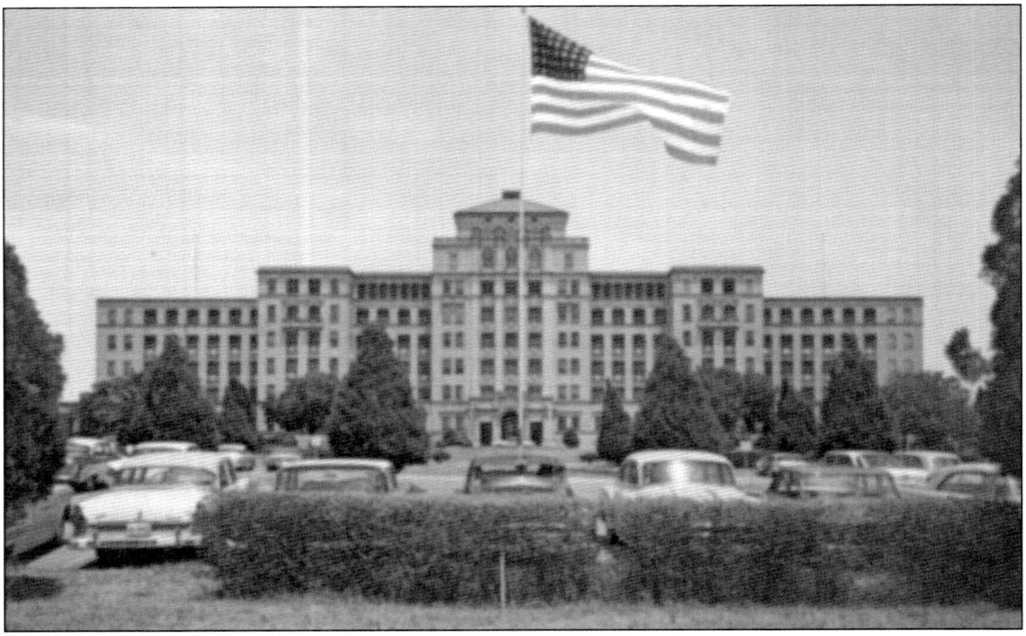

Brooke General Hospital at Fort Sam Houston. Named for internal medicine physician Brig. Gen. Roger Brooke, the hospital has an entrance dominated by a central tower with a low red tile roof and could accommodate over 400 beds. It was constructed in 1938 of brown brick with terra-cotta detailing, and Col. Edwin V. Dunstan is credited with the design while acting as US Army quartermaster. Dunstan was also an assistant professor in civil engineering at George Washington University earlier in his career. This postcard image was taken in the mid-20th century. (PTH/North Texas, McFaddin-Ward House Museum.)

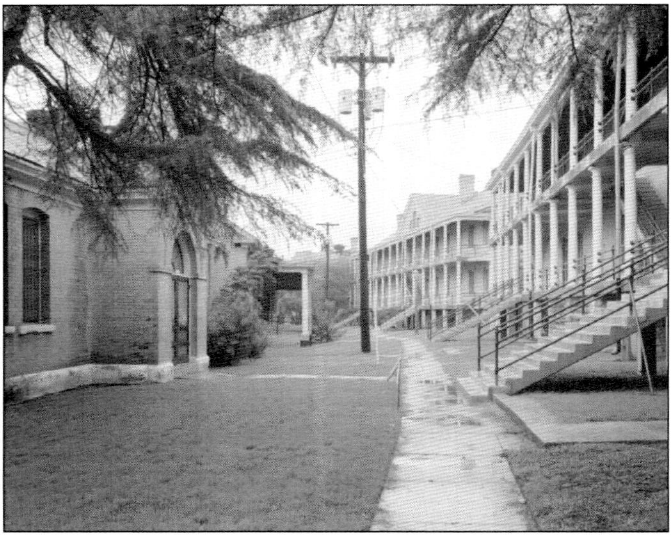

Barracks at Fort Sam Houston. Constructed from standardized plans from the US Army's Office of the Quartermaster General, four identical residence buildings housed soldiers attached to the Fort Sam Houston Calvary Post, seen at right in this photograph. Virtually unchanged on the exterior since they were constructed during the early 20th century, the barracks face the parade ground. The latrine, left, is located at the rear of the barracks. (HABS.)

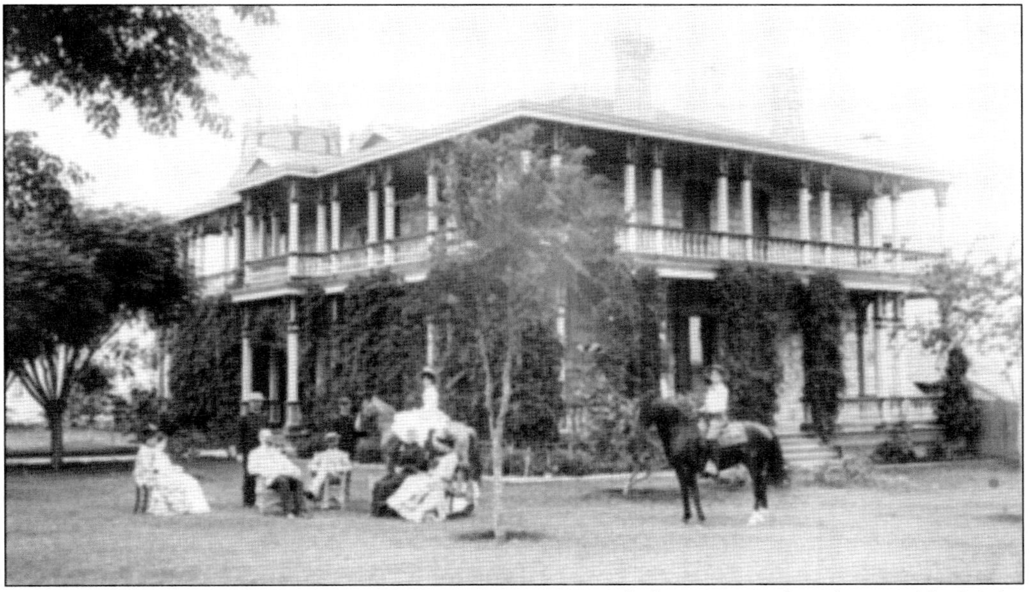

Fort Sam Houston Commander General's Quarters. Locally known British architect Alfred Giles designed this 1881 residence for the Army post's commanding officer. The home is constructed of rusticated limestone blocks of varying sizes and exhibits exquisite wood detailing. The biggest and most elaborate of 15 homes built on Staff Post Road in the 1880s, the home is now known as the Pershing House, for Gen. John J. Pershing, who served during World War I. Above, Brig. Gen. David Sloan Stanley, seated left of center, poses for a photograph with family and friends. The general's daughter, Anna Huntington Stanley, was an American artist known for her Impressionist oil paintings, and is likely one of the women seated at far left. Below, the upper-story porches were enclosed with screens during the mid-20th century. (Above, FSHM; below, HABS.)

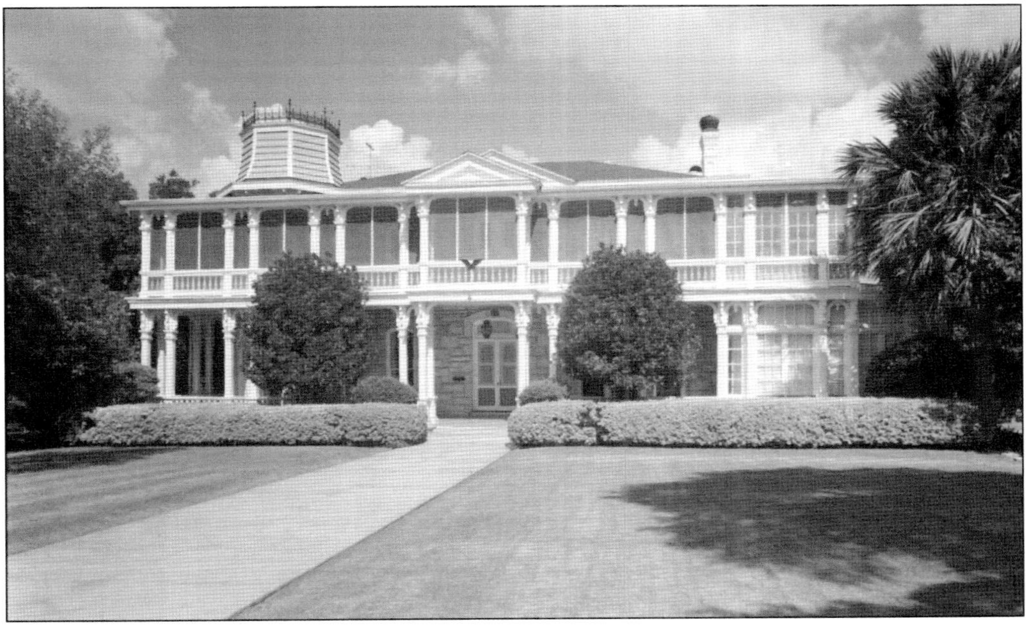

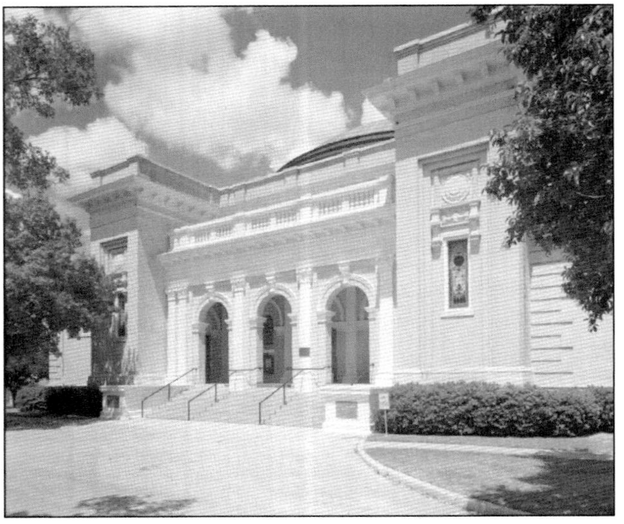

Gift Chapel at Fort Sam Houston. Named for the generosity of donations to see the construction through, the post chapel at Fort Sam Houston was completed in 1909. Designed by local architect Leo M.J. Dielmann, the metal dome is a prominent feature within the building's imposing symmetry and Beaux-Arts influences. Extensive documentation of the chapel is located in the Daughters of the Republic of Texas Library at the Alamo, which includes Dielmann's plans, sketches, and business proceedings. (HABS.)

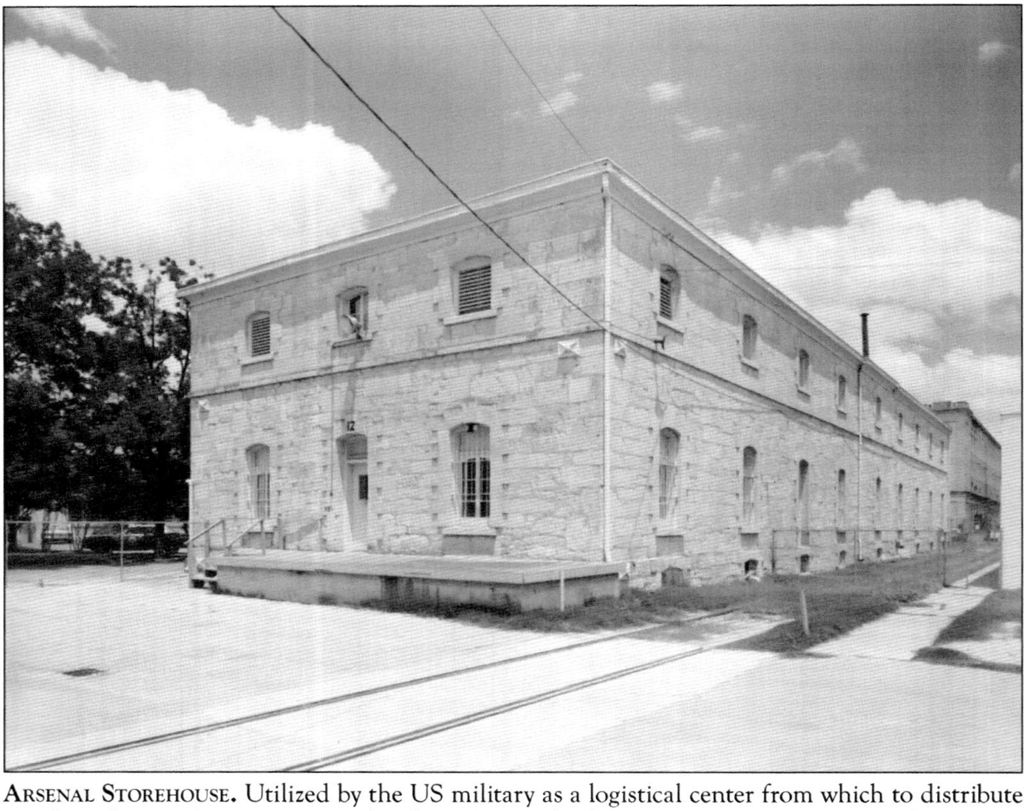

Arsenal Storehouse. Utilized by the US military as a logistical center from which to distribute supplies, the storehouse was completed in 1883 as the first permanent repository to the armory. Remaining Arsenal structures west of Main Street include an office building, horse stable, and magazine. East of Main Street, the HEB Grocery Company rehabilitated a large portion of the Arsenal buildings in the 1980s to serve as company headquarters. (HABS.)

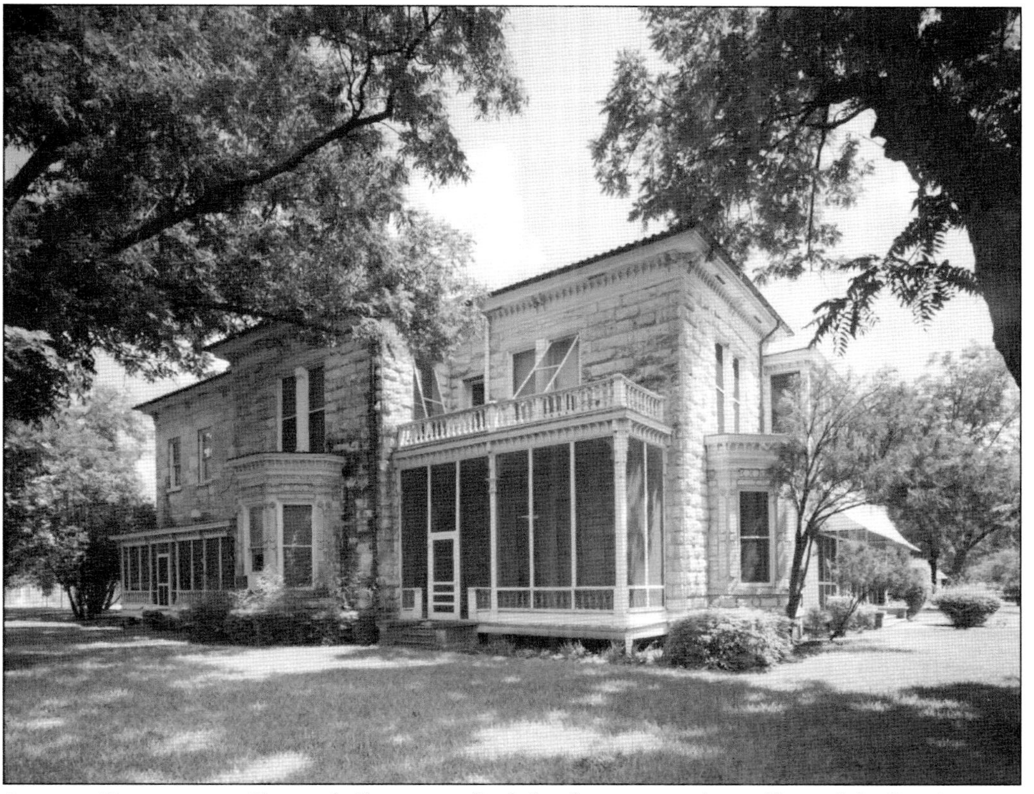

ARSENAL COMMANDING OFFICER'S QUARTERS. Built for the commanding officer of the San Antonio Arsenal, the Italianate residence features rusticated limestone block construction. The former residence of Dr. James M. Devine was originally used for this purpose until the home was demolished and replaced by this structure around 1883. (HABS.)

ARSENAL SERVANTS' QUARTERS. Located just south of the commander's home is this small residential structure. Strictly utilitarian in design, this former outbuilding is the oldest structure within the Arsenal compound and was constructed by Dr. James M. Devine. The modest structure dates prior to 1857 and is finished in stucco. A two-story wooden addition, completed sometime later, extends to the north. (HABS.)

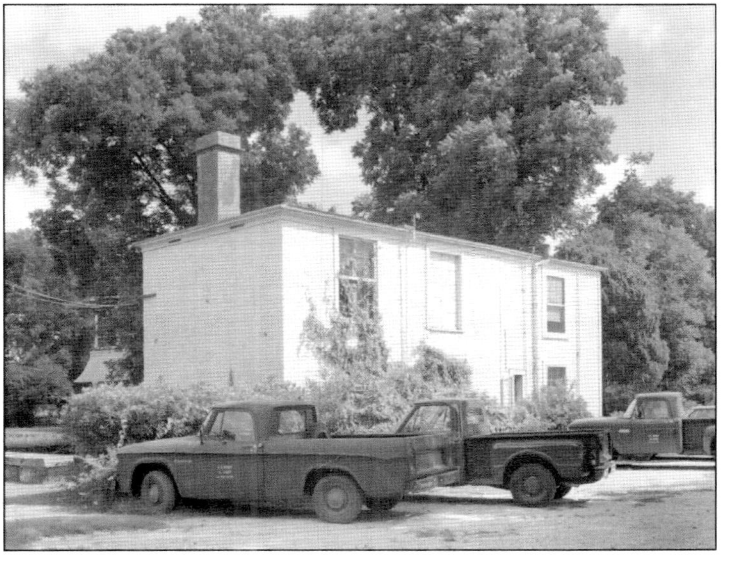

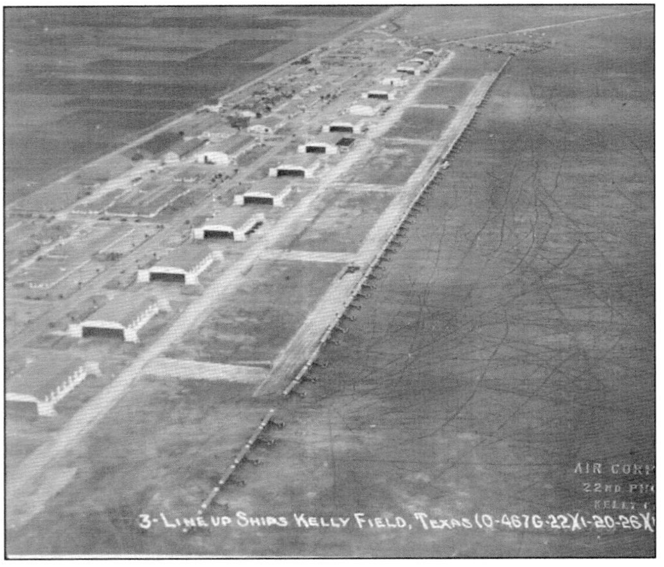

KELLY FIELD AROUND 1920. Lt. George E.M. Kelly was one of the first flight instructors to join Lt. Benjamin D. Foulois in establishing San Antonio's new air school in 1911. Kelly was an immigrant from England and later joined the US Army. Located away from the city center in what was a cotton field, Kelly Field was officially established in 1917. Expeditious construction of numerous wood-frame hangars along the airstrip occurred during this era. (PTH/North Texas, Hardin-Simmons Library Abilene Photograph Collection.)

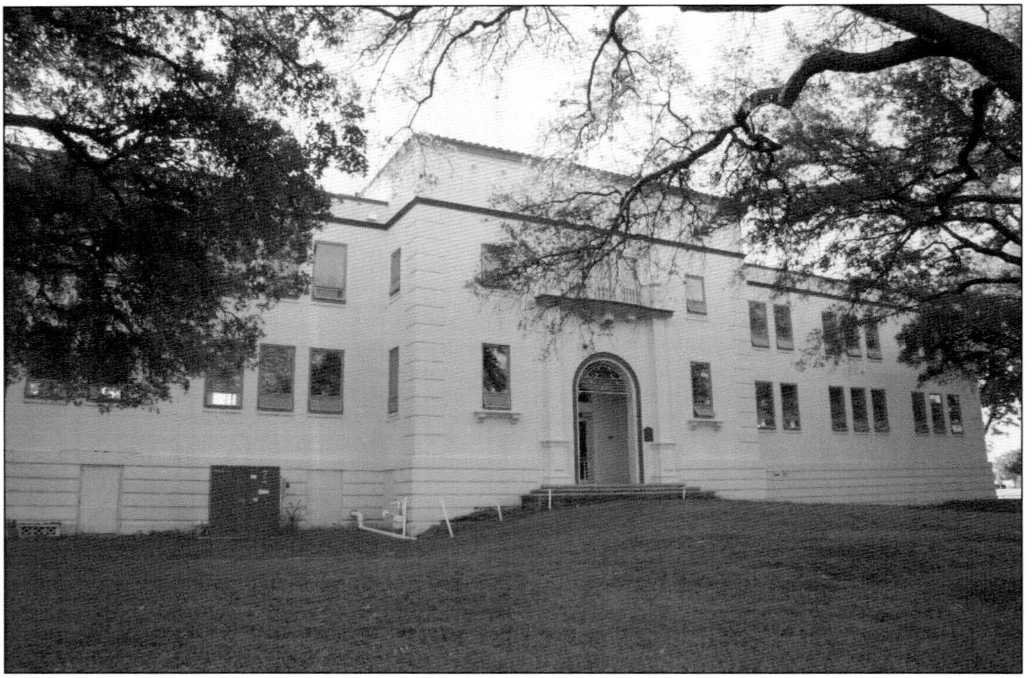

KELLY ARMY AIR CORPS ACADEMIC BUILDING. Constructed in 1940 as an administrative and educational facility for the Army Air Corps Advanced Flying School, by 1943 it was redesignated for use as the Air Service Command. Also housing the base commander's office, the Spanish Colonial Revival building served as the Air Logistic Center. During World War II, Kelly Air Depot was the largest aviation station in the world and was the logistical center for all air, training, and storage detachments. (SAPA.)

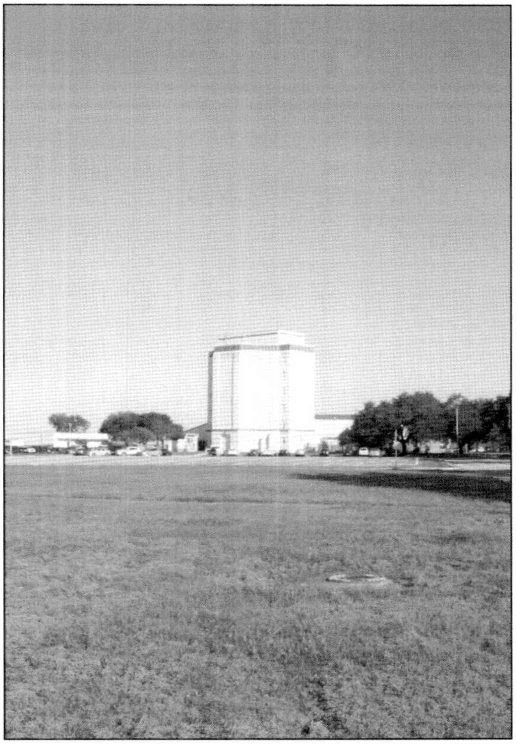

Norden Bombsight Practice Facility at Kelly Field. Developed by Swiss scientist Carl Norden, the complicated sighting instrument was used during World War II for more accurate bomb deployment from the B-17 Flying Fortress and the B-29 Superfortress. Shrouded in secrecy, the device was utilized in thousands of American aircraft. Constructed specifically for bombsight training, this seven-story concrete tower was the facility where bombardiers would simulate operation of the apparatus. (SAPA.)

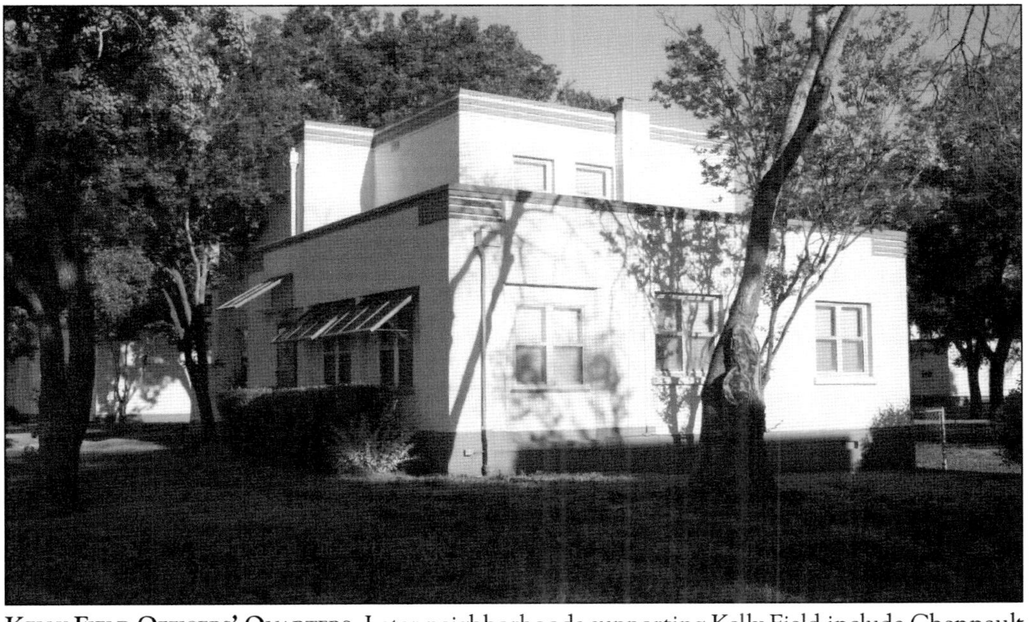

Kelly Field Officers' Quarters. Later neighborhoods supporting Kelly Field include Chennault Circle, named for prominent aviator Claire Lee Chennault from Commerce, Texas. The homes in this neighborhood are constructed of concrete, modernistic in style, and include single and multifamily units. Designed for officers in the late 1930s, the two-story residences include private maids' quarters and rooftop sundecks. (SAPA.)

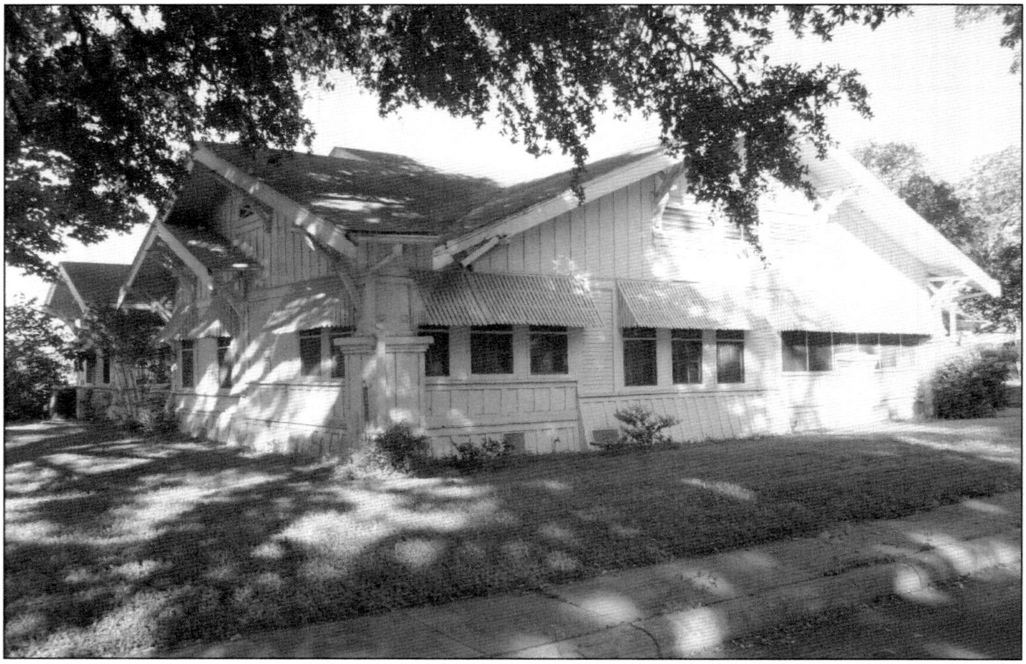

Kelly Field Officers' Quarters Bungalow Colony. Homes in this neighborhood exemplify the American Bungalow movement of the early 20th century. Other communal structures also remain, including bachelor officers' quarters, servants' shacks, streetlamps, garages, and recreational facilities. Containing over 50 architectural components that were constructed between 1920 and 1945, this neighborhood provided housing for the Aviation Camp at Kelly Field, originally established during World War I. Above, an officer's residence exhibits original roof brackets, flared skirting, and a deep porch. Below, the servants' quarters, located behind the main residences, also exhibit Bungalow styling. (Both, SAPA.)

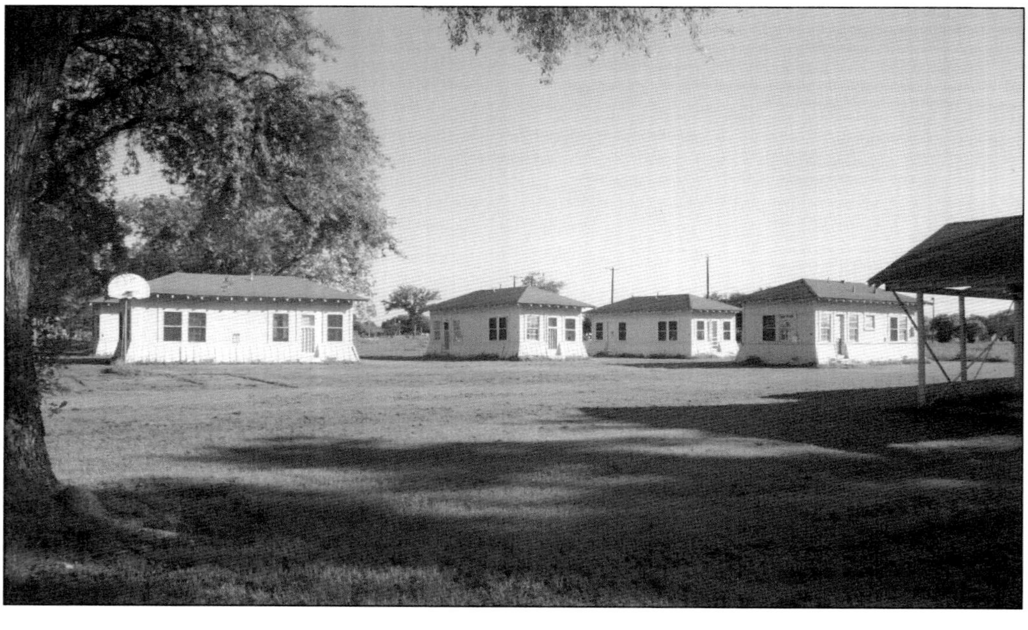

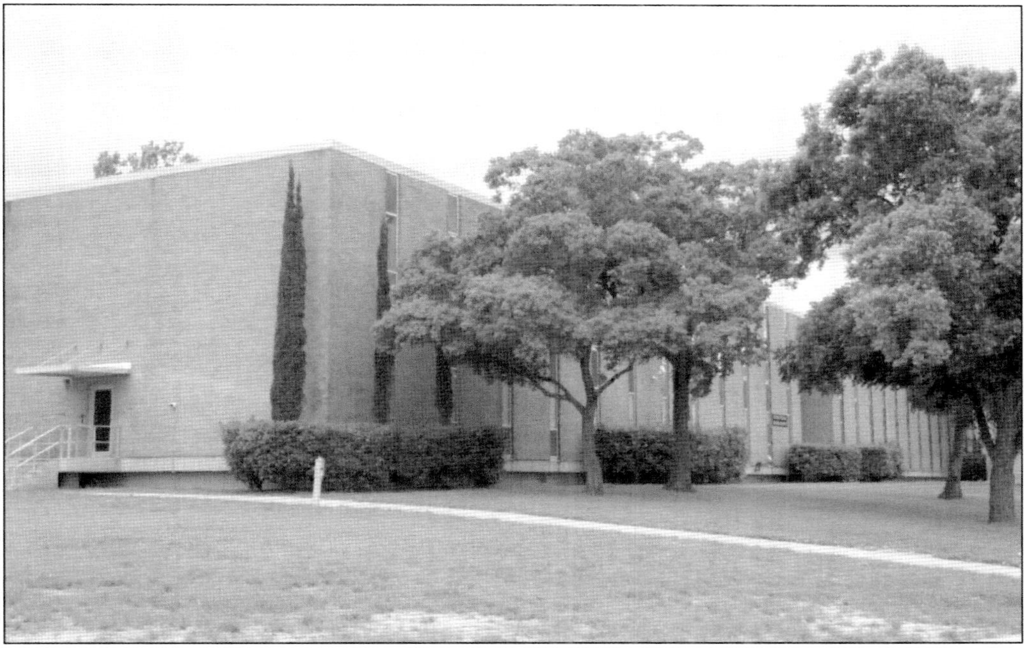

Aerospace Medicine Training Complex at Brooks Air Force Base. Although it was established in 1917 as Brooks Field, later developments involving the US Air Force School of Aerospace Medicine occurred in what is known as the 100-Area Historic District at the decommissioned Brooks Air Force Base. A complex of 15 historic structures, dedicated by Pres. John F. Kennedy in 1963, was constructed to facilitate scientific investigation into the possible dangers and effects of space travel on astronauts during the early years of the nation's space program. Above, the Bedwell Building on Kennedy Circle is exemplary of the training center's architectural style. Below, a stylized service building creates a cohesive appearance within the institutional complex. (Both, SAPA.)

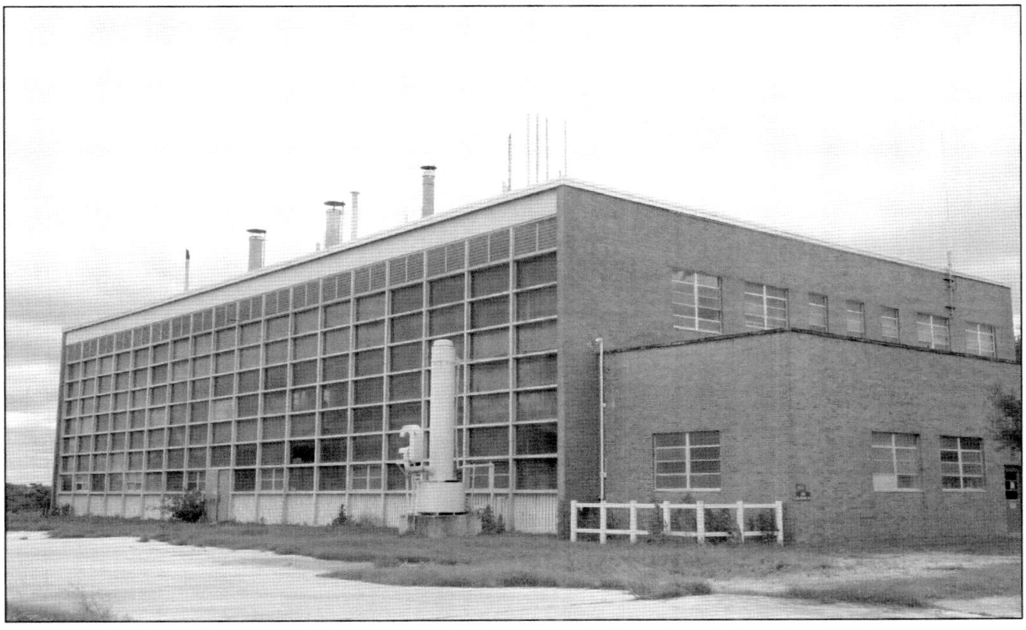

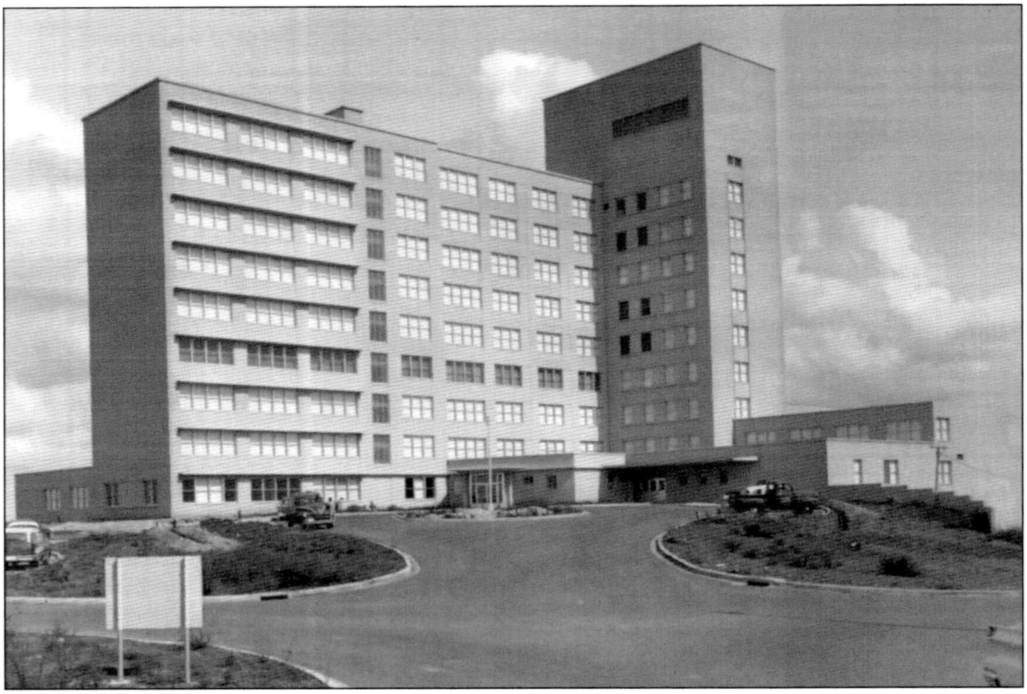

WILFORD HALL AT LACKLAND AIR FORCE BASE. Originally organized as a hospital for the Aviation Cadet Pilot Training Program in 1942, the hospital was later named for Maj. Gen. Wilford F. Hall, who specialized in otorhinolaryngology. By 1957, the hospital had become the above nine-story high-rise, able to accommodate 150 inpatients. Exponential growth within the military branches in the postwar years led to major renovations and expansions, creating the largest medical center in the US Air Force, below. (Both, USAF.)

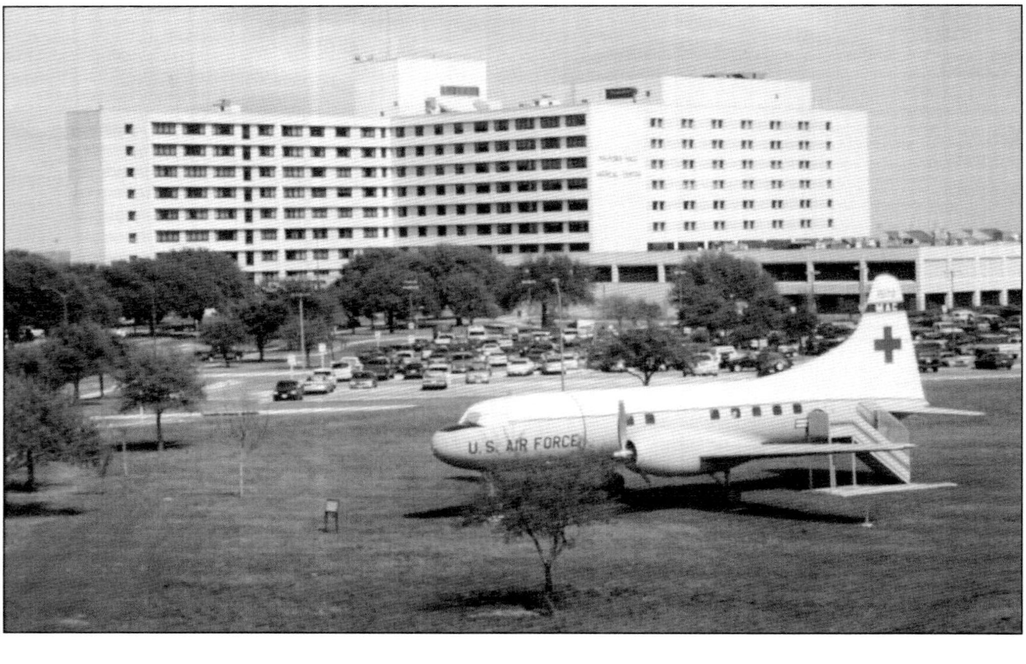

Nine

Theaters and Historic Hotels

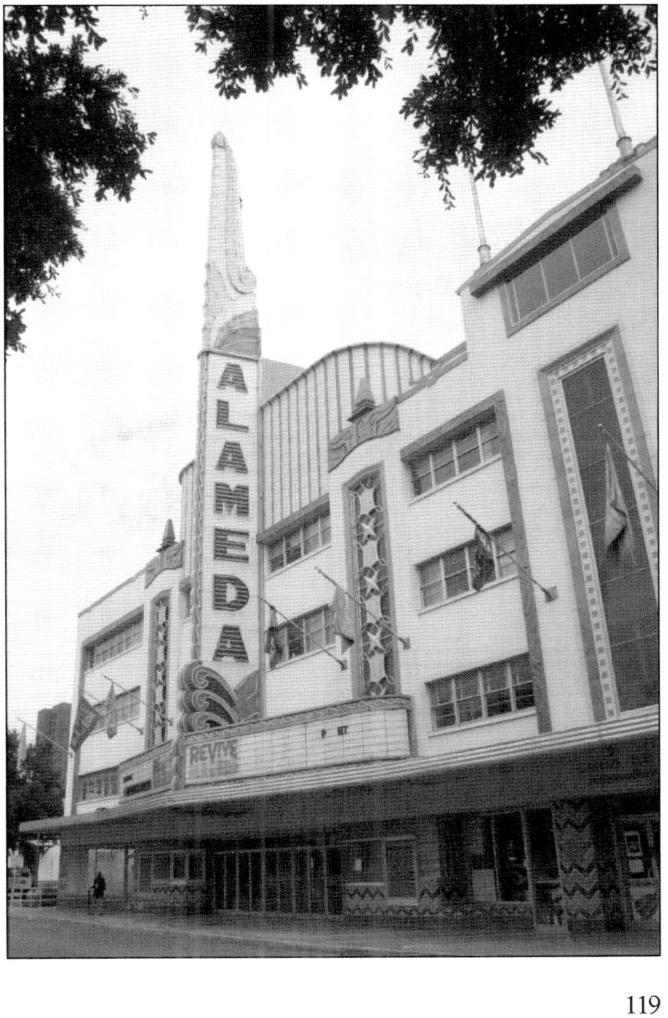

ALAMEDA THEATER. Remarkable for its extensive neon signage, the theater features a decorative facade, and colorful floor finishes designed by local architect N. Straus Nayfach in 1949. Specializing in Spanish-language films, the theater complements the International Building on West Houston Street, the former home of the Mexican consulate. (SAPA.)

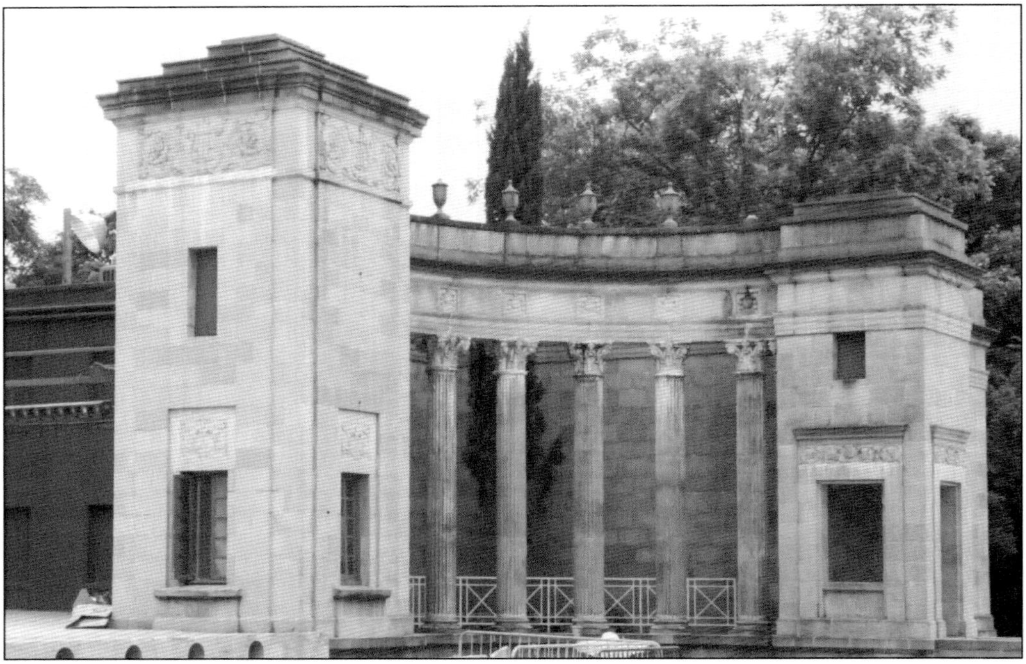

SUNKEN GARDEN THEATRE. Neoclassical in design, the open-air amphitheater was constructed in 1930 and utilized by the San Antonio Civic Opera Company. The stage detail reveals fluted Corinthian columns and floral motifs that surround a lyre. Near the top of the tower are bas-reliefs, seen at far left. (SAPA.)

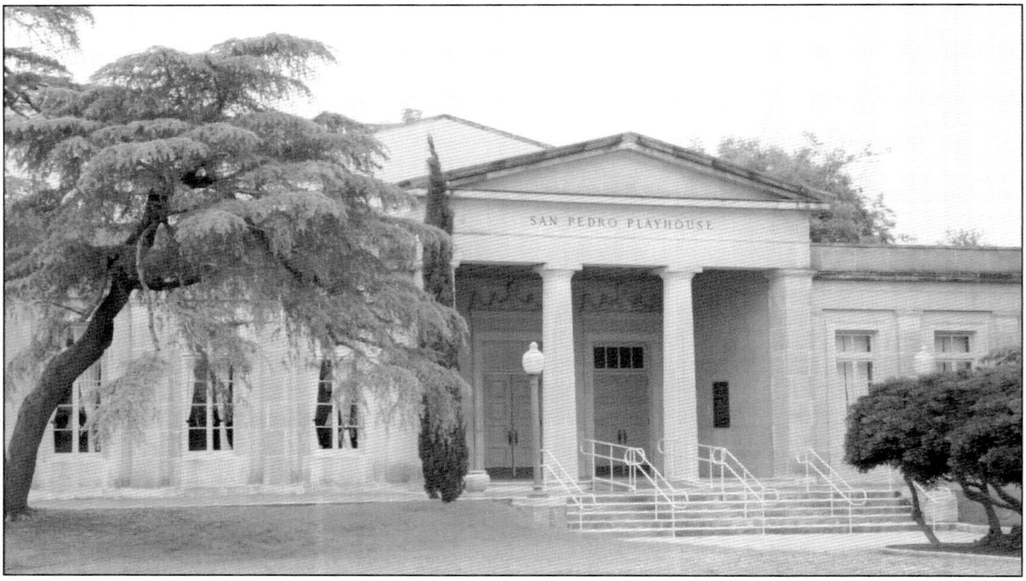

SAN PEDRO PLAYHOUSE. San Pedro Springs Park has origins dating to the 18th century, and claims to be the nation's second-oldest public city park. Constructed in 1929, this Greek Revival theater is a replica of the 1850s Market House that was demolished on Market Street in the 1920s. Local architects Bartlett Cocke and Marvin Eichroht oversaw construction of the theater in the park's northwest quadrant. (SAPA.)

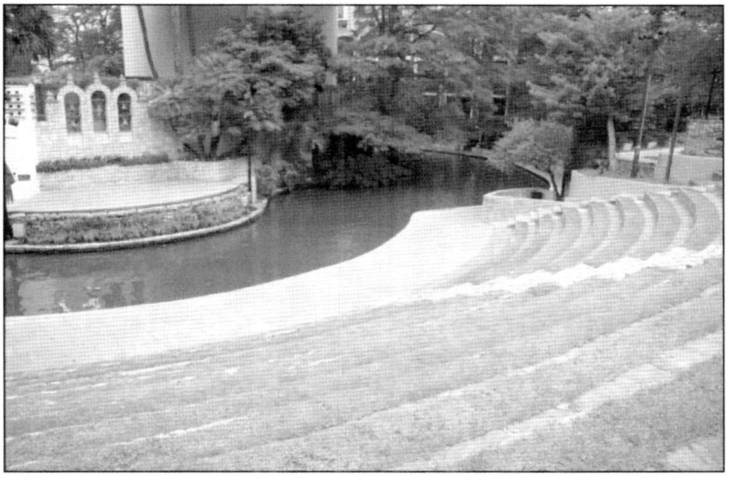

Arneson River Theater. A project completed by the Works Progress Administration around 1940, the open-air amphitheater was named for the engineer responsible for securing funds for the River Walk project, Edwin Arneson. The River Walk, which includes the theater, was designed by architect Robert H.H. Hugman. (SAPA.)

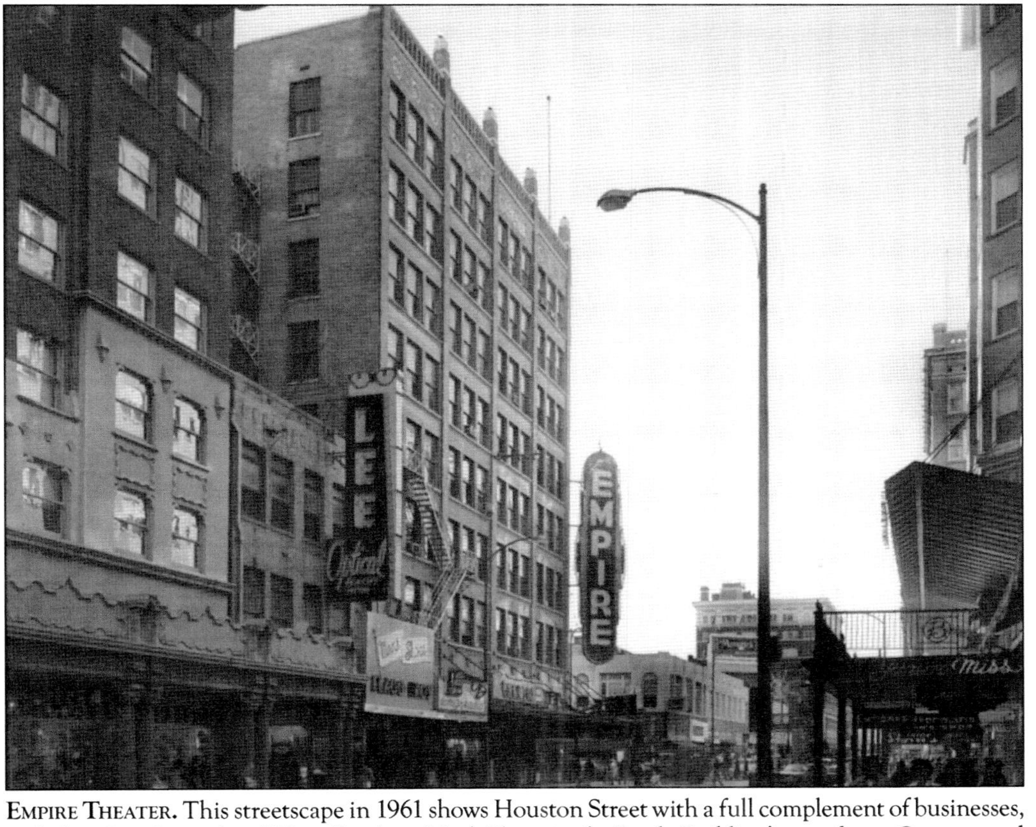

Empire Theater. This streetscape in 1961 shows Houston Street with a full complement of businesses, including Lee Optical and Flagg Brothers Men's Shoes in the Brady Building's storefront. Constructed in 1914 by developer Thomas F. Brady, the vaudeville theater was designed by architects Mauran, Russell, & Crowell of St. Louis, Missouri. (UTSA, Zintgraff Studio Collection.)

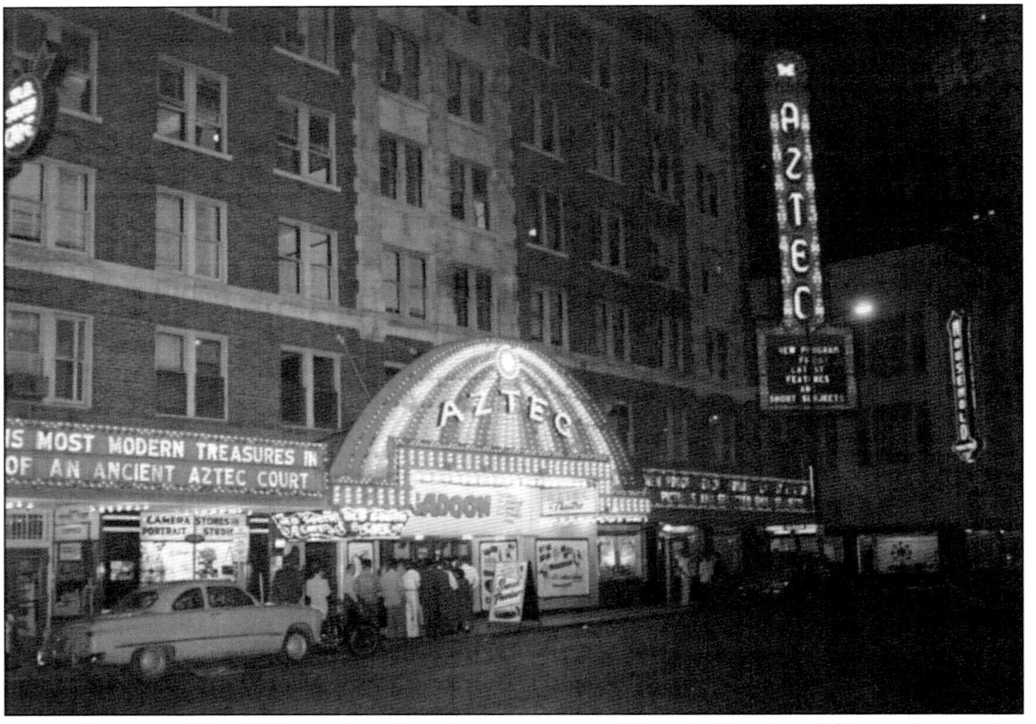

AZTEC THEATER. The 1926 movie palace features a magnificent lobby chandelier and extensive Mesoamerican decor. Below the massive marquee, patrons line the sidewalk for an evening show. A banner for *Brigadoon* is displayed over the entrance in this street scene from the 1950s. (UTSA, Zintgraff Studio Collection.)

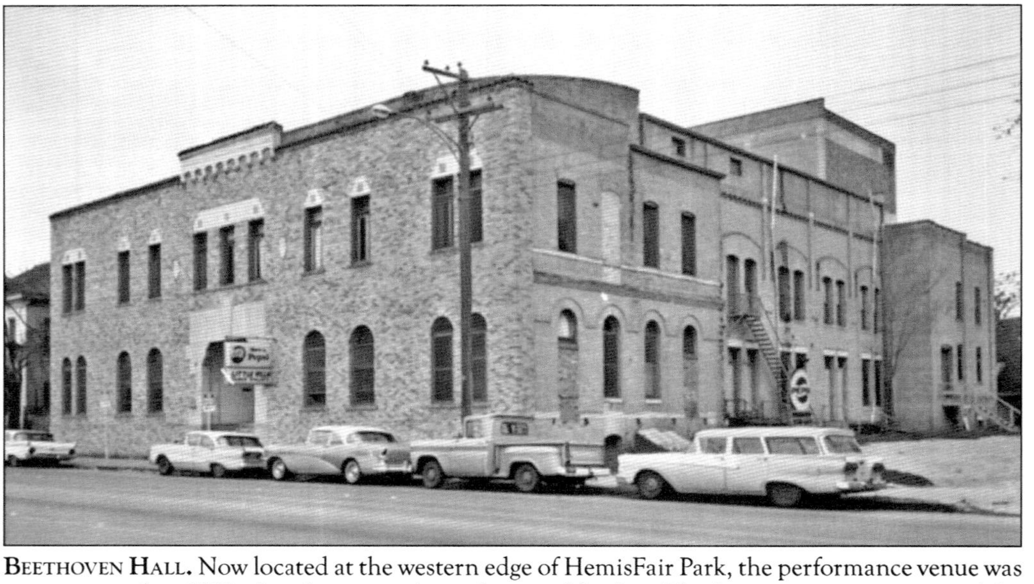

BEETHOVEN HALL. Now located at the western edge of HemisFair Park, the performance venue was reconstructed in 1913 after the original was destroyed by fire. The first structure was created for the Beethoven Maennerchor in 1895. This photograph was taken before the widening of South Alamo Street in the mid-20th century. (San Antonio Development Agency and UTSA.)

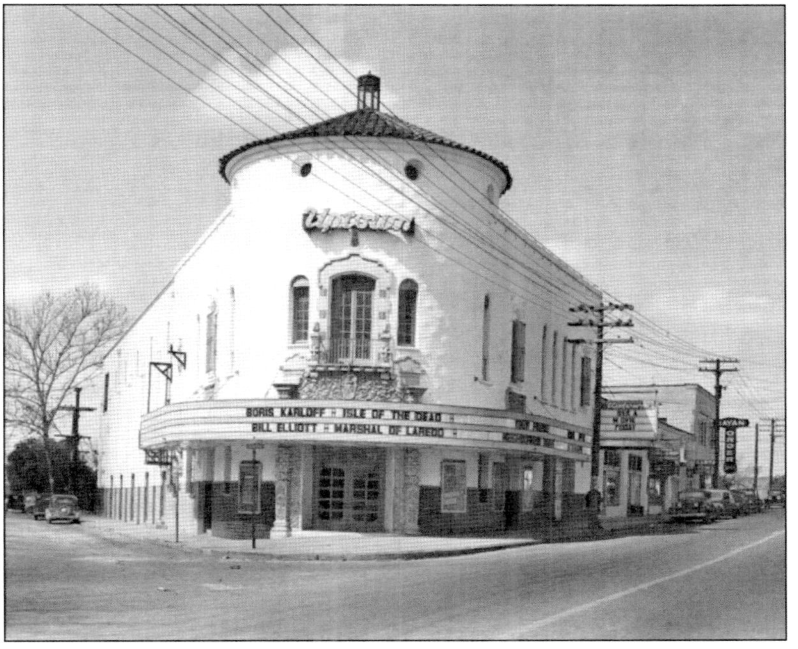

UPTOWN THEATER. Located northwest of downtown on Fredericksburg Road, the Spanish Colonial Revival facade features a prominent rounded corner with a nodule stucco finish. It was designed by architects Adams and Adams, who are recognized locally as participants in developing the Monte Vista neighborhood. (UTSA, Zintgraff Studio Collection.)

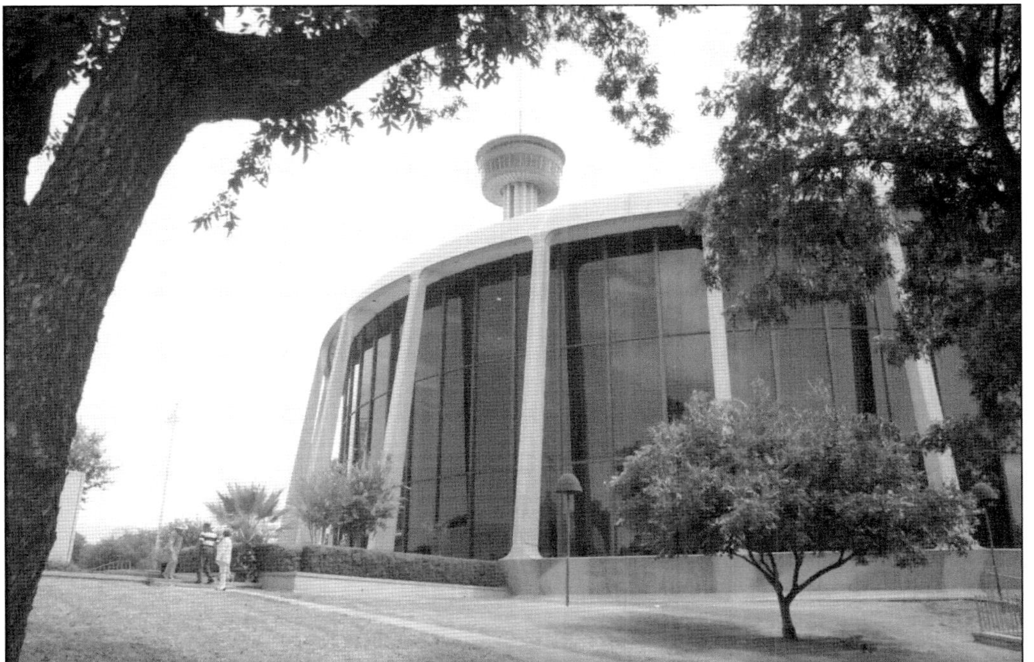

CONFLUENCE THEATER AT HEMISFAIR PARK. Designed by local architecture firm Marmon Mok, the circular glass and concrete structure served as Confluence Theater during the HemisFair World Exposition of 1968. The Tower of the Americas can be seen above the theater at center. (SAPA.)

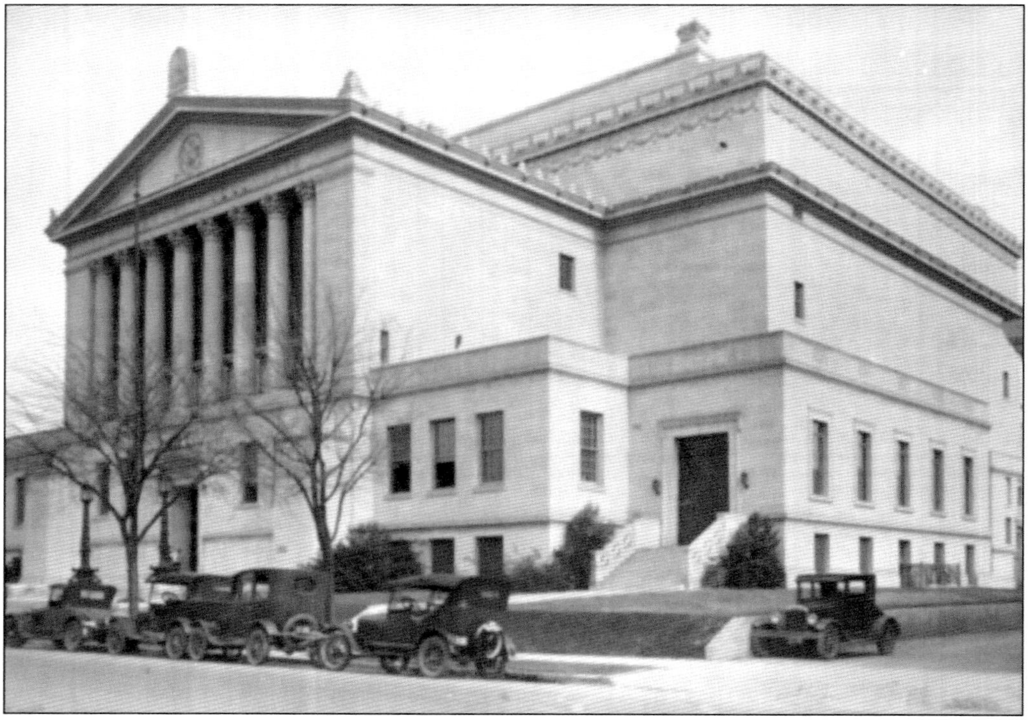

Scottish Rite Cathedral. Completed in 1924 for the Masonic fraternity known as the Scottish Rite, the lavishly decorated meeting hall features a grand ballroom and theater with a projection-capable ceiling, common in movie palaces during the 1920s. The Neoclassical five-and-a-half-story structure, designed by architect Harvey Lindsley Page, dominates the downtown city block. Sculpted bronze entry doors were designed and executed by Italian artist Pompeo Coppini. (UTSA.)

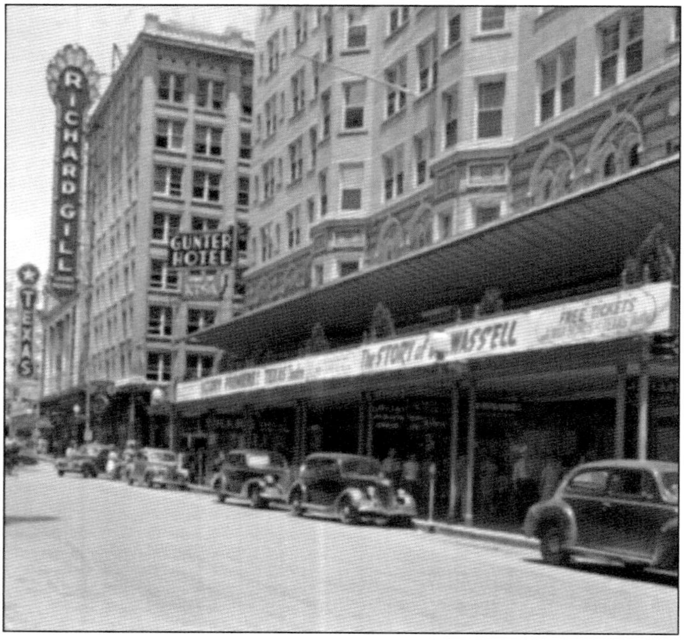

Gunter Hotel and Texas Theater. Built at the corner of Houston and St. Mary's Streets on the site of the former Mahncke Building, the 1909 structure was designed by St. Louis architects Mauran & Russell. The eight-story high-rise is named for Jot Gunter, a well-known businessman and investor throughout Texas. To the far left, the old Texas Theater, built in 1926, is advertised as showing the *Victory!* premiere on a banner on the Gunter Hotel's sidewalk canopy in 1940. (UTSA.)

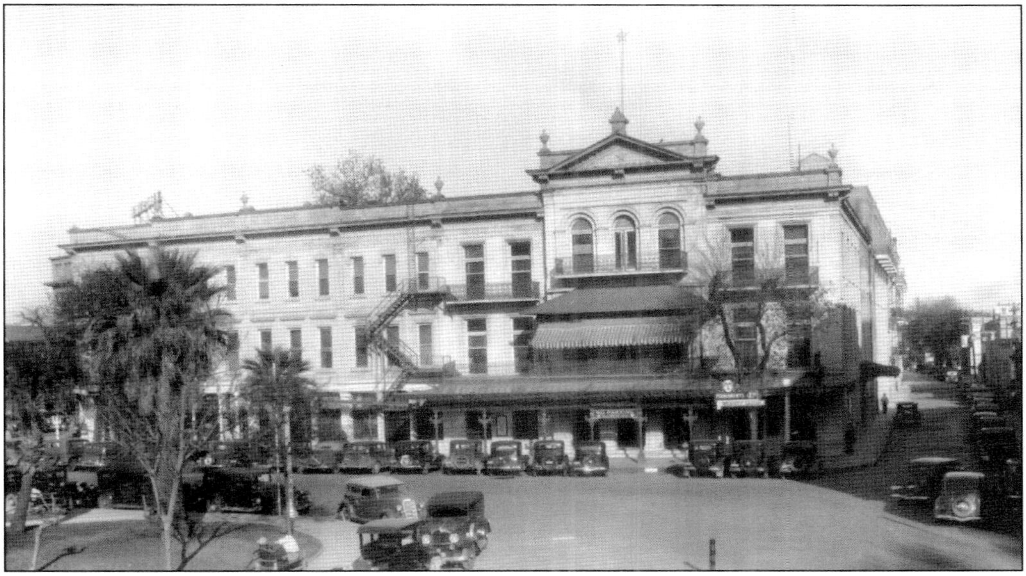

Menger Hotel. Built in the mid-19th century as an expansion to a boardinghouse and brewery, the Menger Hotel has been a famous fixture in Alamo Plaza for generations. Many famous celebrities and several presidents are known to have stayed here. A few early notables include Gen. Sam Houston, Col. Theodore Roosevelt, and Pres. Dwight Eisenhower. In 1887, the fourth floor was added on the south side, seen on the right. (HABS.)

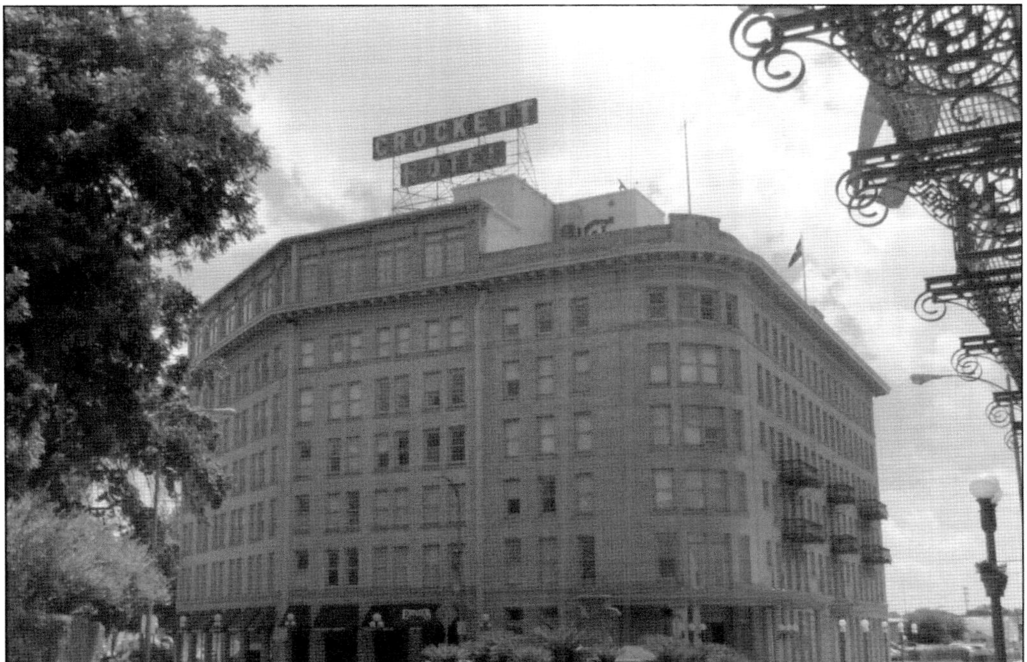

Crockett Hotel. The original six-story structure designed by architects Phelps and Jacob was built in 1909 directly behind the Alamo on Bonham Street. An addition to the north side of the hotel in 1927 was similarly styled but included a seventh floor. (SAPA.)

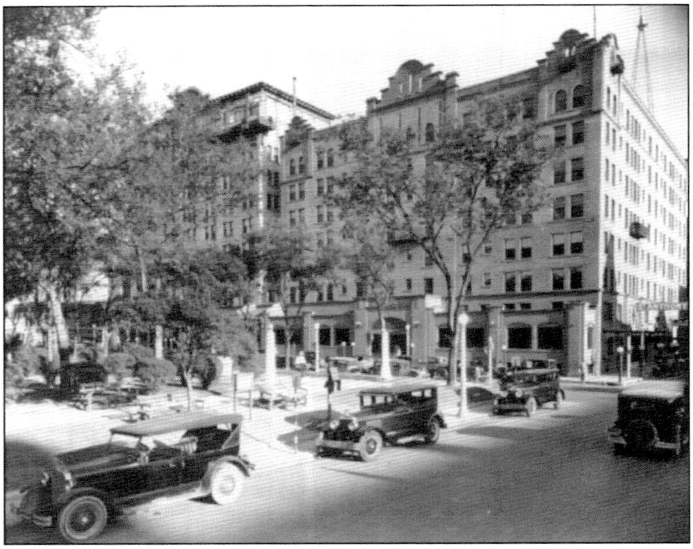

St. Anthony Hotel. The hotel, seen here in the late 1920s, was completed in 1909 overlooking Travis Park. Built by successful local ranchers and then later purchased by banker Ralph W. Morrison in the 1930s, the St. Anthony was San Antonio's first luxury hotel. Innovations included air-conditioning, private baths, telephones, and automatic lighting. (June Jump and UTSA.)

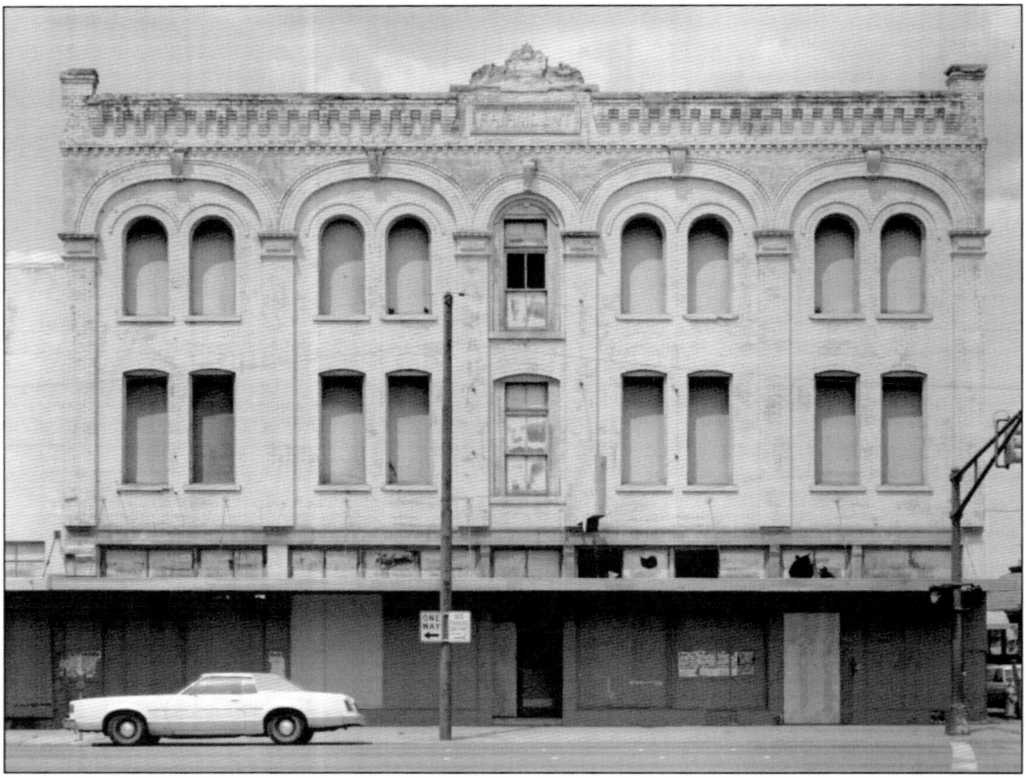

Fairmount Hotel. Formerly located at 857 East Commerce Street, the Fairmount Hotel was constructed in 1906. Designed by San Antonio architect Leo M.J. Dielmann, the hotel is a significant example of typical turn-of-the-century buildings that once lined East Commerce Street toward the Southern Pacific Depot. In a 1985 collaborative effort to save it from demolition, the San Antonio Conservation Society and city government moved the building to South Alamo Street. At the time of its relocation, it was the heaviest building ever moved on wheels at 1,600 tons. (HABS.)

Bibliography

AIA San Antonio, A Chapter of the American Institute of Architects. *San Antonio Architecture: Traditions and Visions*. San Antonio: Trinity University Press, 2007.

airforcehistory.af.mil

atlas.thc.state.tx.us

Gonzales, Sylvia M. *The Life and Works of Walter Nold Mathis*. San Antonio: Villa Finale Museum and Gardens Archives, 2015.

———. *Villa Finale: 401 King William*. San Antonio: Villa Finale Museum and Gardens Archives, 2015.

Hendricks, Barbara Dean and Don Kirk. *The Building Arts of South Texas*. San Antonio: Franklin Scribes, 2015.

lib.utsa.edu

loc.gov

McAlester, Virginia and Lee. *A Field Guide to American Houses*. New York: Alfred A. Knopf, 2009.

nps.gov

Roth, Leland M. *American Architecture: A History*. Boulder, CO: Westview Press, 2001.

saconservation.org

saisd.net

samhouston.army.mil

sanantonio.gov

texashistory.unt.edu